'I received orders from General Ordener just an hour ago,' said the officer. 'We move out at midnight. The infantry will remain here. The General feels speed is of the essence in this operation.'

'Where is the Duke of Enghien?'

'At the Château of Ettenheim, close to here. The only thing we don't know is how many men he has with him.'

'What of the Bavarians and troops of Baden?'

'If possible we are to avoid contact with them.'

'And if that contact is *unavoidable*?'

'Then we fight. Our first and only objective is to return Enghien to French soil. Regardless of the cost or the consequences.' He glanced at his watch, squinting in the darkness to see the hands. 'If I were you, Sergeant, I would rest. In less than two hours, you will have your war.'

Bonaparte's Warriors

———◆———

Richard Howard

time **warner**
paperbacks

A *Time Warner* Paperback

First published in Great Britain in 2000
by Little, Brown and Company
This edition published by Warner Books in 2002
Reprinted by Time Warner Paperbacks in 2003
Reprinted 2004

A CIP catalogue record for this book
is available from the British Library.

ISBN 0 7515 2948 6

Typeset in Plantin by
Palimpsest Book Production Limited,
Polmont, Stirlingshire

Printed and bound in Great Britain by
Clays Ltd, St Ives plc

Time Warner Paperbacks
An imprint of
Time Warner Book Group UK
Brettenham House
Lancaster Place
London WC2E 7EN

www.twbg.co.uk

*Bonaparte's
Warriors*

One

The warmth of the day belied the time of the year. Sergeant Alain Lausard looked up at the sky. The cornflower blue of the heavens was smeared in places by streaks of whispy white cloud but, despite their presence, the sun shone brightly. It was more like a summer's day than one in late September. Only the scattering of fallen leaves and trees waving semi-bare branches gave any indication that the seasons were changing, the only clue that nature was effecting the transition from summer to autumn.

Even as Lausard watched, a single leaf detached itself from a low branch and drifted gently to earth. It fell on the road and was crushed underfoot by the many hooves that trod the thoroughfare.

He glanced behind him at the men of his regiment. Clad in green tunics like himself, the dragoons rode at a measured pace. Many of them seemed as entranced by the glorious autumnal weather as himself. The trees beneath which they passed grew over the road like a canopy, their leaves ranging in colour from light green to yellow and in places brown. They fell like confetti upon the detachment of cavalrymen. The sun-dappled procession continued towards the crest of a low ridge beyond which lay their destination.

Behind the dragoons came a squadron of horse grenadiers, their tall bearskins nodding as they rode. Then came two batteries of horse artillery dragging four- and eight-pounder cannon and, even further back, three regiments of blue-clad infantry, marching at the regulation seventy-five paces a minute. They marched in double files along each side of the road, leaving its middle free for the passage of vehicles. They were singing loudly and Lausard noticed that a number of the men in his unit had also joined in with the raucous cacophony. The strains of 'Dans la Rue Chiffonnière' drifted up to the skies and across the countryside. Birds sitting in the trees took flight at the approaching din. Lausard couldn't blame them, especially when he heard Rocheteau add his own booming tones to the melody.

Bonet, the former schoolmaster, tapped gently on the pommel of his saddle as he sang.

Giresse, the horse thief, and Roussard, the forger, also joined in.

Tabor hummed happily, smiling continually. He couldn't remember the words but it didn't prevent him sharing in the moment.

Up ahead, Captain Milliere grinned and lifted his fist into the air as if to encourage the men to join in.

Karim looked on with amused indifference. The Circassian glanced around at his companions then finally at the sergeant.

'I am grateful they are better soldiers than singers,' Lausard smiled.

Karim nodded.

'Will you not join them, my friend?' the Circassian wanted to know.

'If the enemy heard that racket there would be little need of bayonets or swords. I feel we would be victorious without firing a shot. Surrender would be inevitable. What sane man could bear to hear *that* noise for more than ten minutes?'

The men within earshot laughed.

'Better to hear them singing than crying,' Rostov offered.

Lausard nodded in agreement.

'That's true,' he muttered. 'There have been enough tears these last ten years and I have no doubt there will be more.'

'It hasn't been so bad these past three years, Alain,' Rostov continued. 'There has been peace in France since 1800. Ever since the Austrians were defeated.'

'And where do we find ourselves now?' Lausard wanted to know. 'On the brink of war with England. Preparing to invade.'

'At least it's only twenty-six miles across the Channel,' Delacor said. 'It isn't as if we're sailing to Egypt again, is it?'

'While the English command the seas it may as well be twenty *thousand* miles,' Lausard intoned.

The column began to climb the gentle slope that led to the crest of the ridge. As they reached it there was a strong gust of wind. Lausard inhaled deeply and smelled the salt in the breeze. There was a keenness to the gust that they had not felt before. His horse whinnied protestingly and he steadied it with a pat to the neck. Like the other men, he gazed almost disbelievingly at the sight that lay on the other side of the ridge.

Before him was an encampment the size of a small town.

Huts constructed of wood and tarpaulin had been built to house the thousands of men who occupied them. The camp of Boulogne had been transformed from a military base into something resembling a small provincial settlement. The dwellings were arranged with street-like precision and Lausard could see men moving along the thoroughfares, some in formation, some haphazardly.

Beyond this sprawling conglomeration of buildings lay the Channel itself. Silver-grey beneath the sun, it looked choppy and forbidding despite the calmness of the day. The breeze that blew off it felt, to Lausard, like a warning.

The harbour itself, also visible from the dragoons' position, was crammed with every kind of nautical transport ranging from frigates to flat-bottomed boats and barges, all of which were bobbing about in the water like apples in a barrel.

'There are camps like this all along the coast,' Rostov murmured, not taking his eyes from the sight before him.

'Not all as large as this,' Bonet offered, pushing his helmet back slightly. He pulled a battered copy of *Le Moniteur* from his portmanteau and glanced at the newspaper. 'I picked this up before we left Paris.'

'So read it, schoolmaster,' Delacor told him.

'It says there are over two hundred thousand men awaiting the order to invade England in camps like this all along the coast.'

'Who commands here?' Delacor wanted to know.

'General Soult,' Lausard said flatly.

'Wasn't he wounded in Italy?' asked Rostov.

'He and many others I could mention,' Lausard said in the same tone.

The other men laughed.

'This is to be our home until further notice,' Captain Milliere called. 'I suggest we acquaint ourselves with it.'

The column moved forward.

The camp at Boulogne was the largest of those housing French troops along the coast. Situated at Moulin-Hubert, it contained, like the other encampments, an army corps numbering over twenty thousand men. Each corps comprised between two and four infantry divisions, a brigade or division of light cavalry, between thirty-six and forty cannon and additional detachments of engineers and train troops. The infantry demibrigades of the revolutionary wars had been replaced by regiments. Four regiments to each division. The composition of the corps was kept deliberately fluid both for the benefit of the commanders and also to confuse enemy intelligence.

In addition to the main corps, there was a cavalry reserve composed of two divisions of cuirassiers, four of mounted and one of dismounted dragoons and light cavalry, all supported by twenty-four guns. An artillery reserve, containing a large proportion of twelve-pounders and accounting for almost a quarter of the armies' total cannon, was also available. The most formidable of Bonaparte's reserve was the newly formed Imperial Guard. The unit was an extension of the old Consular Guard and had, like the rest of the fighting force, been streamlined and re-equipped along lines the Corsican had been perfecting for the last four or five years. During that time, the entire composition of the French army had undergone radical change, transforming it from

5

an already powerful force into a weapon of war capable of meeting and destroying any enemy sent against it.

Each of the corps was commanded by the very best and most able of Bonaparte's generals.

General Bernadotte commanded the First Corps at Hanover. Marmont had the Second Corps at Utrecht. Davout, who had set up his headquarters at Bruges, commanded the Third Corps. The men were spread out between Flushing, Ostend, Walcheren Island and Dunkirk. Soult was in command of the Fourth Corps at Moulin-Hubert. Lannes had the Fifth Corps close to Boulogne.

The Sixth Corps, under Ney, was at Montreuil. The Seventh, commanded by Augereau, was at Brest.

Bessiéres commanded the Imperial Guard while Murat had the reserve cavalry, itself numbering over twenty-two thousand horsemen.

Two hundred thousand men. Superbly trained, well equipped and led by generals who embodied the spirit of the revolution. Men of courage and ability. Men who had, for the most part, risen from humble beginnings and attained their posts through their own skill, hard work and loyalty rather than by any fortune of birth.

Bernadotte and Soult were the sons of lawyers. Lannes' father had been a peasant farmer, Ney's a cooper. Bessiéres' father had been a surgeon. Murat was the offspring of an innkeeper, Augereau of a mason. Marmont and Davout were the sons of officers who had served France faithfully.

Many of their men were seasoned veterans of the Italian and Egyptian campaigns. The rest had donned uniform out of patriotic fervour and a desire to serve both their country and the little Corsican who had made it great.

Bonaparte could be rightfully proud of the men known collectively as the Armies of the Coasts of the Ocean.

Lausard glanced around him as the dragoons moved through the encampment. Many of the wooden dwellings had brightly coloured awnings over the doors. Some even had makeshift porches. Smoke rose from a number of the chimneys and, every so often, the men would catch the enticing aroma of cooking food.

Joubert rubbed his large belly as he passed one such building.

As they walked their horses along the wide thoroughfares between the rows of buildings, Lausard glanced up and saw that many of the roadways bore names. He saw Rue Albert Ferrer and, further on, Rue Louis Genet.

'They are the names of men who died in battle,' a voice nearby informed him and the sergeant glanced around to see a corporal of grenadiers nodding towards the signs. The corporal was dressed in a blue forage cap, a white shirt and breeches and a pair of immaculately polished shoes. He was puffing away at a pipe, watching as the dragoons passed him.

Lausard saw that the hut outside which the corporal stood had a garden. Carefully cultivated, it was well planted with potatoes, carrots and cabbages, all of which seemed to be thriving.

The infantryman walked alongside the dragoon sergeant, patting the flank of his sweating horse.

'Have you come far?' he wanted to know.

'From Paris,' Lausard told him.

'It looks as if you dog-faces have got it easy here,' Delacor told him, motioning around at the comfortable dwellings.

The corporal glared at him.

'You'll find out how easy soon enough,' he snapped. 'You'll be drilling until you drop. General Soult has us at it for twelve hours every day. I think he is trying to kill us before we even get to England.'

'How long have you been here?' Lausard wanted to know.

'Ten months. Ever since I returned from Egypt with what was left of my regiment.'

'We know of Egypt,' Lausard told him. 'We were there too.'

'A waste of all our time. Let us hope *this* invasion is more successful. At least the English are not savages like those Arabs were.'

'He's talking about you, Karim,' laughed Carbonne. 'You're a savage.'

The Circassian bowed exaggeratedly in the saddle.

'I am no Arab, thanks be to Allah, all praise to Him,' he murmured. 'And no savage.'

'We have our fair share of savages in this unit,' Lausard said and glanced at Delacor.

The men nearby laughed.

'I noticed that you had a fine supply of cabbages and other produce,' Joubert added, reaching into his tunic pocket and fishing out one sou.

'We are encouraged to grow our own food, to cultivate gardens,' the corporal explained.

'Would you be good enough to accept this as payment for some of your food,' the big man continued, offering the coin.

'Go to hell,' the corporal snapped. 'Even if it was for sale it would take more than that to buy it.'

'But I am starving,' Joubert insisted.

Delacor slapped him on the shoulder.

'Shut up, fat man,' he hissed. 'And don't be giving your money to this dog-face.' He looked down at the infantryman.

'You'll be begging for it soon,' the corporal told him. 'All of you.'

'If we want it, we'll take it,' Delacor snapped.

'I'll be waiting for you,' said the corporal defiantly.

'Then we all look forward to our next meeting,' Lausard informed him, nodding towards the ground. 'In the meantime, it might interest you to know that you are standing in horseshit.'

The cavalrymen laughed.

The corporal looked down to see that Lausard was right. He spat in the direction of the dragoons, watching as they rode on. He chewed angrily on the stem of his pipe a moment longer then turned and headed back towards his hut.

Two

Lausard carefully sponged the eyes of his horse, patting the animal as he did. It was a magnificent chestnut, as alert and energetic as its rider. Unlike a lot of the men who fought on horseback, the daily routine of feeding and grooming a horse was not something the sergeant found tiresome. As far as he was concerned, the animal was as much a part of his armoury as the two pistols, the sword and the carbine he carried. Besides, it had carried him through peace and war, suffered the same extremes of heat and cold as he and generally experienced all that was good and bad through the course of service to the army. He owed this creature, in many ways, as much as he owed any of his human companions. What he was careful to avoid, however, was too much of an attachment to the animals he rode. He had lost count of the number of horses killed under him during battle, or those that had simply died of disease, exhaustion or starvation during his time in the cavalry. Respect for his mount was one thing, but too much kindness, too much caring would only result in more suffering. It was bad enough grieving over dead colleagues without worrying about dead horses too.

The animal pawed the ground with one hoof, sending up a cloud of dust, and Lausard patted it again as he sponged its nose and mouth. It nuzzled the grass and found some choice clumps on which to chew as the sergeant reached into his portmanteau for the currycomb and began working its stiff bristles over the chestnut's gleaming coat. It was a big animal, bred, he assumed, in Normandy or Gascony. This kind of mount was usually secured for the cuirassiers; the heavy cavalry needed beasts well capable of physically carrying troopers clad in steel breastplates and helmets as well as the plethora of equipment they bore. Lausard was glad this one had escaped them. Once the work on the horse was complete, he would polish the saddle and harness itself.

The saddle, including the pistol holsters and seat, was of plain leather. The girth was fabric. The stirrup leathers and martingale were white Hungarian leather, the stirrups themselves were blackened iron for troopers and NCOs but bronzed for officers. The breastplate, securing straps and crupper were of black leather, as were the bridle and reins, the snaffle-bridle and the parade halter. Pistol holster covers were of the same green as the white-lace-edged fabric shabraque and the portmanteau. The regimental number was embroidered on the end of the portmanteau and the corner of the saddlecloth.

Lausard paused for a moment, looking along the line of horses, most of which were being tended by their riders. Others, having finished their tasks, were already firmly ensconced in their billets, the dragoons having been allocated a position between some horse artillery and an infantry battalion that had also arrived that same day. The huts, built close together as if for comfort, were located in a thoroughfare named the Rue Henri Justin. Lausard thought about what the infantry corporal had said that afternoon, about the streets being named after men who had died in battle. He wondered in which battle Henri Justin had met his death. In the savage fighting in Italy back in '96 or '97? At Mondovi, Arcola or Rivoli? Perhaps in the hell that had been Egypt in '98 or '99 or the slaughter at Marengo three years ago? For fleeting seconds he wondered how this man had died. By bullet? Bayonet? Sword? Lance? Had he been ridden down by horses? Crushed beneath the wheels of a wagon? Burned alive in the flaming infernos at Rivoli or Marengo? Or had his life been ended by some other means? Perhaps even by his own hand. Lausard had seen enough men resort to that during the last nine or ten years, driven beyond their limits by what they were forced to endure. And who had he left behind him? A family that still mourned him to this day? A wife? Children? Or had he, like Lausard, been alone? What manner of man had this Henri Justin been? A man like himself? Lausard exhaled wearily. During the last ten years he had begun to wonder exactly what kind of man that was. He wasn't the same person now. It was sometimes as if he existed within this body but was merely looking down upon himself, his old personality watching this new incarnation with the same interest a teacher watches a promising pupil. The aristocrat watching the peasant. The noble watching the thief. The coward watching the soldier. There were so many contradictions within him. Had this dead man who now intruded upon his thoughts, this Henri Justin, had *he* struggled with so many inner demons? Lausard doubted it. Just as he doubted that the man would have left his family to die as he had done. Doubted if he would have betrayed his class and his background just to remain alive. Would he have fled the ravages of the revolution to live among its perpetrators, all to save his own life?

Lausard had sometimes wondered if his own self-loathing might be diminished if he merely came to terms with his situation. Most men would do anything to stay alive. Surely he was not alone there? But how many would allow their families to be murdered to ensure their own survival? He feared the answer was very few. It was that realisation that dug needles of regret and shame into him. His family had lost their lives. He had lost his honour and any shred of self-respect when he fled from them. He had lived with vermin in the Paris gutters because, in his mind, he *belonged* with vermin. From noble to thief. From aristocrat to criminal. From criminal to soldier. It had been a journey that, in Lausard's eyes, could have but one conclusion. From soldier to sacrifice. And again there was the contradiction. He knew his only hope of regaining honour was by death on the battlefield and yet he fought with incredible savagery to preserve a life he felt was worthless. His own. What would Henri Justin have told him to do? This dead man, this man who probably wanted only to live? This man who he would never know.

His musings were interrupted by a familiar voice.

'I wish every man in the squadron was as conscientious about caring for their mount, my friend.'

Lausard turned to see Lieutenant Royere standing behind him.

The officer reached out a hand and stroked the neck of Lausard's mount.

'A beautiful animal,' he mused. 'Unlike the remounts they usually give us.' The officer smiled.

'In times of war when we need good mounts they send us donkeys,' Lausard mused. 'Now, in three years of peace, they supply us with the finest riding stock. When donkeys would, perhaps, be preferable.'

The officer laughed.

'Three years of peace,' he sighed. 'Is that all it has been? How quickly time passes.'

'Peace is of no use to soldiers, Lieutenant, you know that. We exist for war. Conflict at least gives us a purpose.'

Royere shrugged.

'Are our lives truly so empty without it?' he murmured.

Lausard didn't answer.

'It appears you will have your wish again very soon, my friend. The war with England is just a matter of time. Does that please you?'

'I take no pleasure in war, Lieutenant, but I understand it.'

'It is to be war against another monarchy this time. A German king on an English throne.'

'Then *you* should welcome this conflict, Lieutenant. Wasn't that the purpose of your revolution? To remove crowns wherever they are worn?'

'I still retain some revolutionary ethics, my friend, that is true. I thank you not to sneer at them quite so openly.'

Both men laughed.

'And if we win, what will we replace this German king with?' Lausard mused. 'We already have a First Consul for life. What is that if not a king by another name?'

'Bonaparte was appointed First Consul by the French people. He occupies his position because men like you and I put him there.'

'If that is true, we put him there with swords, not with votes,' said Lausard flatly.

'His popularity was won on battlefields, not in the senate or tribunate, I grant you that. But the fact remains, he is a democratically elected leader. The leader that France wants.'

'Your idealism is showing again, Lieutenant.' Lausard smiled. 'Perhaps you would be better off trading your uniform for some robes of state.'

Royere nodded sagely and grinned.

'So, we go to fight a German king on an English throne led by a Corsican at the head of a French army,' the officer remarked.

'And until then, we wait,' Lausard said.

'Alain!'

The shout came from one of the huts close by. The sergeant looked up to see Charvet standing in the doorway beckoning to him.

'The food is ready,' called the trooper.

'Won't you join us, Lieutenant?' Lausard asked. 'It is a humble meal in keeping with the ideals of the revolution.' The sergeant grinned broadly.

'Despite your impertinence, my friend, I would be delighted to join you.'

The two dragoons made their way towards the hut, the smell of cooking wafting invitingly on the evening breeze. The heat of the day had given way to a distinct chill and Lausard was happy to reach the welcoming warmth of the billet.

A fire had been built and a large copper cooking pot

was suspended over it. The smell emanating from it was wonderful. Charvet stood over the pot stirring it with the end of his bayonet. The other men sat around, metal plates gripped in their eager hands.

'Come on, Charvet, I'm starving to death,' Joubert observed, his stomach rumbling threateningly.

'Take your time, fat man,' Delacor chided. 'You've got enough blubber to keep you going for a week, it's the rest of us who are in need of food.'

The other men laughed.

Lausard and Royere took their positions amongst the others. The sergeant sat down next to the young trumpeter, Gaston. Royere seated himself between Moreau and Tabor, both of whom nodded a greeting then watched with interest as Charvet stirred the contents of the pot one final time and began dishing up the repast.

'Not dining with the rest of the officers, Lieutenant?' Rocheteau asked, pushing his plate forward. 'Where is Captain Milliere?'

'He received orders to report to General Soult's headquarters earlier,' Royere told the corporal.

'We'd better make the most of this meal then,' Roussard muttered. 'We'll probably be leaving for England tomorrow.'

'I doubt it,' Lausard offered, accepting his plateful of food from Charvet. 'As long as Nelson has control of the seas, we won't be moving from here.' He bit into a piece of meat and chewed appreciatively. 'This is pork, isn't it?' he asked.

Charvet grinned.

'It's good broth,' Royere remarked, chewing on some carrot.

Rocheteau also smiled.

'I thought we only had dried rations,' Lausard offered.

'We did,' Rocheteau chuckled. 'But some of our comrades in the infantry were kind enough to supply us with some of their own home-grown vegetables.'

'And a tender suckling pig,' Charvet announced.

Lausard grinned broadly. 'When did you steal them?' he wanted to know.

'As soon as it got dark,' Giresse told him.

Royere shook his head.

'You see, Lieutenant,' said Lausard. 'We may be thieves but we eat well.'

'We eat well *because* we're thieves,' Rocheteau added.

The men laughed.

'No one said grace,' Moreau protested. 'We should have thanked God for this food before we ate it.'

'You should thank the grenadiers we stole it from, not your God,' Rocheteau told him.

Moreau clasped his hands together, closed his eyes and some of the other men watched as his lips fluttered soundlessly. Only then did he begin eating.

'After all these years you still believe in a God, Moreau?' Rostov said, chewing on potato.

'So does Karim.'

'Not *your* God,' the Circassian answered. 'I believe in Allah, all praise to Him.'

'What's the difference?' Delacor wanted to know. 'A name? God. Allah. Jehovah. The same thing. Call Him what you will, he has no place here.'

'All men call upon Him in the heat of battle,' Moreau snapped. 'There are no atheists once the cannon open up.'

'If a man is destined to die then no God is going to prevent it. Not yours *or* Karim's.'

'You should ask Bonaparte his opinion of the Church,' Lausard offered.

'He is a heathen,' Moreau said venomously.

'He made France Catholic again,' Lausard reminded his colleague. 'The Concordat he signed with the Pope brought Catholicism to this country.'

'And at what price?' Moreau snapped. 'Seizure of Church lands and properties. Bishops required to take an oath of allegiance to *him*, not to God. Bonaparte himself took it upon himself to *choose* bishops. The ones who would serve him best.'

'That is because most of the others before them were corrupt,' Lausard countered.

'Or in the pay of England,' Bonet added. 'Many were traitors spreading sedition. They used their pulpits for treason.'

'The Church is more corrupt than the government,' Rocheteau mused, finding another piece of meat in his broth.

'And the government itself is merely a puppet of Bonaparte,' Tigana interjected. 'The whole country is run by him.'

'He already rules France, Italy and parts of Switzerland,' Lausard said. 'He plans to rule England next. Perhaps his manipulation of the Church was his first step towards confronting the only place where he has yet to unleash his armies.'

'And where is that?' Moreau wanted to know.

'Heaven itself,' Lausard grinned.

The men around him laughed. Moreau met the comment with an angry glare. He finished his food in silence.

Giresse took a swig from a bottle of wine and offered it to Lieutenant Royere. The officer gratefully accepted.

'Good wine, too,' he observed. 'Where did you get it?'

'The same place as the vegetables,' Giresse told him, grinning.

Several other bottles were passed between the men. Some drank directly from them, others retrieved their tin cups and filled them with wine.

'A toast,' said Rocheteau, raising a bottle. 'To the conquest of England.'

The men drank.

'To women,' Giresse offered, licking his lips.

They drank again, each toast greeted by a cheer.

'Here's to Gaston's virginity,' chortled Delacor.

The young trumpeter turned as red as his tunic and Lausard slapped him playfully on the shoulder.

'To food,' Joubert said, belching loudly.

'To France,' Lieutenant Royere intoned.

'To survival,' Roussard added.

Lausard raised his bottle.

'To fallen comrades,' he muttered. 'To those already dead and those who are yet to fall.'

Three

Napoleon Bonaparte reached out a hand and gently traced the smooth curves of the alabaster vase. It was a magnificent piece of work, identical to the one set on the other end of the mantel above the ornate fireplace. Both had been brought back from Egypt, along with countless other treasures, and used to decorate the Corsican's offices and chambers in the Tuileries. Other trophies of that campaign and the more recent one in Italy also adorned the magnificent rooms. Yet more had found their way into his private quarters inside the palace itself. Flames danced in the grate and, every so often, a servant would hurry in with more wood to ensure the room remained warm. Yet Bonaparte seemed untroubled by extremes of temperature. His mind appeared to be elsewhere, his gaze fixed on the gleaming white vase.

He was dressed in a white linen shirt, breeches and black Hungarian boots. His hair was short, cropped above his collar. His features were a little fuller now, in his thirty-fourth year, than they had been in his twenties, but his cheek bones were still as finely chiselled and his eyes carried a permanent glint. When he moved it was with a short, decisive and almost agitated step and, despite his relatively small stature, his very presence gave him the appearance of someone much larger. It was a presence befitting his position as First Consul of France. Power rested easily on his narrow shoulders. The Corsican thrived on his responsibilities, as adept in his political manoeuvrings as he was at the head of his army. Given the choice, however, he would sooner have been in the field than constrained by the strictures of government.

Bonaparte continued gazing at the vase for a second longer, then turned to face the other men in the room. It was as if a spell had been broken.

'War with England is not only inevitable,' the Corsican said flatly. 'It is to be welcomed.'

There was a murmur from the others but it was Charles Maurice Talleyrand who spoke first. The Foreign Minister cleared his throat and shifted in his seat.

'Would it not be more prudent to continue the commercial war against them longer before committing troops to an armed struggle?' he asked.

'Sanctions against imported English goods will not force them to surrender,' Bonaparte declared. 'French troops in London *will*. I will negotiate a peace from Windsor Castle itself.'

'Sea-borne trade has suffered since war was declared,' Joseph Bonaparte offered.

'And who declared it?' the First Consul countered. 'Not I. Anyway, English sea trade has been impeded too. It has caused a decline in the value of their pound.'

'They feel that the terms of the Treaty of Amiens have been breached,' Talleyrand announced. 'The general feeling within the British government is that your sole motive for granting a peace was to obtain enough time in which to rebuild a fleet in preparation for invasion.'

'I gave them the peace they wanted. After Austria surrendered, they were isolated. They had suffered poor harvests two years running, Pitt's ministry collapsed and they feared we would invade as early as 1801. It was *they* who needed the peace, not us. And yet their Prime Minister, Addington, chose to open negotiations only after Nelson had attacked Copenhagen and their campaign in Egypt was gaining strength.'

'The terms of the treaty were very favourable to France,' Talleyrand reminded him. 'We agreed to restore the Kingdom of the Two Sicilies and the Papal States but to retain Nice, Savoy, Piedmont, the territories on the left bank of the Rhine *and* Holland. In addition to guaranteeing the independence of Portugal and the Ionian Islands.'

'I am well aware of what we agreed to do, Talleyrand,' the Corsican snapped. 'And, in return, the English agreed to return the Cape, Egypt, Malta, Tobago, Martinique, Demerara, Berbice and Curaçao.'

'They wanted remuneration for the maintenance of prisoners of war and the restoration of the Prince of Orange,' Joseph interjected.

Bonaparte laughed bitterly.

'You see,' he said. 'They demanded money to reinstate another monarchy. If I remember correctly they also wanted the restoration of the King of Piedmont. They wanted rulers in lands that belonged to France.'

'They would have been nominal figureheads with no power,' Talleyrand said wearily.

'That is not the point,' the First Consul bellowed. 'They chose to dictate to me when *they* were the ones so desperate for peace. They insulted everything France had striven to obtain during the revolution by their insistence on reinstating monarchs in countries conquered by Republican armies.'

A heavy silence descended, broken only by the crackle of flames from the fireplace. The other men in the room looked at each other then at the First Consul, each reluctant to speak. They were somewhat relieved when the Corsican himself continued.

'And remember,' he muttered. 'They are the aggressors, not us. Addington has done everything short of issue an ultimatum. He has placed an embargo upon all French shipping in English ports.'

'And you demanded the arrest of all British nationals resident in France or passing through here or any of our territories,' Talleyrand said.

'What did you expect me to do?' snapped the Corsican. 'Sit by idly while the English dictate how this war unfolds? Besides, most of those arrested have been spies anyway.'

'There is no proof of that,' Talleyrand protested.

'I have it on very good authority that *chouan* agents are operating from Jersey,' remarked Joseph Fouché. The Minister of Police sipped at his glass of wine and smiled thinly.

'Word from Davout, in command of the Third Corps, is that these English spies come like flies to rotting meat,' Bonaparte continued. 'He hangs them daily when he catches them.'

'Addington still argues that his country has been provoked into war,' Talleyrand said.

Bonaparte merely shook his head.

'He cites the invasion of San Domingo by General

Leclerc,' the Foreign Minister continued. 'The sale of Louisiana to the United States.'

'Eighty million francs that were sorely needed in our coffers to help finance this war,' the Corsican interrupted.

'Nevertheless, Addington and the English feared you were planning some kind of manoeuvre in America itself.'

'The American President, Jefferson, made it quite clear that if France remained in Louisiana he would side with the English *against* us in the event of war,' Bonaparte snapped.

'It was Colonel Sebastiani's mission to the eastern Mediterranean and the proposed expedition to India that Addington objected most strongly to. The British were convinced those incidents signalled our continued interest in Syria and Egypt. Sebastiani's comment in *Le Moniteur* that it would require only six thousand men to reconquer Egypt did little to appease English fears. It was only with the greatest reluctance that they ordered the withdrawal of their troops from that country.'

'Then why did they not also evacuate Malta?' the First Consul demanded. 'The British have used nothing but a series of legal technicalities to justify their continued occupation of the island. As long as they possess it, they hold the upper hand in controlling the Mediterranean. That is a flagrant breach of the terms of the Treaty of Amiens.'

Talleyrand got to his feet and walked across to the fireplace where he took up a position close to the Corsican. For long moments he regarded the First Consul quietly and, when he finally spoke, his voice was soft.

'I have made genuine attempts to find grounds for conciliation and the prospects of a lasting peace between

England and France,' he said quietly. 'If you feel my efforts have been a failure then I will happily resign but I must say to you, my friend, that my attempts have been thwarted at every turn by your own determination *not* to allow peace to be maintained.'

Bonaparte put his hand on the Foreign Minister's shoulder.

'The Treaty of Amiens was only ever intended to give me time to mobilise and prepare for what was an inevitable conflict,' he said. 'A First Consul cannot be likened to these Kings-by-the-grace-of-God, who look upon their states as a heritage. My actions must be dramatic, and, for this, war is indispensable. I have too much at stake to let foreigners take the initiative.'

'But it is not just England,' Talleyrand continued. 'Russia and Austria are both unhappy with our influence in Germany and the Austrians continue to take issue with our presence in Italy. If they so chose, the English could easily find allies to join them in a war against us.'

Bonaparte nodded almost imperceptibly.

'If that is how it must be,' he announced, 'then I will meet the threat of three enemies.'

'The people of France want peace.'

'The people of France want victory. I will give them what they desire.'

Four

The first rank of dragoons moved forward like a green tide.

Moving at a hundred and twenty paces a minute, harnesses jingling, the cavalry made their way across the large expanse of open ground. Lausard chanced a look to his left and right and noticed how straight the line was. Riders completed their movements almost robotically. Years of training and fighting had turned them all into consummate horsemen, able to obey commands at the trot, the canter and the gallop without a second thought.

The first squadron, of which the sergeant was a part, continued at a walk until an order was bellowed, then the speed increased to the two hundred and forty paces a minute of the trot. The ground began to shake as the massed ranks continued to move forward. Twelve paces behind came the second squadron, also formed into eight lines sixty files wide. Another twelve paces further back came the third squadron. Then the fourth. The entire unit moved with a fluidity born of practice both on battlefields and parade grounds. Men guided their mounts effortlessly.

A blast from the trumpets signalled that the unit was to increase to the four hundred and eighty paces a minute of the gallop. They thundered on until another signal told them to change formation. Like some huge amoebic mass, the dragoons filtered into a closed column, twenty files wide and thirty-two deep. The other three squadrons did likewise, the entire formation turning one hundred and eighty degrees behind the galloping figures of Captain Milliere and Lieutenant Royere. Further signals from the trumpeters slowed the column from a gallop to a trot once more then, quickly, to a walk.

High above, the sun moved slowly across the cloud-flecked sky and some of the horses were lathered by their exertions. Lausard guessed that these manoeuvres had been going on for well over four hours now. They had followed the same pattern for the entire duration of the exercise. The regiment had advanced in line by squadrons, then into column and back again. He couldn't remember exactly how many times the action had been repeated but guessed it was more than thirty. There had been only brief respites between movements, once to allow the horses to drink. The exercises were being carried out in full dress with the dragoons carrying a full complement of equipment. Much more of this and both men and animals would be exhausted.

No more than two hundred yards to their right, a regiment of cuirassiers had been engaged in similar drill. Lausard had looked more than once at these imposing figures. Big men on big horses, the watery sun glinted off their bearskin-trimmed steel helmets and polished cuirasses. Their blue saddlecloths flapped in the breeze. The leather at the top cuff of their boots was reinforced. When they rode, they rode knee to knee, in action and in training. Their effect, when launched against an enemy, was designed to be that of a mounted battering ram. Their trumpeters, in brightly coloured jackets, dashed ahead of the lines and columns blasting out the notes that signalled formation changes. To a man they rode greys and the distinction between them and their companions was striking. Almost without exception, the horses ridden by these heaviest of cavalry were black and dark brown. Lausard wondered what they would have looked like to enemy forces as they bore down upon them at the charge.

He looked in the direction of a small hill and saw several officers there, some dismounted, most watching the proceedings before them through telescopes. One walked with a slight limp as he wandered back and forth before his staff and it was this particular officer upon whom Lausard fixed his gaze.

General Nicolas Jean de Dieu Soult was dressed in a gold-trimmed blue tunic and sported a black bicorn with a large white feather attached to the tricolour cockade. His wound had been inflicted in the last Italian campaign and he stopped his pacings every so often to massage the injured leg, finally climbing into the saddle of his horse when the discomfort became too intolerable.

'I've got a feeling the General might have more chance of killing us than the English at the moment,' murmured Lausard, nodding in the direction of Soult who was himself gesturing in the direction of the cavalry and speaking animatedly to one of his staff.

'Twelve hours drill a day, three times a week,' gasped Rocheteau. 'The man's insane. He *will* kill us.'

Lausard managed a grin.

'A man can never have too much training, Corporal,'

Captain Milliere offered as he rode up alongside the leading dragoons.

'No wonder the dog-faces were complaining about him,' grumbled Delacor.

'I'll bet they've all got sore feet,' chuckled Tabor.

'Well I've got a sore arse,' Delacor snapped. 'I've never spent so much time in the saddle. Not even on campaign.'

'I don't mind this,' Roussard interjected. 'At least while we're drilling we can't get killed.'

'Don't count on it,' Rocheteau snapped. 'We'll all be dead of exhaustion within a fortnight.'

Some of the other men laughed.

The column continued across the huge open area, more than one man glancing across to watch the cuirassiers thundering along at a gallop, swords raised high above their heads.

'They're quite a sight aren't they, Alain?' Giresse noted.

'They're probably thinking the same about us,' Lausard mused.

'We'll go round once more,' called Captain Milliere.

'Are we finished then, Captain?' Joubert wanted to know. 'I'm hungry.'

'You're always hungry, fat man,' Delacor snapped.

'The General has other delights for us,' Milliere told him. 'Sword and bayonet sharpening. To be followed by practice with each weapon. Cartridge making. Target practice and drill on foot.'

'Perhaps you were right, my friend,' Lausard grinned, slapping Rocheteau on the arm. 'General Soult *is* trying to kill us.'

Karim wiped the scimitar with a damp cloth and examined the razor-sharp steel closely, running his hand along the flat of the blade. That task completed, he slid it carefully back into its engraved scabbard and drew his regulation weapon from its sheath. The dragoon sword was standard issue to all heavy cavalry: three feet long with a single cutting edge, wicked point and steel guard. It was designed for cutting or stabbing but the men had found, over the years, that the maximum damage could be inflicted by driving the point into an enemy. It wasn't unusual for men to survive a number of cuts but to be speared by the lethal steel was a different matter.

The reverse was true of the scimitar Karim carried. Despite the lightness, even the perceived fragility of the blade, the curved sabre was incredibly strong and as sharp as a razor. A cut was just as likely to sever a limb and, on more than one occasion, Lausard had seen men decapitated by one blow from the superb blade. The sergeant watched as the Circassian slid the dragoon sword back into its scabbard and sat forward in his saddle.

Ahead of the dragoons there were four lines of wooden stakes. Twenty in each line. About six feet apart, each was roughly five feet tall. Some were padded, others had infantry shakos propped jauntily atop them. One or two even had pumpkins jammed on to the tops. Lausard and his men had performed the exercise often enough. They had to ride between the sets of stakes, striking at each one in turn. First to the left, then to the right. The sergeant watched as Rocheteau set off, urging more speed from his horse as he drew nearer the stakes. The corporal struck at them with practised skill. He missed two on his first pass. On the way back he missed just one.

First Roussard then Tabor rode the gauntlet of stakes with similar success.

Delacor missed three of the wooden markers but managed to cut one of the pumpkins.

One by one, each of the men made their circuit of the stakes with varying degrees of success.

Tigana, realising he was going to miss the final stake, merely rode his horse into it. There was a great roar of laughter from the watching dragoons.

Captain Milliere grinned.

'There is nothing wrong with that,' he called. 'Your horse is as much a weapon against the enemy as your sword or carbine. If you can't *cut* them down, *ride* them down.'

Tigana smiled triumphantly.

'It's a wonder he didn't try to steal the stakes.'

Lausard turned in the saddle as he heard a familiar voice.

Sergeant Delpierre rode up, scratching at one of the pockmarks on his face.

'Still pretending to be soldiers, Lausard?' he chided.

'We *are* soldiers,' the sergeant said quietly.

'You're scum. You always have been and you always will be. Criminals. Thieves, rapists, murderers, horse thieves, heretics. You are an insult to that uniform.'

Lausard regarded him evenly.

'Would you dare to challenge one of us?' he asked, nodding towards the lines of stakes.

'A wager?' Delpierre grunted. 'How much?'

'Three francs that you cannot hit as many stakes as one of us.'

'Which one of you?'

'Myself.'

Delpierre grinned crookedly.

'Give the signal, criminal,' he hissed, drawing his sword.

'Let me see the money,' Lausard told him. 'I don't trust you.'

Delpierre dug in his surtout pocket and pulled out three coins. Lausard did the same. The two men handed the money to Rocheteau.

'The most strikes wins,' Lausard said. 'I'll go first if you prefer.'

Delpierre urged his horse forward and set off at a canter towards the first line of stakes. He steadied himself in the saddle then put spurs to the animal. It thundered on and he began striking at the stakes one at a time. Pieces of wood flew into the air with each impact. He carved a chunk from one of the shakos, hacked a lump from one of the pumpkins and then turned his horse and rode back up the next line, sword flashing in the watery sunlight. His strokes were impressively accurate and he was smiling as he reined in his mount before Lausard.

'Two misses,' Rocheteau informed him.

'Your turn, criminal,' Delpierre said flatly. 'Or would you rather just give me the money now?'

Lausard said nothing. He coaxed his horse forward, gradually building speed as he drew nearer the first line of stakes. He pulled the sword clear of the scabbard and struck at the first length of wood. Quickly he brought the blade back again, cutting into another stake. He carved the peak from the first of the shakos he encountered. The speed and power of the strokes were extraordinary. He turned his horse and rode back, hacking at the next row with similar expertise. The men cheered as he reined in his mount.

'Two misses,' Rocheteau announced.

'What is to become of the money?' Giresse enquired. 'You are equal.'

'You were lucky, Lausard,' Delpierre hissed. 'Let us keep our money until another time.'

'Would you accept a challenge from me, Sergeant?'

Delpierre turned to see Karim lead his horse forward.

'The Arab,' Delpierre sneered.

'I am Circassian and I repeat my question.'

'Go on. Do your best, *Sandman*,' the sergeant grinned.

Karim bowed his head then sat upright in the saddle and, to the astonishment of the watching troops, took the reins in his teeth. He drew both the scimitar and his sword then, with one weapon gripped tightly in each of his fists, set off at a trot, gradually building speed as he neared the stakes. He guided his mount straight down the middle of two parallel rows of stakes and, as the mesmerised dragoons watched, he struck at both sides simultaneously. Lausard grinned as he watched the Circassian hack through the wood with ease. He split one of the pumpkins in two with the scimitar then wheeled his horse, sheathed his sword and hurtled back towards the waiting cavalrymen. But this time, using the scimitar alone, he struck down with dizzying speed and accuracy, carving into the stakes from the top. By the time he rejoined his watching companions, they were cheering wildly. Karim spun the scimitar and sheathed it, his gaze directed straight at Delpierre.

'No misses,' Rocheteau called loudly and the men cheered once again.

'Pay up,' Lausard said. 'Give the money to Karim.'

Delpierre glared first at Lausard then at the Circassian.

He gripped the coins in his fist for a moment then tossed them on to the ground.

'You want the money, you pick it up,' he sneered.

Lausard drew his sword with incredible swiftness. The coins had barely hit the mud before he had the point of the weapon pressed against Delpierre's throat.

'*You* pick them up,' he said quietly.

Delpierre tried to swallow but, as he did, he felt the cold steel against his windpipe.

'You would threaten one of your own?' he muttered. 'Side with an Arab against one of your own countrymen? What kind of man are you, Lausard?'

'The kind that would stick you like the pig you are. I am *not* like you, Delpierre. The only things we share are our nationality and our flag. Don't ever presume to think there is anything more that unites us. Now pick up the money.'

Very slowly, Delpierre dismounted and retrieved the coins. Karim took them gratefully, watching as the other man swung himself back into the saddle.

'One day I will kill you,' he told the sergeant.

'You will try,' Lausard murmured.

Delpierre tugged on his reins and rode off, the laughter and jeers of the other dragoons ringing in his ears.

Only then did Lausard sheath the sword.

The rhythmic sound of marching feet filled the air and Lausard looked across in the direction of an infantry regiment as it drilled. Divided into its requisite number of battalions, while one marched the others performed musket manoeuvres. Arms were held at port. At the shoulder. At 'Present'. Every movement was carried out with practised precision by the men as officers and NCOs bellowed orders and drums beat. Occasionally horns would be used to signal a change of speed, from the normal seventy-five paces a minute to the faster 'double pace' that could be anything from a hundred and eight to a hundred and twenty paces a minute. This was used for change in formations and for deployment before the enemy. Lausard now watched as the infantry deployed from line to square, the usual method adopted when facing cavalry. The two centre companies remained steady while the three on either flank fell back, forming the sides and rear of the formation. The two front ranks kept their muskets, complete with the seventeen-inch bayonets, at waist or chest height, the steel perimeter forming an impenetrable metal hedge, while the two ranks behind would fire into the attacking horsemen. If necessary, the front ranks would kneel, pressing the butts of their muskets against the ground and tilting the bayonets up to form this *chevaux de frise*, but, as was being practised, the battalion could still advance if necessary while continuing to protect itself from enemy horsemen. The movement was completed with seamless skill and the sergeant was further impressed to watch the entire mass of blue-clad men move across the training ground while retaining their shape. As he gazed at the spectacle he saw a familiar figure riding close by the square, the large white plume on his bicorn blowing in the breeze.

General Soult shouted a few orders of his own at the infantry and Lausard watched as they broke up, still marching, from square into column, again without a break in their step.

'At this rate, the dog-faces are going to run out of shoes before they run out of bullets,' Delacor said and the men around him laughed.

'It looks as if Marshal Soult is trying to kill *them* too,' Rocheteau echoed.

Again the others laughed.

'Would you change places with them?' Roussard wanted to know. 'Would you rather be an infantryman than a cavalryman?'

'And have to do all that marching? Never,' grunted Delacor.

'But they have no horses to worry about,' Giresse offered. 'Once we have finished our drill we must ensure our horses are cared for. They need only relax and put their blistered feet into cooling water.' He sighed wistfully.

'And they have only one set of equipment to clean,' Carbonne added. 'We have our own uniforms *and* the saddles and harnesses of our mounts to take care of.'

'Well, *I'd* rather ride anyday,' Joubert offered.

'That's because you'd rather have a horse carrying your fat arse than carry it yourself,' Delacor snorted.

'I wouldn't want to be in the infantry,' Gaston added. He patted his horse's neck with pride and the animal tossed its head as if in agreement.

'I bred horses all my life,' Tigana said. 'I feel as much at home with them as I do with men.'

'I *stole* them all my life but *I* feel more comfortable with women,' Giresse intoned.

The men laughed loudly.

'What about you, Alain?' Rocheteau asked. 'Would you prefer to fight on foot?'

'What are we?' Lausard asked, a slight smile on his face. 'We are dragoons are we not? Trained to fight on horseback *and* on foot. We have the best of both worlds.'

'Or the worst,' Rocheteau grumbled.

'Look at it this way,' the sergeant said. 'The infantry only get blisters on their feet. We get them on our arses too.'

The men laughed.

'We have twice as much equipment to look after,' Lausard continued. 'We have to find food for our horses as well as ourselves. We have to ensure they are watered and cared for. We have more responsibilities than the infantry. To answer your question, no. I would not change places with the infantry nor with any man in this army. And, when the time comes, when we are charging towards enemy infantry, riding them down, cutting them to the ground, tell me then where you would rather be.'

'There is another advantage to being horsemen,' Roussard added. 'If we have to, we can run away quicker.'

A great roar of laughter erupted from the men.

Even Lausard joined in.

Some of the infantry, still drilling, glanced across to see what the noise was. More than one of them wondered why the squadron of dragoons passing by were laughing so uproariously.

Five

General Louis Alexandre Berthier ran a hand through his hair and regarded the maps and drawings before him with a combination of amusement and irritation. Dressed in a blue jacket, sumptuously decorated with gold braid and lace, he looked as imposing as his title suggested, and as comfortable and relaxed in a uniform as most men would be in a smoking jacket. The Minister of War was in his fiftieth year and much of that time had been spent in the service of his country. Like his father before him, he had joined the royal army at a young age and, from his thirteenth birthday onwards, had been involved with the military in some way, shape or form. He took a pinch of snuff and stood back from the maps, aware that the eyes of the First Consul and the other men in the room were upon him.

'I trust you have decided to dispense with some of these more fanciful ideas for the invasion of England,' Berthier said, finally turning towards the Corsican.

'Such as?' Bonaparte wanted to know.

'The suggestion of building a tunnel beneath the Channel for one,' the Minister of War said dismissively.

Bonaparte smiled.

'Just as I have dispensed with the notion of invasion by steam-powered boats,' he grinned. 'Or by balloon. I see you were not impressed by these ideas, my friend.'

Berthier shook his head.

'So what are we left with?' Bonaparte murmured. 'What I had always envisaged. An amphibious landing. I estimate it would take no more than ten hours to land a hundred and fifty thousand men on the shores of England, using flotillas to transport them across the Channel.'

'Speed is of the essence,' Berthier remarked. 'If the English discover our landing sites it would make getting ashore very difficult.'

Bonaparte shook his head.

'The coast is unprotected by fortifications and undefended by a regular army. What men they have there are scattered along the coast,' he declared. 'They would not be able to unite quickly enough to prevent our advance upon London. Once their capital is seized they would have little option but to surrender.'

'They are a proud people,' Talleyrand interjected. 'Their patriotism would raise another hundred thousand troops should a call to arms be made.'

'It would be too late by then,' the Corsican responded. 'Once in London, our objective would be fulfilled. They could raise half a million men and still be unable to deflect us from our goal.'

'Have you considered the possibility of partisan activity?' Berthier wanted to know. 'We have already seen evidence of what a powerful tool it can be. The "barbets" in Italy caused problems to our men in '96 and '97.'

The Corsican raised a hand dismissively.

'Did they alter the outcome of the war? No. They were an annoyance, nothing more. It would be the same with English partisans.'

'How do you propose to make the crossing of the Channel when Nelson still commands the seas?' Joseph Bonaparte wanted to know.

'A squadron will be collected in the Antilles,' the First Consul began, running his finger over a map. 'From there it will come under full sail to Boulogne to provide protection for the flotilla.'

'And what do you expect Nelson to do while our ships cruise the Channel?' Joseph persisted. 'Sit back and sip tea?'

'Another fifty vessels sailing from Toulon, Brest, Rochefort, Lorient and Cadiz will unite at Martinique. The English will not allow a force of that magnitude to menace their possessions in the two Indies. While Nelson's fleet seeks them out off the Cape of Good Hope, the ships assembled at Boulogne will secure the landing on the English coast.'

Berthier exhaled deeply.

'Something troubles you, my friend?' Bonaparte stated.

'I have no doubt our armies are superior to those of the English,' the officer stated. 'But I do not share the same confidence in our navy.'

'Ten hours,' the First Consul hissed. 'That is all we need. Do you doubt their ability to secure even such a short time for us?'

'Nelson pursued us half way to Egypt when we invaded and that was the other side of the world. If he had caught us, he would have destroyed us. *You* know that. Our navy

41

could do nothing to protect us then. And yet now we are to face him in his own waters?'

'Not if this plan works,' Bonaparte snarled, his voice rising in volume. 'What I mentioned earlier is only a part of it. There are French ships of the line rotting at anchor in ports all over the country and I am happy for them to do so. The price of keeping them there is small compared to the price the English must pay maintaining their blockading squadrons. As long as they keep these "watch-dog" forces in position, they leave other parts of the ocean free to be exploited.'

Berthier nodded but the Minister of War remained unconvinced.

'Even if the navy manage to secure the Channel,' he said, 'the war with England would need to be concluded swiftly.'

'I agree,' Talleyrand interjected. 'Signs grow daily that we will face opposition from both Russia *and* Austria. The moment you set foot in England may be the signal for one or both of them to attack France herself. Should that happen, you risk losing everything you have won during the past ten years.'

'You think I am not aware of that?' the Corsican snapped. 'Until the murder of Tsar Paul, I need not have feared any intervention from Russia but this son of his, Alexander, he is now counselled by the very men who helped destroy his father.'

'There seems little doubt that Alexander knew of the plot against his father,' Talleyrand interjected. 'He seemed both unable *and* unwilling to prevent it.'

'He wanted power. He wanted his father's crown. Why *would* he have prevented it? His ambition appears to know no bounds. Not even those of family loyalty,' Bonaparte hissed. 'He is as keen to expand his empire as ourselves or Britain.'

'British and Russian foreign policy has had a tendency to conflict during the past few years,' Talleyrand offered. 'Alexander's interest in Turkey, the Baltic states and Malta in particular have bred suspicion between their statesmen. Britain is largely reliant upon the Baltic for supplies of timber, tar, hemp and other supplies for their navy. They had no wish to find them in a country under Russian rule. The irony with Malta is that, as you know, by the terms of the Treaty of Amiens the British were to return the island to the Knights of St John.' The Foreign Minister smiled. 'It is somewhat unfortunate for them that the Grand Master of that order should happen to be the Tsar of Russia.'

Bonaparte and the other men in the room laughed.

'So how great a threat to France is this boy Tsar?' Berthier wanted to know.

Talleyrand shrugged.

'Russia has an interest in both Italy and Germany as well as Malta, the Levant and the Mediterranean,' said the Foreign Minister. 'The Peace of Luneville made ourselves and Russia coexecutors of Germany as well as making Russia the guarantor of that country's neutrality. The Tsar is not happy with the territorial adjustments we have made in that region nor with the seizures of territory in the Po valley in Italy. He has been further troubled by Colonel Sebastiani's mission to the Levant. Russia feared it was a sign we intended to occupy the Morea or Montenegro.'

'Is that why Alexander felt it necessary to seize Corfu?' Bonaparte snapped.

'Quite possibly.'

'What of the Austrians?' Berthier asked. 'Have they as many grievances?'

'If anything, they have *more*,' noted the Foreign Minister, smiling. 'They have two lost wars and two unfavourable peace treaties to avenge. They lost a great deal of territory in Italy and Germany. It is the Rhineland area they are particularly aggrieved about.'

'It is the destruction of that archaic monstrosity the Holy Roman Empire they truly mourn,' the First Consul offered. 'Its principalities were controlled by them. Reducing those from three hundred and fifty to thirty-nine damaged their hold on that part of Europe. The fact that we are now protectors of those remaining thirty-nine doubtless also troubles them.'

'Like Russia, they also fear our expansion in Italy,' Talleyrand added. 'Particularly the annexation of Piedmont and Elba and the seizure of Naples. The fact that the former Queen of Naples is mother-in-law to the Emperor of Austria himself no doubt added to the pain of its loss.'

There was more laughter inside the room.

'So, what is to be done?' Berthier asked, looking at the First Consul. 'If we move against England we risk inviting two other enemies against us. Do you really want to fight a war on two fronts, possibly three?'

'I will fight wherever I have to for the sake of France,' Bonaparte told the Minister of War. 'I trust you will be at my side wherever that fight may be.'

'You need never doubt that,' Berthier told the Corsican.

Bonaparte put a hand on the general's shoulder.

'Europe is like a powder keg waiting to explode,' the First Consul said quietly. 'When it ignites, the blast will be felt around the world. Let us be grateful it is *we* who hold the match.'

Six

To a soldier of Alain Lausard's experience the sound was unmistakable. As he rolled out of his wooden bed the shattering noise filled the air again and again.

The sergeant knew, even before he reached the door of the hut and dashed out into the chill of the February morning, that the sound was cannon fire.

For fleeting seconds, he had wondered if he was dreaming. Sleep never came easily to him; it hadn't for longer than he cared to remember and, even when it did, he slept fitfully and lightly, likely to be awakened by the slightest disturbance. This had served him well during his years in the field, but there was nothing slight about the disturbance that now catapulted him from sleep.

Rocheteau was at his side, also having recognised the tell-tale blasts.

All along the Rue Henri Justin, men were spilling from their billets, wondering, like Lausard, where the thunderous explosions were coming from.

For fleeting seconds, Lausard wondered if the artillery might be undertaking some early morning practice but as

45

he squinted through the mist he realised that was not the case. Besides, he had heard the retorts of his own side's four- and eight-pounders enough times to recognise those blasts. These were different. Furthermore, they came in a kind of rolling volley. The sound also seemed more distant.

Captain Milliere emerged from the hut nearby dressed in just his boots and breeches. He looked at Lausard as if expecting the sergeant to identify the source of the fire that had shaken him and so many other men from their slumbers but the NCO could only shake his head.

There was a ridge about one hundred yards ahead and, beyond it, lay the beach that sloped gently down to the freezing water of the Channel itself. It was towards this ridge that Lausard now ran, with Rocheteau in pursuit.

As he drew nearer he saw several blue-clad artillerymen dashing back and forth in the mist, one of them carrying a swab, several others staggering under the weight of cannonballs.

There was another thunderous volley and Lausard heard a sound all too familiar.

The high-pitched scream of a cannonball.

It cut through the air, carving a path in the mist before thudding to earth less than ten yards behind him. Rocheteau spun round just as three more of the deadly missiles sped to earth, one of them striking a wooden hut occupied by sappers. The projectile splintered wood and sent lumps of it spiralling into the air. The next brought the roof down. Two sappers stumbled from the wreckage of the hut, one of them clutching at a head wound. By now, Lausard was hauling himself up the reverse slope and he and Rocheteau reached it almost simultaneously. Behind them, trumpeters were blowing frantically to rouse the remaining men from their billets as another volley of shot came hurtling out of the mist and thudded into the camp. Another hut was hit. Elsewhere, geysers of earth erupted into the air as the canonballs buried themselves in the ground.

The crew of the four-pounder loaded the piece and waited, portfire lit.

'Why the hell don't they fire?' Roussard wanted to know, suddenly appearing beside Rocheteau and the sergeant.

'Because they can't see anything,' Lausard said flatly, staring into the impenetrable mist.

Even as he spoke, a breeze picked up, parting the mist like a veil.

Lausard found himself gazing at a British frigate that was making its way through the choppy water less than one hundred yards from the beach. Beyond it were two other, larger ships of the line and Lausard could see men moving about both on the decks and also in the rigging. Even as he watched there were more loud explosions and one of the ships let loose with another volley of shot. Men nearby ducked down as the cannonballs came hurtling through the air. The crew of the French four-pounder lit their fuse and there was a thunderous roar as the cannon spat out its load. The shot missed, sending up a geyser of water where it landed. They hastily reloaded and now, all along the ridge, the French artillery were beginning to return fire. At first there seemed to be no cohesion to the gunners' efforts but, slowly, they began to fire by batteries and the thunder of four- and eight-pounders filled the air as surely as the broadsides being fired from the English ships. The cloying stench of gunpowder began to replace the crispness of the early morning air.

To Lausard, it seemed as if the majority of the firing was now coming from the guns close to him. The three English ships seemed to have been surprised by the ferocity of the French reply and appeared content to drift along merely watching the troops who had gathered along the heights. He watched as two battalions of infantry, moving with clockwork precision, loaded, aimed and fired their muskets in the direction of the ships. The blast was deafening and it soon grew in volume as more blue-clad foot soldiers joined in. A great cheer rose from the massed ranks as part of one of the frigate's sails was shredded by the clouds of musket balls. The infantry continued firing, many of their shots falling short, but a sufficient number peppering the closest of the three vessels.

Rocheteau smiled as he saw the ships turning away, seeking the safety of the deeper water and the distance that would take them out of harm's way.

The corporal of the nearest four-pounder knelt and sighted the gun, adjusting the screw at the base of the bronze barrel to alter the trajectory of the shot. When he was satisfied, he stepped back and one of the other gunners lit the fuse with the portfire. The gun spewed out its load, the recoil sending it hurtling back six or seven feet.

Another huge cheer greeted this shot. Even Lausard managed a grin as he saw a portion of the main mast of the nearest ship blasted away. Part of the sail collapsed on to the deck, covering the men beneath like a huge shroud.

The infantry battalions opened fire again, huge clouds of smoke mingling with the mist that drifted off the Channel. Lausard looked around and saw a familiar figure seated on a magnificent bay. General Soult looked on with delight as the infantry poured more volleys after the ships. One of the staff officers with him stood in his stirrups and waved his hat in the air triumphantly.

'If he continues making them drill for twelve hours a day they'll turn those Charlevilles on *him*,' Lausard murmured with a smile.

'Go on, run, you bastards,' roared Delacor, shaking his fist at the English ships.

They were now disappearing from view into the ever-thickening mist, grateful for its camouflage.

Some of the other dragoons had joined Lausard and Rocheteau in gazing out to sea and they too watched as the ships slipped from sight and range.

'A warning?' Bonet offered.

Lausard nodded almost imperceptibly.

'To remind us it is they who rule the seas,' he mused.

'We kicked their arses,' Delacor insisted. 'We have nothing to fear from them.'

'I wish you were right,' Giresse murmured.

'If *our* navy could stop them, I'd feel much better about this crossing,' Roussard added. 'If they catch us in mid-channel . . .' He allowed the sentence to trail off.

The infantry shouldered arms and marched back to their billets, saluting General Soult as they passed.

By the time Lausard looked seaward again, the ships had completely disappeared.

Throughout the last twelve years of his life, Alain Lausard had found that time seemed to have lost its meaning. Each day was more or less indistinguishable from the last and had been for as long as he could remember. When he had lived in the gutters of Paris as a thief the days had been depressingly similar. Waking in some rat-infested building, scratching an existence in the streets and markets, preying on those who had as little as he. After his arrest, he had faced the soul-destroying monotony of imprisonment. Cramped in a twelve by twelve cell day in day out, knowing his only release would be a trip to the guillotine. The army had rescued him, like so many of those he fought alongside. They had released him from one form of captivity into another. He had exchanged the tedium of a cell for the regimentation of a fledgeling army, but it was a change he had welcomed. The days had become endless bouts of training. After that, his world assumed two very distinct patterns: the crushing tedium of marches and bivouacs, and the savagery of fighting. Since 1801, the time that had always passed so slowly for him had seemed to stop altogether. For Alain Lausard, peace brought the curse of inactivity. Unlike other men, he did not welcome it. As he sat on his bunk polishing his scabbard he looked around at the other men of his squadron billeted with him. Like himself, they had all been criminals at one time or another; some would say they still were. But, to Lausard, they were companions now. Bonet, the former schoolmaster. Moreau, the religious fanatic. Giresse, the horse thief and womaniser. Roussard, the forger. Delacor, the rapist. Rocheteau, the thief. Carbonne, the former executioner. Charvet, the gambler. Rostov, the political prisoner. Men like himself? Twelve years ago, no. But now they were as brothers to him. All of them, he knew, felt the same frustration as he. For five months now they had been at the camp of Boulogne, their lives a routine of drill, rest, then more drill. The time had advanced with excruciating slowness. Winter had passed and they were now in late February of 1804. Lausard was beginning to wonder if they would still be in this camp when the next winter arrived. And for the other two hundred thousand men of the Army of England, it was the same tale. All they could do was wait.

It was comfortable in the camp, Lausard didn't deny that. Many of the men, his own companions included, seemed content to remain. To some it was better to suffer the daily rigours of drill and the boredom of confinement than to face cannons and bayonets. It was not a sentiment Lausard shared. Only on a battlefield did *he* feel truly alive. Something had perished inside him long ago. It had died as surely as his family had died beneath the blade of the guillotine. Only in the heat of battle could he forget the pain of that loss. Only when faced with even greater suffering could he purge himself of an agony that gnawed at his soul like a rat at a piece of carrion. And he knew that pain would continue until his own death released him from it.

He looked around at the men he had come to know as companions.

Several of them were playing cards, using cartridges as currency.

Joubert was chewing on a dried-up carrot, watching the game.

Sonnier was cleaning his carbine.

Gaston was brushing his red trumpeter's tunic with meticulous care. Once he had finished he began polishing the silver buttons with a piece of rag.

Charvet was mixing flour and water to make dough, watched by Carbonne and Tigana. Every now and then he would hold up the dough proudly. His father had been a master baker and Charvet was proud of the skills he had inherited.

Giresse was sketching, using a piece of charcoal. Lausard finished his task and wandered across to inspect the former horse thief's work.

It was a magnificent representation of a mounted dragoon, riding at the gallop, sword held above his head.

'Is that you?' Lausard asked, smiling.

'Alain, if it was me there would be a woman in the saddle with me,' Giresse grinned without looking up.

'If it was Roussard he'd be riding in the other direction, *away* from the enemy,' Delacor interjected.

'Joubert would be eating the horse,' Rocheteau added.

The men laughed.

'You have a great talent, Giresse,' Lausard told the trooper.

'There is magic in these fingers. Any of the women fortunate enough to have met me will tell you that.' This time he laughed.

Bonet was also busy with a piece of paper and a quill, the feather scratching across the parchment as the former schoolmaster wrote in his elegant hand. As he worked, Tabor sat beside his bunk watching, eyes scanning words that were as indecipherable to him as if they had been in a foreign language.

'Why don't you teach the half-wit to read instead of wasting your time with that?' Delacor sneered, glancing round at Bonet and the big man.

'Perhaps I should teach *you* to read,' Bonet answered.

'I read well enough, schoolmaster. I don't need you to help me.'

'Can you write?' Bonet wanted to know.

'I have no need to write. I would not waste my time as you do.'

'What are you writing, Bonet?' Lausard asked.

'As you know, General Soult is very keen on concert parties,' the former schoolmaster said. 'I thought I would contribute a short play for the next one. It's about a soldier who wants to marry his childhood sweetheart before he goes off to war, only to discover she is the daughter of his commanding officer.'

'More plays acted by men in skirts,' Rocheteau rasped. 'I'm sick of these concert parties.'

'I'm sick of seeing men in skirts,' Giresse added. 'We saw enough of those in Egypt. I want to see *real* women.'

'Take care what you write, Bonet,' Lausard told him. 'The General is choosy about what he allows us to watch. I heard that he refused to permit one play to be performed because it contained the part of a cowardly French soldier. As far as General Soult is concerned, there *are* no cowards in the French army.'

'I am beginning to wonder if any of us will ever have the opportunity to prove that,' Rostov offered. 'We have been here for longer than I care to remember. When will Bonaparte give the order for us to invade?'

'As long as English ships can cruise the Channel unchallenged as they did this morning,' Lausard explained, 'there will be no invasion.'

'So we sit here and rot,' rasped Delacor.

'We are soldiers. We obey orders,' Lausard told him flatly.

'And the latest order is that we are all to be docked one day's pay a month to finance that infernal bronze monument that our General wants to erect to Bonaparte,' Delacor snarled.

'It is to commemorate the invasion,' Bonet said, without looking up. 'No one had any objection to it when they thought the government were paying for it.'

'I fear it will be a waste of all our money,' Lausard said, heading for the door.

'Where are you going, Alain?' Rocheteau wanted to know.

'I have no idea, my friend,' the sergeant answered, smiling. 'If you see Bonaparte, be so good as to ask him where *any* of us are going. Or, more to the point, *when*.'

He closed the door and stepped outside, leaving laughter echoing behind him.

Seven

The sound of marching feet echoed through the still night air, drifting up towards the window where Napoleon Bonaparte sat. He gazed out into the blackness, the shouting of orders rising with the tramp of boots from the Tuileries Palace courtyard. Inside the bedroom two lamps burned, their low flames colouring the walls a burnished yellow and imparting a bronzed look to the silk curtains that hung around the large bed. It was from beyond those curtains that the voice came, a voice still musical to the Corsican's ears.

'What troubles you?'

The words floated on the warm air like fine perfume.

Bonaparte turned in their direction and saw Josephine sitting on the edge of the bed, slender legs drawn up beneath her. Even in the subdued light of the room he could make out the piercing, almost hypnotic blueness of her eyes. Her olive skin looked ebony in the gloom, a stark contrast to the paleness of the sheets.

Even after eight years of marriage, his passion for this

woman was as intense as it always had been, and the sound of her voice, as mellifluous to his ears as any he had ever heard, held him spellbound.

'It is late and yet still you do not sleep,' she said softly. 'Is the burden you carry so great?'

'I carry the burden of a nation,' he said wearily.

'Through choice. And it is the choice of that nation that you should be where you are today.'

Bonaparte managed a smile.

'And where is that?' he mused. 'I sometimes wonder if I enjoy only improvised greatness.'

'You are First Consul of a country that loves and respects you.'

'France reveres me. My enemies despise me. My own Generals envy me. There is not one among them who does not think himself as deserving as I.'

Josephine rose from the bed and made her way across to her husband. She slipped both arms around the Corsican's neck and hugged him to her.

'They all insist they are Republicans,' he continued. 'And yet, at one time, they spoke of dividing France between them as if it were some captured principality, not the country of their birth. That is why the people gave *me* power. They know that France's greatness is dependent upon a strong leader.'

'And you are the only one who has that strength. Why do you doubt yourself now?'

'I do *not* doubt myself. But it saddens me that I cannot trust those whom I should be closest to. Men like Moreau and Bernadotte. Men who have fought for France, fought for *me* and yet still harbour their own dreams of power and advancement.'

'Is it not the nature of all men to seek power?'

He nodded almost imperceptibly.

'Perhaps I was a fool to expect loyalty from them all,' he said quietly. 'Power and position bring their own burdens. It appears that one of those is solitude.'

'You will never be alone as long as I live,' she told him, kissing his head.

Bonaparte turned and pulled her to him, inhaling her scent. For long moments they remained locked together then he took a step back, tracing a pattern on her cheek with an index finger.

She held his hand and kissed it tenderly.

'I fought to replace a monarchy with a Republic,' he said, turning back towards the window, peering down at the grenadiers who guarded the entrances to the palace. 'I led armies across Europe, across the world, to remove kings and now I am left, it seems, with little choice but to reinstate a form of leadership I myself would have opposed to the death ten years ago. If I die tomorrow, who will succeed me? My brothers? Lucien and Joseph quarrel over the succession as if it were some kind of family heirloom.'

Josephine took a step away from him, tears in her eyes.

'If we had a child there would *be* no problem, would there?' she said softly, her voice cracking slightly. 'Do you blame me for not presenting you with an heir?'

'No. I blame you for nothing. Your own daughter may yet provide me with the solution I seek.'

Josephine looked puzzled.

'The son of Hortense and Louis, my brother, would be able to succeed me, were we to adopt him,' the Corsican said. 'A nephew would be the next best thing to a son. He would carry the name Bonaparte. His accession would provide the continuity required to ensure the solidity of France that *I* have fought to build.'

'And you think the people would accept one not directly of your blood as their ruler?'

He shrugged.

'There is danger in submitting this matter to a plebiscite,' he admitted. 'When one speaks of succession, one speaks the language of kings.'

'So what is the answer?'

'If necessary, I will take by force what I dare not solicit. I will appoint an hereditary successor, if necessary. I have striven for too long and worked too hard to see my efforts erased by the return of some Bourbon princeling. France will accept my decision for as long as I give her victories. This entire administration was founded on bayonets, not votes. It was won on battlefields, not in council chambers.'

'Why do you fear the return of the Bourbons?'

'I fear anything that undermines the stability of France. There are many countries in Europe now housing those who would happily see France restored to a monarchy. Many who fled during the revolution have been merely biding their time, waiting for me to make a mistake. Waiting to restore that which I and so many others fought to remove forever.'

Josephine wandered back towards the bed and lay down, pulling the sheet over her.

'The greatest threat still comes from within France herself,' Bonaparte said quietly. 'Fouché brings me news daily of assassination plots against me.'

'I do not trust Fouché,' Josephine said dismissively. 'Even *I* have been the subject of his spying and deceit.'

'I do not like the man but someone has to do that job.

I must have a Minister of Police and he is a very able man. Whichever level he has to work at. Be it with Royalist spies or those plotters who hide in sewers.'

'Perhaps you are right. Few men seem more suited to crawling through sewers than Fouché.'

'Word has it that he has three penniless princes working for him as well as several exiled Jacobins. One of his most accomplished spies is head gardener at General Macdonald's estate.' The Corsican smiled. 'He seems to be keeping a foot in both camps.'

'And you are prepared to overlook that?' Josephine asked sharply.

'He has access to information others are not even aware of.'

'Only by the grace of God were you not killed four years ago on the way to the opera. That infernal machine that exploded and killed so many. Why did Fouché not know about *that*?'

'He knew who was behind it. A man who is in this country now. A man who plots against me as we speak. Georges Cadoudal. He landed at Biville more than a year ago.'

'Then why has he not been arrested?'

'He is dangerous but he is no fool. There are many willing to hide him. Fouché has had two of his agents under arrest for over twelve months. Under torture, one of them implicated Cadoudal and also mentioned several exiled dukes including those of Artois and Enghien. It is as I said: there are those who will not rest until they see a monarch restored to the throne of France. And only my death can leave the way open for that.'

The First Consul began pacing slowly back and forth, his face cast in even deeper shadow as the candles in the bedroom burned lower.

'At first, I sought genuine conciliation with the Jacobins,' he said quietly. 'Cambacérès was appointed as Second Consul but that was not enough for them. They are men dedicated to violence. They know no other way and so I met *their* violence with my own. Those found conspiring against me I had shot or deported. The same is true of the Royalists who oppose me. I attempted conciliatory measures by appointing Lebrun as Third Consul and how did they receive my olive branch?' There was a note of scorn in his voice. 'With rebellion in the west of France. With conspiracies. Cadoudal himself is little more than a *chouan* leader. Master of the same cowards who preyed upon their own countrymen back in '99. And, behind it all, there are the English. Fouché informed me only today that Cadoudal intends to join forces with the English agent, Drake, who is himself plotting to raise the Rhineland in revolt. They plan to prepare the way for the return of the Duke of Enghien, a Bourbon, at the head of a corps of émigrés.' He turned to Josephine and held out his arms. 'But first, they must remove *me*.'

She eyed him warily.

'I wanted no divisions in this country,' Bonaparte said. 'No Jacobins and Royalists. No Catholics and atheists. No pre-revolution and post-revolution. All I wanted was Frenchmen and France. One people united within one country. The most powerful country in the world. That is what I wanted and that is what I will have. It is a dream I will see fulfilled. And if there is blood to be spilled, I swear it will be that of those who oppose that dream.'

Eight

Sergeant Alain Lausard drew the sword in one fluid movement and held it at arm's length. He was dressed in the short green surtout favoured by dragoons when on campaign, a pair of grey overalls and his boots. His long brown hair was tied back, not in a queue but merely held in place by a strip of leather.

Opposite him, Lieutenant Royere drew his own sword and tapped it gently against the outstretched blade of the NCO. The officer nodded slowly, a signal that he was ready.

Lausard struck first, aiming at the other man's chest but his strike was parried and Royere hit back, bringing his sword down with tremendous power. Lausard blocked it and ducked beneath the swing, cutting at the officer's legs. Royere jumped to avoid the stroke then rolled and stood facing his opponent once again. The blades grated together as both men regained their breath then began again. Thrust was met by counter thrust, every blow parried or ducked. Lausard began to feel sweat running down his face from the exertions and he used the sleeve of his jacket to wipe the droplets of moisture away.

The lieutenant was panting heavily as he struck at Lausard then stepped away, driven back by the counterattack. Each countered blow sent juddering impacts up the men's arms and, more than once, sparks flew from the blades as they crashed together. Royere lunged forward, realising that Lausard was going to avoid the thrust with ease, but the officer's momentum carried him past his opponent. Lausard tripped him, watching him sprawl on the ground. He stepped towards the fallen officer, aiming the tip of his blade at Royere's throat. However, as he did, the officer managed to swing his own weapon around so that it was pressed against Lausard's groin.

The two men, both sweating profusely and gasping for breath, burst out laughing.

'An honourable draw, my friend?' Royere asked, feeling the tip of Lausard's blade against his flesh.

The sergeant nodded, careful to avoid moving any closer to the sword that rested against his genitals. He extended a hand and helped the officer to his feet. Both men sheathed their swords, still chuckling happily.

'So, you intend to enter the competition arranged by General Soult, Lieutenant?' Lausard said as they walked back across the camp.

'It will help to pass the time,' the officer told him. 'Besides, there is a purse worth ten francs for the winner. I trust you will not be entering yourself?'

Lausard smiled and shook his head.

'Is there any form of competition General Soult has *not* arranged?' the sergeant mused. 'Karim won five francs yesterday in a horserace.'

'That does not surprise me. I have never seen a man ride more brilliantly.'

'Sonnier is entering a competition for top marksman tomorrow.'

'Do none of these pursuits interest you, my friend? You would be as likely to win as any man I know.'

'I am not interested in games, Lieutenant. Shooting at targets. Racing horses. Fighting with swords.' He shook his head. 'The only thing I wish for is the order to board the craft that will take us to England. I have more interest in facing men than targets. However, I fear the longer we are here, the less likely that is to occur.'

'I agree with you. I think that if Bonaparte had truly intended to invade then he would have done so before now. With *or* without English domination of the seas.'

'You doubt the intentions of our First Consul, Lieutenant?' Lausard smiled. 'Is that not sedition?'

'This is now a country of free speech, my friend. Made so by the success of the revolution and the efforts of Bonaparte. I am entitled to voice my opinions.'

'For an intelligent man, Lieutenant, you display an extraordinary amount of naivety. Speech in France is only free if it is within the boundaries set by Bonaparte himself. He controls the newspapers. He even controls the Church. The press are nothing more than a mouthpiece for his views and pulpits have become political platforms for those too ill-educated to read. He has been tuning them for years. Priests no longer serve God, they serve Bonaparte. It is *his* gospel they spread.'

'Even if that is true, and I suspect there is some foundation in your cynicism, would you not prefer the restrictions of a First Consul to those of a monarchy?'

'What is the difference?'

'Bonaparte was democratically elected to his position, not *presented* with it by some accident of birth.'

Lausard nodded.

'You are right, Lieutenant, and, if Bonaparte could hear you speak, he would be proud of your patriotism,' he said.

'Why do I detect sarcasm in your tone, Sergeant?' Royere grinned. 'You fight for France with as much fervour as any man in this army.'

Lausard laughed.

'I thank you again for the practice,' Royere said, tapping the hilt of his sword.

Lausard hesitated before the door of his billet.

'Won't you come inside for a moment, Lieutenant? There's something I'd like you to see,' the NCO murmured, guiding the officer towards the hut.

As he pushed open the door and ushered the officer inside, Royere saw that more than a dozen faces greeted his arrival and, as Lausard stepped alongside him, the lieutenant smiled as the men inside the hut burst into song. 'Where could one better be than in the bosom of his family?' was sung with gusto and varying combinations of tuneless enthusiasm by the watching dragoons, every one of whom seemed to be holding a cup or mug in his hand. Indeed, Lausard accepted one for himself then pushed another towards Royere who took it gratefully as the singing finally stopped.

'Happy birthday, Lieutenant,' Lausard said, raising his cup in salute.

The other men echoed the sentiment and Royere grinned broadly.

'I didn't know that you knew,' the officer admitted.

'You forget, Lieutenant,' Lausard told him. 'We are a reconnaissance squadron.'

'*And* we asked Captain Milliere,' Rocheteau added. 'Happy birthday, Lieutenant.'

The other men shook hands with the officer who accepted their congratulations with a smile, thanking each one. As he drank he sniffed the air and detected a quite delicious aroma of cooking food. There was a large metal pot suspended over the fire towards the rear of the hut, the smoke escaping up the makeshift chimney. Tabor was stirring it happily.

'Chicken?' Royere observed.

'Cooked with red wine, onions, carrots and potatoes,' Rostov told him, sniffing the contents of the pot.

'Where did you get chickens?' the officer wanted to know.

'The fifth hussars have some, or rather *had* some,' Giresse chuckled. 'I liberated them.'

'And the infantry of the 29th had a particularly fine vegetable garden,' Rocheteau added.

The men laughed.

'These are the best scavengers in the entire army,' Lausard told Royere proudly. 'As I said to you before, Lieutenant, thieves we may be. Hungry we are not.'

'But before the meal,' Charvet called, pushing his way through his companions, 'you must see your cake. Prepared to my father's recipe.' He emerged with a cake on a metal plate. There was a single large candle stuck in it, already lit.

'Here's to the cake,' called Joubert, raising his mug.

'Here's to Lieutenant Royere,' Lausard said.

The men echoed the toast and the officer nodded gratefully.

'Thank you all,' he said, smiling. 'I will not forget this birthday.'

'By the grace of Allah, all praise to Him, may you have many more,' Karim interjected.

'Let us hope it isn't your last,' Roussard murmured.

'Shut up, you miserable bastard,' Delacor snapped, slapping him on the back of the head. 'We'll have our next celebration in London.'

The men raised their drinks in salute once more.

Lausard looked at Royere and raised an eyebrow questioningly.

'Perhaps we should save a piece of the cake for General Bonaparte,' Tabor said. 'I hear he is coming to review us soon.'

'Where did you hear that, you half-wit?' Delacor wanted to know.

'I was speaking to one of the men in the second squadron and he said that the First Consul was visiting here to see that all was ready for the invasion.'

'Perhaps he's coming to give the order for us to leave,' Rocheteau offered.

'We'll see,' murmured Lausard.

'Don't save him any cake, there's barely enough to go around as it is,' Joubert whined.

'There isn't enough for *you*, fat man,' Giresse said. 'Lieutenant Royere is taking the cake with him when he leaves.'

Joubert looked desolate as he watched Charvet remove the impressive confection.

The men around him laughed.

'Let us eat,' Lausard announced. 'And Rostov,' he called, 'a double helping for the Lieutenant. He will need all his strength for the fencing competition tomorrow.'

Royere smiled.

Once again, the men broke into song and the sound that filled the hut was a joyous one.

As evening turned slowly to night, hastened by the dark clouds that gathered forebodingly over the Channel, Lausard saddled his horse. He threw the green shabraque over its back then fastened the girth and breast straps securely before swinging himself into the saddle and guiding the animal, at a walk, through the sprawling mass of buildings that was the camp of Boulogne. Wherever he was, either on campaign or, as now, in a billet, Lausard usually took the air at the end of the day whenever possible. He enjoyed this time and preferred to savour it alone. Although more than comfortable in the company of the men of his squadron, Lausard still found solitude a pleasing companion. Sometimes he fooled himself into thinking that his wanderings would prepare him for sleep but, as he had found over the last few years, sleep was something elusive. Perhaps this was for the best, for sleep brought dreams and the kind of dreams it brought were not welcome in Lausard's subconscious.

He guided the chestnut along the Rue Gerrard Larrey, past a number of huts where men sat outside on their makeshift porches. Two cuirassiers, dressed in blue and grey fatigues, raised hands in greeting to him as he passed and Lausard returned the gesture.

Further down the thoroughfare, infantrymen were returning from drill, muskets sloped, sweat pouring down their faces despite the chill in the air. He could hear many voices, he smelled many different aromas as he passed the endless array of huts and other buildings that housed the men of the Fourth Corps. The occasional pop of muskets rang through the air. Sometimes the best way to clean the barrel of a Charleville was simply to discharge it into the air.

As he reached one of the parade grounds, Lausard urged his horse into a trot, then a canter, guiding the eager animal towards the range of low hills that all but hid the turbulent waters of the Channel from view. He noticed that several ten-inch mortars and six-inch howitzers had been sited on the crest of the hills, presumably to deal better with any form of sea-borne attack the like of which they had experienced before. These huge weapons were capable of hurling their deadly projectiles over one thousand yards and, although Lausard had previously only seen them used for siege purposes, he was well aware of the damage they would do to enemy shipping. Several of the blue-clad crews were covering the guns with tarpaulin to protect them against the dampness in the air. Lausard rode past them and down the incline towards the beach, the smell of the sea now strong in his nostrils. He walked his horse up and down the sand, the water lapping within yards of the animal. He could hear waves breaking gently on the shingle further out but could see nothing. The blackness that was gathering over the Channel was growing steadily more impenetrable. On a clear day the cliffs that formed a rampart to the English coast were visible but, in the gloom, he could see no more than a few yards ahead. Lausard continued up the beach for another five minutes then turned the chestnut towards a narrow defile that led up towards the camp.

From his position on the low hill he saw that many of the windows of the huts, lit from within by candles and oil lamps, were spilling a welcoming light into the night. The encampment looked more like a well-established village than a gathering place for fighting men about to embark on the invasion and conquest of another country. That the venture would be successful, Lausard had little doubt. Despite the rigours of the two Italian campaigns and the horrors they had endured in Egypt, the sergeant knew that a combination of Bonaparte's skills as a general and the ability of the French army as a whole would see them victorious. In fact, he reasoned, it was probably *because* of the privations he and those like him had faced in previous campaigns that his mood was so optimistic. Most of the men that comprised the Army of England were either veterans of at least one previous campaign, or they were well-drilled recruits led by able officers and commanded by good generals. Besides, they would encounter none of the natural savagery they had encountered in the previous two campaigns. None need fear the kind of searing heat Egypt had presented them with or dread the numbing cold they had endured crossing the Alps. And yet, for all that, as Lausard guided his horse back towards the billet he felt uneasy. He told himself it was merely anticipation. The months of waiting had gnawed away at him. All he wanted to do now was fight, to face destruction as he had so many times before and experience that incredible sensation he knew so well. A man was never so alive as he was when courting death. So why did he feel this sense of unease, he asked himself. He left his horse in the makeshift stables, ensuring it had enough feed then, trying to push his uncertain thoughts aside, he made for the thoroughfare beyond. Even before he reached the door that led from the stable he smelt something familiar, a cloying, almost fetid odour that clouded the crisp night air.

'Why the hell don't you get yourself some decent

tobacco, Karim?' the sergeant said, waving a hand in front of his face.

The Circassian, who was puffing happily on a pipe, merely looked at Lausard.

'It is a Turkish blend. I always smoke it,' he mused. 'I brought four pounds of it with me when we left Egypt.'

'If Bonaparte smells it he'll have to cancel the invasion. The English will smell it days before we actually land and they will be waiting.'

Karim smiled and took another puff on the pipe.

'They probably will be anyway,' he mused. 'They know we are here. They must know *why* by now.'

'And tomorrow Bonaparte arrives here. For what? To lead the invasion? To issue orders?'

'Who can say? We can do nothing other than wait.'

'Waiting has become a part of our lives during the last four years, Karim. I have no reason to believe that the waiting will end tomorrow.'

Nine

Napoleon Bonaparte paced back and forth, his steps short and agitated. His expression was dark, his eyes blazing. The other men in the room watched the Corsican, aware more than ever of the atavism of the man. All of them knew that this kind of long silence usually presaged an outburst of some kind and none doubted that one was imminent.

'Can there be any doubt as to the validity of this information?' the First Consul finally said, spinning around to face Fouché.

'None,' the Minister of Police told him. 'Querelle was captured by my men a matter of days ago. He implicated Moreau, Pichegru and Cadoudal. There is no mistake.'

Bonaparte paused beside his desk for a moment then suddenly swept his hand across it, sending the items there hurtling on to the floor. A wine glass shattered. Pieces of paper went flying into the air.

'Traitors,' he snarled. 'I have done nothing but good for France and her people and this is how I am treated. With attempts upon my life. Plots against me. Conspiracies intended to remove me from power.'

'Pichegru was a gunner in the Bourbon army in his early days,' Fouché interjected. 'His loyalty has always been suspect.'

'He also fought *against* the enemies of France during the revolution,' Talleyrand offered. 'Was it not he who was responsible for the capture of the Dutch fleet at Texel? He led cavalry across frozen water to do so.'

'Do you seek to excuse his actions?' the Corsican rasped, turning on his Foreign Minister.

'I was merely stating a fact,' said the other man. 'I too find his actions indefensible in this case.'

'An ex-Royalist and a *chouan*,' Bonaparte said, his voice low. 'I could understand *their* grievances. Cadoudal has been trying to kill me for four years but why has Moreau allowed himself to become a party to this treachery? He fought with courage and skill against the Austrians on the Rhine. Is his ambition so great now that he would see me murdered for the sake of his own advancement?'

'It has long been known that he has Royalist sympathies,' Fouché told the First Consul. 'The restoration of a monarchy would be perfectly acceptable to him.'

'And is there any doubt who has been chosen to lead that restoration?' Bonaparte snapped. 'The Duke of Enghien.'

'We have no irrefutable proof of that. The Duke . . .'

Bonaparte interrupted angrily.

'What need is there of proof?' he snarled. 'Isn't he a Bourbon, and the most dangerous one of them at that? Your own intelligence informed you that these conspirators were awaiting the arrival of "a prince". We need look no further than Enghien himself.'

'I suggest we secure more evidence against the Duke before embarking upon any course of action,' Talleyrand suggested.

'What do you need to convince you, Talleyrand? We have the word of prisoners, the evidence collected by Fouché's secret police and spies. Will you only believe when Enghien marches into Paris with troops? When he uses my dead body as his throne to preside over a new monarchy?' Bonaparte glared at the Foreign Minister. 'I am *not* prepared to wait. I have evidence enough. Enghien is the enemy we must strike at. He is the body of the Hydra. Those like Pichegru, Moreau, Cadoudal and their minions are merely the many heads of that Royalist beast. If we cut off a dozen, more will grow back in their place. To crush this rebellion once and for all, we must destroy the very heart of it. That heart is the Duke of Enghien.' He turned to look at Fouché. 'Where is this traitor now?' the Corsican demanded.

'At the Château of Ettenheim, in Baden, not far from Strasbourg,' the minister told him. 'He resides there with his wife, Charlotte de Rohan-Rochefort. Supposedly he has supporters, possibly even troops, at Offenburg. They gather daily.'

'I want him arrested immediately,' the Corsican said flatly. 'I will order troops to cross the border and bring this Bourbon back to France.'

Fouché looked at Talleyrand as if willing the Foreign Minister to speak. Neither man seemed anxious to question the First Consul's decision but it was Talleyrand who finally spoke.

'Baden is within the boundaries of Germany,' he said. 'A country designated as neutral.'

'I know where Baden is, Talleyrand.'

'If you cross its borders you contravene a neutrality act embodied within the Treaty of Amiens.'

'A treaty that is being violated every day by the English,' Bonaparte snorted indignantly.

'Russia herself is guarantor of that neutrality,' Talleyrand continued. 'If you proceed with such a course of action you run the risk of provoking the Tsar.'

'Are you telling me now that I should fear the wrath of a mere boy?' Bonaparte snapped. 'Alexander himself attained his throne because of treachery. Now a country he presumes to protect shelters a man who would destroy France.'

'I agree with Talleyrand,' Fouché offered. 'Such an act would cause unrest within France herself as well as the rest of Europe.'

'Do not presume to tell me what my own people would think of my intentions. Do you believe they would rather Enghien returned to restore a monarchy that they suffered so cruelly under?' He glared at both men, his voice rising steadily in volume. 'The man is a traitor. By bringing him to justice I am striking a great blow that is absolutely necessary.'

'Then be aware of the repercussions you face,' Talleyrand insisted. 'If you violate neutral territory you *invite* Russia to move against you. The results could be catastrophic. If he was on French soil or in enemy territory then I myself would urge you to act, despite the lack of evidence against him. If enough evidence was gathered after his arrest then the law would prescribe his execution. If you kidnap him from his current position, you compromise the interests of France and give Russia and England the fuel they need. Even now the English are looking for allies against France. Arresting Enghien on neutral soil would inevitably push them closer to the Tsar who would take your actions as a personal affront.'

'I am prepared to take that chance,' Bonaparte declared. 'I will have that princeling in my grasp soon enough. No matter what it takes.'

'Even at the cost of peace?' Talleyrand asked. 'You would risk everything for which you have fought, for the sake of one man?'

'Enghien is but one of many who would oppose me. Perhaps it is time an example was made. Those who might follow him will lose the stomach for their treachery when they see what befalls their figurehead.'

Talleyrand shook his head wearily.

'You would take France into war for the sake of your vendetta against the House of Bourbon?' he said accusingly.

'This is no vendetta,' Bonaparte snarled, rounding on him. 'This is justice. Enghien does not merely challenge my authority and position, he seeks to undermine the very stability of France herself. I will not permit that.'

'But we have no proof of this,' Fouché insisted.

Bonaparte turned and headed for the door.

'You can debate this matter among yourselves, gentlemen,' he said, dismissively. 'My mind is made up. I leave for Boulogne in one hour.'

'What you intend is a crime,' Talleyrand offered.

'It is more than a crime,' Fouché added. 'It is a mistake.'

'I will let history be my judge,' Bonaparte told them. 'This matter is no longer of any concern to you. From this point onwards, it is a military operation. I myself will select the troops to carry out this mission.'

He swept out of the room.

Ten

Lausard had woken early that morning. As usual, he had slept fitfully, his own dreams waking him as often as the chorus of snoring that filled the small hut. The third time he had woken he'd found the room in darkness. The sergeant peered out of the window near him and saw that dawn was still an hour or two away. He'd been surprised, therefore, to hear the rattle of the drums sounding '*La Diane*'. After a moment or two, the steady beat was joined by the blaring of trumpets as cavalry as well as infantry were summoned from their slumbers. Lausard reached for his watch. It was 4.03 a.m., an hour earlier than the men were usually called to order. He shivered momentarily then reached for his tunic and boots. All around him a cacophony of grunts, groans and complaints greeted the all too familiar sound.

'It's still the middle of the night,' croaked Rocheteau, rubbing his eyes.

'What's going on?' Bonet wanted to know.

'Time to get up, schoolmaster,' Lausard told him. 'Perhaps Bonaparte has arrived early.'

Joubert was still lying on his side snoring loudly.

Delacor kicked him in the backside.

'Come on, fat man,' he snapped. 'Time to shift your carcass.'

'Call me again when the food is ready,' Joubert moaned and turned over once more.

Delacor hooked his fingers beneath the wooden bed and lifted, tipping Joubert on to the floor. The other men laughed as he floundered helplessly for a moment before scrambling to his feet.

Karim was already prodding the dying embers of the fire with the end of his bayonet, stirring it up to bring some warmth into the room. Charvet checked that the camp kettle was full and hung it over the fire. Karim fed a few pieces of wood into the glowing mass and it began to grow.

The sound of the drums still filled the morning air.

'You know who's behind this, don't you?' Giresse grunted, pulling on his boots. 'General Soult. He probably wants us to drill for even longer today as Bonaparte is coming to review us.'

When the water in the kettle was warm, Karim tipped some into a cup and retreated back to his bunk where he pulled his razor from his portmanteau. He also withdrew a small piece of soap which he dipped into the warm water, making a thin lather that he smeared over his cheeks and chin. He then began scraping the blade across his skin.

'Why are you always so particular about your appearance, Karim?' Delacor asked.

'It's a pity *you're* not,' Rocheteau said, sniffing the air and grinning.

The other men laughed.

'I used to be *very* particular about my own appearance,'

Giresse added. 'When a man is as popular with women as myself, it is only good manners.'

'Well, you won't have to worry about women for a while then, will you?' Rostov said. 'God knows when we'll ever see any again.'

'When we reach England,' Delacor offered. 'There'll be enough for all of us.'

Lausard watched as the men dressed, all except Moreau who was kneeling at the foot of his bunk with his hands clasped together and his head bowed.

'What's he wasting his time doing?' Rocheteau asked, buttoning his surtout.

'Leave him,' Lausard said quietly.

Moreau finally straightened up.

'What were you asking your God for, Moreau?' the sergeant wanted to know.

'I was thanking Him for another day.'

'Another day stuck in this place,' snorted Roussard. 'Another day of drill. Of meaningless exercises. You should be cursing Him, not *thanking* Him.'

'Keep your blasphemy to yourself,' said Moreau.

'You should have asked Him if Bonaparte is coming here today to give the order for the invasion of England,' Lausard offered. 'No one else seems to know when it's going to happen.'

'What do you think he *is* coming for, Alain?' Rocheteau asked.

'A review? To hand out more medals? Who knows?' the sergeant said disinterestedly. Lausard wandered over to the camp kettle. The water was boiling now and he watched as Charvet filled several cups with coffee grounds then poured the water on to them. He handed one to Lausard who sipped at the steaming cup.

There was a loud knock at the door which, a moment later, was opened. Captain Milliere stepped in and the men saluted.

'Sergeant Lausard,' said the officer, 'I want to see you and Corporal Rocheteau in my quarters in fifteen minutes.'

'Yes, sir,' Lausard said, saluting sharply.

'By the way,' the officer continued, 'when the rest of you men are dressed, you are to remain in your billet until further orders. Do not join the other troops. There will be no drill for our regiment today.'

Then Milliere was gone, slamming the door behind him.

'What the hell *is* going on?' Rocheteau wanted to know, fastening his sword belt around his waist.

Lausard could only shake his head. He sipped at his coffee and wondered.

The officers' quarters in the camp of Boulogne were barely distinguishable from those of the rank and file. A few colonels and certainly one or two generals of brigade had larger and more imposing dwellings with bigger gardens, but for the most part there was a uniformity about the camp that, Lausard mused, would have pleased the advocates of revolutionary ethics. No man, despite his position, appeared immediately more important than the next if his billet was anything to go by. So it was with the quarters occupied by Captain Milliere. The hut occupied by himself and Lieutenant Royere was built of the same wood as the other dwellings that made up the camp. Nothing outside gave it the appearance of belonging to men of rank. Lausard approached the door, Rocheteau alongside him. The wooden shutters were still closed. Lausard knocked and was ordered to enter.

As he and Rocheteau stepped inside they found half a dozen men waiting for them. Captain Milliere was seated at a table, a bottle of wine before him. Lieutenant Royere stood behind him. Opposite, their backs to the dragoons, were two aides-de-camp dressed in gold-trimmed blue jackets, a man whom Lausard recognised from his uniform as a major and another individual who also sported a blue jacket heavily embroidered with gold. His gold epaulettes also marked him out as someone of considerable importance. He was a tall man with dark hair and, as he turned to face Lausard, the sergeant recognised him immediately.

General Soult ran appraising eyes over the two NCOs, both of whom saluted sharply.

'Stand at ease,' Soult told them.

Lausard met the general's gaze and waited for him to speak again. He was aware of Soult's gaze. The general finally got to his feet and walked across to the dragoons. He brushed a small speck of dust from Rocheteau's shoulder and muttered something under his breath. Then he passed to Lausard, murmuring approvingly about the state of his uniform.

'You are a credit to your regiment,' he said, standing before them. 'Do not let these high standards drop.'

Milliere looked at the men and nodded almost imperceptibly.

'You were thieves, were you not?' Soult said flatly. 'You, your corporal and most of your squadron.'

'That is true, sir,' Lausard answered. 'We *were*. But then again, show me a man has never stolen *anything* and I will show you a liar.'

Soult laughed sharply, a sound that echoed around the room and was picked up by the other officers.

'Has this man heard of my fondness for art?' the general mused, looking around at the other officers before returning his attention to Lausard. 'You are quite right, Sergeant. We have all been thieves in our day. Some of us still are. Some enemies even call our beloved First Consul the thief of Europe, so it would appear we are in good company.' He poured two glasses of wine and offered them to the dragoons, both of whom accepted. 'Be seated,' he instructed and Lausard and Rocheteau pulled up chairs opposite the general. 'As you know, General Bonaparte arrives here later today to review the troops. I believe you once met him, Sergeant.'

'Yes, sir. In Italy back in '97.'

'He would probably remember you. He has an incredible memory. He prides himself on knowing and remembering the names of all the men he has met, from humble infantrymen up to generals.'

'He might have cause to remember *me*, sir. He stripped me of my rank.'

Soult laughed loudly again.

'Which it took you little time to regain, I see,' he mused, pointing at the three chevrons on Lausard's jacket sleeves. 'You are obviously a brave man.'

'A thief is better off knowing no fear, sir.'

Soult nodded, a smile on his face.

'So, while you were enjoying the sunshine of Italy, I was consigned to the rain and cold of Germany and Switzerland,' the general chuckled. 'Until four years ago. I was wounded at the siege of Genoa.'

'We both received wounds at Marengo, sir,' Lausard informed him.

'Many did, Sergeant. But enough of these reminiscences. They are for old men to speak of to their grandchildren. They have no place here. I received word from General Bonaparte last night. My orders were to select a unit of cavalry for a mission that would be explained to me at a later date. A mission, I hasten to add, that I would not be associated with. That is to be the province of the Marquis de Caulaincourt and General Ordener. The First Consul requires a very special kind of soldier for this mission. Captain Milliere and your squadron were recommended to me by some of my staff.'

'May I enquire if the First Consul requested men who were expendable, sir?' Lausard wanted to know.

'Meaning what?' Soult demanded.

'It would not be the first time myself and the men in the squadron with me have been called upon to perform *special* duties. Our use seems to be limited to tasks others are unwilling to perform.'

'You should be honoured that you have been chosen by the First Consul,' Soult insisted.

'If I knew what we had been chosen *for*, perhaps I might manage some measure of gratitude, sir.'

'You have been chosen because of your outstanding abilities as soldiers. Be grateful for *that*,' Soult rasped. 'When I know the details of the mission I will relay them to Captain Milliere. He will then tell you and your men.'

'Why did you need to see *us*, sir?' Lausard wanted to know. 'If, as you say, you will be passing on the information to the Captain, why was this meeting necessary?'

'I was interested in the *kind* of man who would be undertaking this mission.'

'And may I ask what kind of man you see, sir?' Lausard enquired.

'A man like myself,' Soult told him. 'I am from humble stock like yourself, Sergeant. My father was a lawyer. I myself was a baker's assistant before I became a soldier. What did you do before you joined the army?'

'You already know that. I was a thief.'

'Before *that*,' Soult said, his tone darkening slightly.

Lausard met the general's gaze. He was grateful the officer could not read minds. What would he have thought had he known he was addressing a man who had once been considered part of the upper classes. Not, as Soult thought, the same 'humble stock' as himself. Lausard realised he shared nothing with the general except his allegiance to France.

'I never knew my father, sir,' Lausard lied. 'My only recollections are of the Paris gutters.'

'You have come a long way, Sergeant,' Soult told him. 'Be grateful you will not have to return to that way of life again.'

'I hope you are right, sir,' said Lausard.

The general ran appraising eyes over the two dragoons once more. 'You are dismissed,' he said, turning his back on them.

The NCOs rose to their feet, saluted and marched towards the door.

'Sergeant,' Soult called, a slight smile on his face. 'If your fighting abilities match your insolence, this mission should be of little consequence to you.'

Lausard saluted once more then closed the door behind him.

Napoleon Bonaparte stood motionless on the slope and smiled as he regarded the mass of troops before him. They were drawn up in regimental columns, vast phalanxes of men sporting all manner of different coloured uniforms. The blue-clad infantry, muskets at the 'Present' position, were placed between cavalry regiments and batteries of artillery. Lausard and the dragoons were dressed in their familiar green tunics, the hussars in a dizzying combination of reds, yellows, greens and blues, some wore fur kolpacks, others sported shakos. The cuirassiers were in their dark blue jackets and gleaming steel body armour. Mounted chausseurs, also dressed in green, with red pelisses slung over their shoulders, brilliant red plumes waving on their headgear. Horse grenadiers, dressed, like their infantry counterparts, in blue jackets faced with white and with towering bearskins ruffled by the wind. All of these magnificent troops sat astride their mounts or stood in rigidly straight lines gazing at the low hill upon which their First Consul stood. Lausard could see the Corsican walking back and forth slowly, hands clasped behind his back. Behind him, the men of his staff sat motionless on their own horses. Lausard also saw General Soult and his own aides. A huge man dressed in the uniform of a Mameluke held the harness of Bonaparte's white Arab to quieten it.

'Soldiers of France,' Bonaparte shouted, forced to use all his lung power to make himself heard. 'We stand on the threshold of fresh conquest. No more than twenty-six miles across that water,' he gestured behind him towards the Channel, 'lies England. Our most persistent enemy. Very soon you will embark upon the invasion and subjugation of that country. Something I know you will achieve with ease. The English will not stand against you. They *cannot*. You are the finest fighting force in the world, led by the ablest commanders. You have conquered all who have dared to oppose you. You have helped to make

France great, to extend her borders and her possessions. I know you will not fail when the time comes. I know I can depend upon every one of you. Let us all prepare for our newest victory.' He took off his bicorn and waved it in the air. The gesture was the signal for an eruption of sound that Lausard was sure could be heard in England. Every man watching roared his approval, including many of the dragoons. Men raised their headgear into the air, suspended on swords and bayonets or waved in their hands. Officers spurred their horses back and forth across the heads of the columns, driving the troops to even greater frenzy.

The paroxysm of adoration continued and Bonaparte strode back and forth smiling delightedly, accepting every cheer as an actor would welcome the applause of a grateful audience.

As Lausard watched he saw one of the staff officers step forward, open a large wooden box and stand before the Corsican who reached inside and withdrew one of the many objects there. They glinted in the watery sunlight. Crosses of the Legion of Honour. There were several dozen troops from various regiments gathered together at the foot of the hill on which Bonaparte stood and, at a given signal, they approached the First Consul in an orderly line. The Corsican held the the white enamel cross on its watered-silk red ribbon in the palm of his hand and turned to Soult, a smile on his face.

'It is with baubles that men are led,' he remarked.

The first soldier to approach him was a private of foot grenadiers. He saluted stiffly, trying to prevent himself from quivering as the First Consul approached. The Corsican slapped the man on the shoulders then carefully pinned the Legion of Honour to his breast and kissed him on both cheeks. The grenadier saluted again, the red plume on his bearskin shuddering with each movement. The same procedure was repeated with the lieutenant of hussars who followed. Then the corporal of the 29th Line infantry. It continued almost robotically as each man was presented with the coveted prize.

'Do you think they'll give any of *us* medals?' Rocheteau murmured, watching the ceremony.

Lausard didn't speak. He merely looked on, his expression a combination of indifference and bemusement. The line of troops waiting to receive their decorations now stretched half way up the low hill on which Bonaparte waited. Lausard watched the little Corsican embracing each man and attaching the medals to their tunics. All around, the frenzied cheering of the watching troops continued.

'I wonder how much they are worth?' Giresse mused.

'It isn't their financial worth that's important,' Bonet offered.

'It is if you're going to steal one,' Rocheteau chuckled and some of the other men also laughed.

'What is the purpose of this?' Roussard wanted to know. 'This entire charade?'

'To boost morale,' Lausard told him. 'Bonaparte is as skilful at manipulating men's minds as he is at manoeuvring divisions in the field.'

'I wonder where he intends to have *us* manoeuvre on this mission he would send us on?' Rocheteau wanted to know, a note of disdain in his voice.

Again Lausard had no answer. He leant forward in his saddle slightly, readjusting his position. He and the other dragoons had already been in the saddle for over an hour, their horses standing immobile as other formations moved into position before the Corsican. Now the sergeant leaned on the pommel of his saddle, temporarily taking the weight off his backside and the base of his spine.

'Perhaps we are to be some kind of advance invasion force,' said Carbonne.

'With what purpose?' Delacor snapped. 'To capture England ourselves?'

'When our mission is over, perhaps we will receive a medal then,' Rocheteau grinned, still transfixed by the steady stream of men receiving the Legion of Honour.

'If we're still alive,' Lausard said quietly.

The procession continued up the hill towards the waiting Corsican.

The dragoons of the first squadron, led by Captain Milliere and Lieutenant Royere, left the camp of Boulogne at just after eleven p.m. Lausard checked his own watch and confirmed the time with Rocheteau. The men had been told to take all of their belongings because it was unlikely they would be returning to the camp. Roussard feared it was because they would all be killed during the course of the mission and a number of the other men shared his concern. They passed through the line of pickets that guarded the outskirts of the camp then joined the road leading to St Omer and away from the coast. They moved through the night with impressive speed, resting for an hour every ten miles. They did not bivouac during the night but rode on. Milliere had told them they were to rendezvous with an infantry unit around dawn where the entire force would come under the command of General Ordener. He would lead them to their final destination.

'When are we expected to reach our objective, Lieutenant?' Lausard asked the officer as the cavalry crossed a ford, the quick flowing water of the stream lapping around the horses' hooves.

'I have no idea, my friend,' Royere told him. 'Myself and Captain Milliere have been given no idea what *or* where that objective is.'

'God help us,' Moreau intoned.

'Why should He?' Sonnier muttered. 'He has seen fit to ignore us so far.'

'I doubt if even your God knows where we are destined for, Moreau,' Lausard observed.

'General Ordener will lead the mission once we meet up with his infantry,' Royere said.

'I hope *he* knows where we're going,' Lausard murmured.

The dragoons rode on through the night towards the waiting dawn.

Eleven

The gardens of the Tuileries Palace were in transition. Caught in seasonal limbo, the landscape was struggling to escape the rigours of winter and embrace the coming of spring. Many bushes and trees already had an early flush of leaves, while some of the flowerbeds sported shoots that pushed their way up through the dark earth to greet the new season. But for the most part the gardens in mid-March were still awaiting the onset of warmer weather before they displayed their myriad colours to all those who looked on. From his position high up in the magnificent building, Napoleon Bonaparte peered out at the gardens. When he walked in them now he was escorted by more than a dozen grenadiers of the Imperial Guard. These huge men in their massive bearskins, each the veteran of three campaigns, acted as Bonaparte's personal bodyguard in addition to the hundreds of troops that guarded the outskirts of the palace itself.

'I am still a prisoner in my own house,' the Corsican remarked, watching as a small detachment of guards, dressed in long blue overcoats, marched majestically

along one of the gravel pathways through the gardens.
'Still threatened by enemies who would stop at nothing
to destroy me.'

'Not for much longer,' Fouché told him confiden-
tially. 'Moreau and Pichegru have already been tried
and Georges Cadoudal himself is in custody along with
forty other conspirators. You will soon have nothing to
fear from any of them.'

Bonaparte turned to face his chief of police.

'So you say,' he murmured. 'I hear that sentries are presenting arms every time Moreau appears before them.'

'They still remember him as a good general,' Talleyrand
interjected. 'Perhaps we all underestimated his popularity.
That is also evident by the number of lawyers who refused
to have any part in his prosecution.'

'So, these lawyers are content to turn their backs on
a traitor?' Bonaparte snapped. 'To forget their duty to
France?'

Talleyrand sipped at his wine.

'This conspiracy raises a question that must be addressed,'
the Foreign Minister offered. 'Even if its ramifications are
unpalatable.'

Bonaparte looked at his minister quizzically.

'The matter of succession,' Talleyrand continued.

'Talleyrand is right,' Fouché added. 'This plot of
Cadoudal's is not the first and it may not be the last.
It is time provision was made for the long-term stability
of France.'

'And how do you propose to secure that?' the Corsican
wanted to know.

'Before your appointment as First Consul this country's government resided in the hands of the Senate,
the Tribunate and the Legislative Corps,' Fouché said.

'The loyalty of some was suspect and it still is, you know that.'

'They were still powerless to obstruct my decisions,' the Corsican reminded him. 'When did they ever manage to prevent me pursuing a course of action that I deemed necessary for the well-being of France and her people? They opposed the Concordat with Rome to no avail. They even rejected the first draft of the Civil Code but that too was finally approved. They cannot offer the necessary resistance to the strength of my position as First Consul.'

'But France is only strong as long as *you* are strong,' Talleyrand remarked. 'If some disaster were to befall you, if one of the plots against you had succeeded, then where would France be? Returned to the ministrations of lawyers? Of those you despised and fought so hard to remove? The only answer is hereditary rule. You must take upon yourself a position even greater than that of First Consul. You must ensure that all you have striven for, all you have given to France and her people, does not perish with you. The only way is to find a situation that allows you to designate your own successor. Just as the Roman Emperors did.'

'I have considered that too, Talleyrand,' said the Corsican. 'If it meant the future solidity of France, I would be prepared to accept the position of Emperor. Head of an Empire the like of which has not been seen since Charlemagne in the ninth century. I would be prepared to take on the burden that would come with the title of Napoleon the First. And I have no doubt that the people would support me in this.'

'It may appear to some like the restoration of a form of monarchy,' Talleyrand offered. 'It would be important to stress that was not the case.'

'We are all products of the revolution,' Bonaparte assured him. 'To allow such counterfeit royalism would be to betray our own ethics and those of France. The people would never stand for it.'

'I feel they will tolerate anything that guarantees them stability,' Fouché said. 'The next step is to approach the Senate. First for confirmation of the plan and then for ratification.'

Bonaparte raised a hand.

'This is something the people must decide,' he insisted. 'Just as they elected me to the office of First Consul, it is they who must place the crown of Emperor upon my head.'

'A plebiscite?' Fouché murmured.

'I am the expression of general will in France,' the Corsican exclaimed. 'I have nothing to fear from my own people and everything to gain. I see a new order, rather than a relic of the past reinstituted by hypocrites,' he mused. 'It is certainly the most logical path to take. The creation of an Empire would also remove the threat posed by these murderous conspirators.' He looked at Fouché. 'What news of the most vile of these traitors? What news of Enghien?'

'The troops selected to arrest him are within less than a day's march of the Bavarian border,' the Minister of Police said. 'Latest intelligence reports confirm that they are nearing the Kiel bridge.'

'There is still time to stop them,' Talleyrand offered.

'Stop them?' Bonaparte rasped. 'And allow the Bourbons access to that from which they were ejected? The people carried those fat pigs from the throne to the guillotine eleven years ago and now you expect me to show mercy to one of their kind?'

'For the sake of France.'

'What I do, I *do* for the sake of France,' Bonaparte bellowed. 'And if Russia seeks war because of it then so be it. When that time comes they may find themselves confronted not by a general but by an Emperor.'

Gaston skinned the rabbit with his usual skill then tossed the carcass towards Karim who gutted the dead animal and washed it in the stream. The water was cold and the Circassian watched as it slowly turned red around the flayed rabbit. Further down stream, several infantrymen were washing their tunics in the swiftly flowing water and one of them gestured angrily in the direction of the dragoons as he saw them cleaning the rabbit. Wherever possible, troops in the field were encouraged to keep their uniforms clean. In the event of sustaining a wound, the last thing they needed was for pieces of filthy, germ-laden clothing to be carried into the laceration along with the lead of a musket ball or the cutting edge of a sword. Officers were particularly at risk because they also wore gold embroidered epaulettes and braid on their uniforms and it wasn't unusual for the fibres to become embedded in flesh with little hope of removing them. Infection was then just a matter of time.

Behind them the ground rose gently towards a thick outcrop of trees. Beyond, the road stretched away through the countryside like a scar across unblemished skin. The dragoons and the infantry who had accompanied them for the last four days were camped on the slopes. Most were seated around camp fires. The temperature had dropped sharply with the onset of night and Karim was sure that this particular night felt colder than others during the march. He and the young trumpeter made their way

95

back up the slope carrying the rabbit that was now ready for the pot which awaited it.

'I wonder why we've been allowed to make camp fires?' Gaston mused, glancing at the yellow and orange beacons that littered the hillside. Smoke rose into the air where it was rapidly dissipated by the growing breeze.

'We have no enemy to hide from,' Karim told him.

'None that we *know* of,' Gaston murmured.

The Circassian shrugged.

At the top of the slope was a large tent, the temporary abode of General Ordener. Gaston could see the commanding officer standing outside the tent, arms folded, talking to three of his staff officers. The men were chatting amiably and once or twice Karim even heard sounds of laughter from the group.

'At least someone is happy,' Gaston remarked as the dragoons made their way back up the slope.

'About time,' Charvet called as he saw the two men approaching. He was stirring the contents of a pot with the end of his bayonet and there was a delicious smell rising from it. Karim tossed the rabbit to him and he dropped it into the pot.

Bonet was lying with his head resting on his saddle, reading a copy of *Le Moniteur* that he'd had for more than a week.

Tabor was cleaning the buttons on his tunic, breathing on them then rubbing them vigorously with a piece of cloth to make them shine.

Several more of the men were playing cards.

Lausard sat silently, gazing around at the troops spread out across the hillside.

Karim sat down beside him. Gaston pulled up his collar against the breeze.

'So quiet,' Lausard observed. 'This is more like a field exercise than a mission.' He emphasised the last word with something akin to scorn.

'Things will change when we cross the border,' Bonet offered. 'We are entering neutral territory. I don't think the Bavarians will take too kindly to that.'

'Do you think they will fight?' Roussard asked.

'What would *you* do if someone invaded your country?' Bonet mused.

'So, are we at war with Bavaria?' Tabor wanted to know.

'Of course not, you half-wit,' snapped Delacor.

'Not yet,' Bonet added ominously.

'Then why are we here?' Tabor persisted.

'To arrest a man,' Lausard told him. 'Just as General Ordener said.'

'Three hundred cavalry and infantry for the sake of one man?' Rocheteau mused. 'He must be very special.'

'Or very well guarded,' Roussard said. 'Do you think there will be fighting, Alain?'

Lausard could only shrug.

'He is an enemy of France and of Bonaparte himself,' the sergeant said sardonically. 'Isn't that what we were told? We have come here to arrest a traitor.'

'He's an aristocrat, isn't he?' Rocheteau said flatly. 'He deserves what's coming to him. He's lucky he ran when he did otherwise he'd have been sneezing into the basket like all those other overfed bastards who lost their heads back in '93.'

'I found most of them to be very brave,' Carbonne offered. 'When I worked as an executioner, I must have seen off ten or twenty every day but they all faced their deaths with courage. I respected them for that.'

Lausard said nothing.

'Good riddance to them all. Their money and their position couldn't save them then, could it?' Delacor snapped. 'And I don't care if this Duke we've come for *does* decide to fight. We either kill him here and now or return him for execution. It makes no difference to me how he dies.'

'The newspaper says that there are many in France who still seek to undermine Bonaparte's rule,' Bonet offered. 'That there have been plots to kill him. They say the English are behind most of them.'

'That is because he has turned his back on God,' Moreau offered, crossing himself. 'He thinks himself higher than God.'

Some of the other men laughed.

'Then perhaps God should assassinate him,' Rocheteau chuckled.

'I thought your God was a merciful one,' Lausard said mockingly. 'Shouldn't He forgive Bonaparte for what he has done?'

'He has destroyed the Church,' Moreau countered. 'Weakened its authority.'

'He should be applauded for that, not condemned,' the sergeant declared.

Moreau waved away Lausard's comments.

The men passed around two bottles of red wine, each of them sipping at the rich liquid before handing it to their nearest companion.

'This is quite some picnic,' Rocheteau smiled. 'It's a pity all our missions aren't like this.'

'Let's see if it's still a picnic once we've crossed the border,' Lausard said, accepting a bottle. He cradled it in his hand for a moment then drank deeply before passing it to Rostov.

'What news of General Moreau's trial?' the Russian wanted to know. He prodded Bonet with the toe of his boot.

'He and General Pichegru are heavily implicated in a plot against Bonaparte,' the former schoolmaster read. 'The prosecutors are calling for the death penalty against them both.'

'It sounds as if Bonaparte has more enemies *inside* France than he has on her borders,' Rostov observed.

Charvet gave the pot one last stir then began cutting up the cooked rabbit, distributing pieces to the waiting men, then ladling the broth into their bowls as they held them up. Joubert savoured the delicious aroma for a moment then began eating.

'Giresse. Delacor. When you've finished eating, go and relieve Tigana and Sonnier,' Lausard instructed. 'Tell them there's some food for them.' He consumed his own share quickly then got to his feet.

'Where are you going, Alain?' Rocheteau wanted to know.

'For a walk,' Lausard told him flatly.

The men watched as he made his way up the slope.

Lausard picked his way between the camp fires on the hillside; smoke rose thickly from many of them. Some of the other dragoons nodded as he passed and Lausard returned their greeting as he drew nearer the crest of the ridge. As he reached the edge of the woods he slowed his pace, moving through the dense underbrush until he emerged on the far side of the trees. Two sentries, carbines at the ready and with bayonets fixed, saw him and moved towards him but the sergeant raised a hand and both men withdrew. The night air smelled of pine, dewy grass and damp wood and Lausard drank in these aromas as he stood gazing out over the Bavarian countryside. The hills sloped away gently to form a flat plain. He could just make out the lights in houses half a mile or so away. They looked like so many fireflies in the gloom. The dark waters of a river coursed across the plain and, spanning that expanse, Lausard could make out the black outline of the Kiel bridge and the wide road that led to it.

Beyond that crossing point lay the electorate of Bavaria and, within that state itself, the Grand Duchy of Baden. Somewhere amidst the rivers and dark forests was the man they sought. The Duke of Enghien. Enemy of Bonaparte. Enemy of France. Aristocrat. The word was seldom used now, Lausard mused, except in a derogatory manner. Despite the passage of more than ten years of revolutionary government, the upper classes, who had been slaughtered so wantonly and so willingly by the common people of France, were still hated. Anything associated with hereditary wealth was anathema to those who had sought the eradication of an entire class during the savagery of revolution. The irony of the present situation was not lost on Lausard. He, a former aristocrat, now formed part of a detail whose sole purpose was the capture and arrest of a man who had been part of the very same social caste as himself prior to the frenzied rule of the guillotine. In the time before his world had been turned upside down, Lausard realised that, in other circumstances, he might have met this duke. Might have hunted with him. Attended lavish balls or banquets in his company. But that was the world he used to know. That world did not exist any longer, at least not for him. It had ceased to exist when he had fled from it to find another way of life in the gutters of Paris. When he had run from his responsibilities like a spineless coward, leaving his family at the mercy of mob rule while he saved his own worthless life and submerged himself among those he would normally have found repellent. What puzzled him even more, and had done ever since he joined that netherworld, was how easily he had adapted to it. Many times he had amazed himself at how seamless had been his transition from rich and privileged nobleman to starving and deprived thief. And from there to prisoner. The lowest of the low. Condemned even by those inhabiting the new and odorous world he had chosen to frequent.

Lausard continued gazing out over the German countryside, aware of the contradictions within him, wondering if he would ever reconcile them. To those around him, those he called friends and comrades, he was a common soldier. Nothing more. A man like them. The Duke of Enghien would see him as such were they to meet. Only Lausard himself knew that the man he had been despatched to help arrest might find comfort in the knowledge that at least one of his would-be captors was of the same background as he. Lausard wondered if a glimpse of the world he had once known would leave him mourning its passing or celebrating its abolition. He took one more long breath then turned and headed back towards the trees.

'A fine night.'

The voice startled him momentarily but he showed no sign of alarm.

'Yes, Captain,' he answered, saluting as Milliere emerged from the underbrush.

'It is beautiful countryside, is it not?' the officer remarked. 'A pity to spill blood on it.' He grinned.

'Is that what we must do, Captain? Spill blood?'

Milliere rubbed his chin thoughtfully.

'Hopefully not,' he mused. 'We were sent as soldiers. Not executioners.'

'Sometimes there is precious little difference.'

'That is true but I wish that this man we seek was somewhere else other than here.'

Lausard looked puzzled.

'When we cross that bridge, Sergeant,' said Milliere, pointing towards the large dark shape spanning the river, 'we pass over more than just water. We ride into war.'

'The man we are here to arrest is an enemy of France, Captain. Isn't that what General Ordener told us? Isn't that what Bonaparte himself believes? That is why we were selected, isn't it? He knew the dangers. He needed men like us.'

'The dangers do not lie in the arrest of the Duke of Enghien but beyond that. You are no fool, Sergeant. You know as well as I that we enter neutral territory to carry out our orders. There isn't a man present who doesn't realise it. But how many understand the greater implications of our actions?'

'Bonaparte obviously does.'

'I have no doubt of that. Just as I suspect he knows this act will precipitate war.'

'We are soldiers, Captain. War is where we belong. It is our reason for existing.'

Milliere shook his head almost imperceptibly.

'We exist for the advancement of Bonaparte,' the officer sighed. 'I accept that. I have no quarrel with it. I am proud to be part of his army. Proud to be a Frenchman. But that does not prevent me from being tired of war, does it? More than four years have passed since we last raised arms against others. Tell me that time was not wondrous.

But now we are close to shattering that peace again.' He shrugged. 'Do not misunderstand me, Sergeant. When the time comes I will obey every order I am given. I will sacrifice my life for France. I will kill any man who opposes Bonaparte. I will ride at the head of my squadron into the mouth of hell itself if necessary. But also understand, that does not prevent me from mourning the loss of the men around me. I have seen too many men die on battlefields these past eight years to welcome more bloodshed. Do I sound like a coward to you?'

'Certainly not, Captain. I know the very opposite is true. I respect your feelings but forgive me for not sharing them. The prospect of war is not something I relish but, if it should come, and I know it will, I shall embrace it. Perhaps one day I will be able to tell you why the very thing you find so abhorrent gives me a reason to live.'

The two men regarded each other silently in the gloom for long moments then Milliere nodded.

'I received orders from General Ordener just an hour ago,' said the officer. 'We move out at midnight. The infantry will remain here. The General feels speed is of the essence in this operation.'

'Where is the Duke of Enghien?'

'At the Château of Ettenheim, close to here. The only thing we don't know is how many men he has with him.'

'What of the Bavarians and troops of Baden?'

'If possible we are to avoid contact with them.'

'And if that contact is *un*avoidable?'

'Then we fight. Our first and only objective is to return Enghien to French soil. Regardless of the cost or the consequences.' He glanced at his watch, squinting in the darkness to see the hands. 'If I were you, Sergeant, I would rest. In less than two hours, you will have your war.'

Twelve

The sound of horses' hooves reverberated through the night as Lausard and the other dragoons walked their mounts across the Kiel bridge. The men were on foot, leading their animals by the bridle but it hardly seemed to matter such was the noise that rose from the wooden bridge. As they passed over the swiftly flowing water, Tabor looked over the parapet of the bridge into the dark river that rushed beneath. The clank of many swords also added to the cacophony and Lausard wondered why General Orderner had even bothered to emphasise the need for silence when it would have been just as simple to *ride* the animals across. However, as the first members of the squadron reached the far bank they mounted, steadying their horses as the others continued their passage. Ordener himself, a plain black bicorn perched on his head, walked his grey back and forth, pausing occasionally to glance at a map held by one of his aides. The dragoons formed a column and set off towards the lights of the village Lausard had seen from the hillside.

'Welcome to Bavaria,' Bonet muttered as the column moved off. 'There's no turning back now.'

'Shut your mouth,' snarled Sergeant Delpierre, slapping him on the arm. 'Silence in the ranks. You know the orders.'

'Then why don't *you* follow them and keep quiet?' Lausard hissed at his fellow NCO.

Delpierre shot him a furious glance then rejoined the column further back.

Karim and Tigana spurred their horses towards the head of the formation and Lausard saw them leaning close to Ordener as he gave them orders. A moment later, they galloped off in the direction of the village. The rest of the dragoons followed at a walk, silent but for the sound of jingling harnesses and the occasional snorts of their mounts. It was as if the animals too were aware of the need for quiet. The column moved steadily along the road, finding that it narrowed slightly the closer they came to the village. Lausard could see lights much more clearly now and he guessed the small settlement was less than a thousand yards away. The road forked, the left-hand tributary leading directly to the gaggle of buildings, the right disppearing into some cedar trees, the branches of which were stretched across it like clasping arms. The dense canopy of leaves only made the right-hand fork look more forbiddingly dark but the dragoons needed cover and Lausard glanced ahead to see what Ordener had decided. The general raised his arm and, without hesitation, gestured for the dragoons to take the road through the trees. They moved on, the blackness closing around them like a velvet glove. Lausard heard very little sound inside the wood. No birdsong, only the invisible nocturnal ramblings of hunting animals seeking prey. The undergrowth grew up to the very edge of the road, hedges scratching at the flanks of mounts on the periphery of the column. The road turned gently to the left and, through gaps in the trees, Lausard could see the lights of the village fading into the distance. The wood began to thin out slightly and the sergeant could see that beyond it lay more open ground that he assumed was farmland. Hedges and stone walls separated the fields, most of which were still bare of crops due to the season. From somewhere ahead he heard the thudding of fast-moving hooves and involuntarily touched the hilt of his sword. Sonnier felt for his carbine. Rocheteau slid a hand inside his tunic and allowed his fingers to play over the hilt of his knife. Delacor prepared to pull the axe from his portmanteau should it be needed.

The men relaxed slightly when they saw that the sound came from two approaching horsemen who reined in their mounts as they reached the head of the column.

Karim and Tigana steadied their mounts as they drew alongside Ordener.

'There are Bavarian troops about a mile ahead, sir,' the Circassian said flatly.

'How many?' Ordener wanted to know.

'Fifty or sixty lancers,' Karim told him. 'It looks like a patrol and they are coming this way.'

'We should not even be on their soil,' the general mused. 'The last thing I want to do is slaughter one of their patrols, as easy as that would be. Is there any way of avoiding them?'

Tigana nodded.

'Half a mile ahead there is another river,' Tigana told

him. 'Guarded on both banks by trees. An entire army could hide there and not be seen.'

'An army,' Ordener muttered. 'It will suffice for a squadron then. Lead us to this place, quickly.'

The two horsemen rode off and the other dragoons followed at a trot, covering the ground with ease.

'Why are we hiding from sixty men?' Delacor wanted to know.

'You heard the order,' Rocheteau told him. 'There is to be no killing.'

'And what do you think the Bavarians would do if they found us?' Delacor grunted. 'I say we should wipe them out.'

'Just ride,' Lausard snapped, urging his own horse on.

The column moved quickly along the road, the trees on either side growing more dense. Lausard could see another bridge, much smaller than the first they had crossed. In fact, he wondered if the tributary that flowed beneath it should even rightly be called a river. General Ordener raised an arm and waved to his left and right. The column of dragoons immediately split, half of the men guiding their mounts into the trees on one side of the road, the remainder seeking refuge on the other. Lausard found that once the initial barrier of trees had been passed, there was little undergrowth and the horses could manoeuvre freely. Moving with as much care as possible, the dragoons edged deeper into the enveloping woods and brought their animals to a halt. Somewhere in the branches above them an owl hooted and a number of the horses neighed in protest. Rostov calmed his mount with a couple of pats to its neck. Elsewhere, some of the troopers dismounted and held their mounts by the muzzle, reassuring the nervous animals. Lausard heard more hooves beyond the confines of the wood and realised the sound was coming from the road. He ducked low in his saddle and gazed through the trees.

As he watched, twenty horsemen cantered past. They were clad in light green tunics and grey overalls. The pennants of their fifteen-foot lances fluttered as they rode. They were followed a moment later by twenty more. Some of the hedges at the side of the road had been broken down when the dragoons forced their way through but, Lausard reasoned, any damage would be impossible to spot in the blackness and at the speed the lancers were moving. His horse tossed its head impetuously and he gripped the reins hard to quieten it. Several of the other dragoons were having problems controlling their mounts, the animals having been disturbed by the cloying confines of the forest. Another group of lancers cantered past and Lausard listened as the sound of their horses' hooves gradually died away into the distance. He kept his gaze fixed on the road, squinting to see as best he could. He could see nothing and there were no other sounds apart from the odd movements and noises made by the dragoons' mounts. He reached for his watch and glanced at it. A minute passed. Then two. Karim finally led his horse slowly out of the woods and into the road. Lausard watched as the Circassian rose in the stirrups and looked both left and right along the thoroughfare. He waited for a moment then looked again. It seemed to be taking an eternity.

'All clear,' he called finally, and, with a collective sigh of relief, the dragoons led their mounts back out of the trees and on to the road. They hastily reformed into a column then, at General Ordener's command, they moved off across the bridge.

'We should have killed them,' Delacor rasped.

'There'll be time for killing soon enough,' Lausard told him.

The column moved on.

In the darkness Lausard thought that the Château of Ettenheim appeared to have been hewn from one massive lump of rock rather than assembled from many stones. It was a suitably imposing edifice but the dragoons' most pressing concern was with the presence of troops rather than the architectural splendour of the building that confronted them. A number of the château's windows were lit, casting dull yellow light into the gloom. Lausard squinted through the darkness but could see no signs of armed men.

'This aristocrat seems very certain of his safety,' Rocheteau whispered.

'Why shouldn't he be?' Lausard remarked. 'He's on neutral soil. He has no reason to suspect men are coming to arrest him.'

'Sergeant.'

The voice belonged to Captain Milliere.

'You and five of your men are to accompany myself, General Ordener and Captain Varrier of the Gendarmes into the château itself. The order has been given to surround the building. We will provide the guard for the General when he actually arrests the Duke.' The officer looked at the men closest to him. 'There are strict orders from the General. No casualties are to be inflicted upon *any* personnel present.'

Lausard jabbed a finger in the direction of the first five dragoons near him and they guided their horses towards the ornamental gardens leading up to the main front of the château. Other troops hurried to complete the order that, in less than ten minutes, would see the building completely surrounded. Lausard saw General Ordener sitting motionless on his horse. Next to him, wearing a large bicorn with white edging, was Captain Varrier. The gendarme officer was gazing in the direction of the château while he unfastened the twin pistol holsters on his saddle.

'I thought we were to take the Duke alive,' Lausard offered.

'We are,' Varrier told him. 'But he may need some *encouragement* to accompany us.' He pulled one of the pistols free and checked that it was loaded. Satisfied that it was, he joined the other men as they advanced.

They were within fifty yards of the building now and still Lausard could see very little movement in or around the château. Every now and then a figure would pass one of the windows and he thought he saw shadows moving outside the main entrance but, other than that, there certainly didn't seem to be any escort present to act as a bodyguard for the duke. They slowed their horses as they reached the gravelled area before the building and Ordener dismounted, eyes ever watchful.

The dragoons followed his example, all except Joubert whom Lausard patted on the shoulder.

'Watch the horses,' he whispered and the big man nodded. 'If you see anyone, fire your pistol once into the air.'

They were within a few feet of the main door now and Ordener approached it.

He heard movement on the other side and then, suddenly, the door opened. The Frenchmen steadied themselves. The man who opened the door was, by the look of his clothes, a servant of some description. He wore a heavily embroidered frock coat, silk stockings and finely polished shoes. For interminable seconds, he stood gazing at the French troops, the colour draining from his face. Then he opened his mouth to say something, possibly to warn those inside. Rocheteau took no chances. He stepped forward and drove a fist into the face of the attendant who dropped like a stone. He dragged the unconscious man outside as Ordener, Varrier and the others hurried past him into the château itself. They found themselves in a spacious hallway, from which an ornate staircase led up to a gallery hung with several paintings. Wooden doors led off to the right and left.

'Spread out,' Ordener said sharply. 'Find Enghien.'

Scarcely had the words left his lips when one of the doors to the left began to open and the men saw a figure emerging. Lausard stepped behind the door and cupped his hand tightly around the mouth of the newcomer. It was a woman, a maid in her early twenties. As he held her, he could see her eyes bulging wide in terror and he felt her struggle against him. Delacor eyed the young woman with a slight grin, running appraising eyes over her.

'Where is your master?' Ordener asked.

Lausard could feel her shaking uncontrollably.

'I'm going to take my hand away from your mouth,' he said, close to her ear. 'Do not scream.'

She moaned loudly as he removed his hand and tears began to coarse down her cheeks.

'Where is the Duke of Enghien?' Ordener demanded.

All she could do was point towards the staircase.

'Is he alone?' Varrier wanted to know.

The maid could not speak.

'Has he soldiers with him?' Varrier rasped, taking a step towards her.

She shook her head.

'Watch her,' the gendarme told Delacor as the other men made for the stairs.

'Alain, you can't leave a rapist alone with her,' Rocheteau protested.

Delacor shot the corporal a furious glance.

Lausard hesitated a moment, grabbing the dragoon by the arm.

'You take care of her,' he snapped.

'Oh, I will,' Delacor grinned, touching the girl's cheek with his rough hand and licking his lips.

'You hurt her and you have me to answer to,' the sergeant told him, fixing his companion with a withering stare. 'Do you understand me?'

Delacor nodded and shook the woman loose, watching as the men reached the landing.

Ordener, Milliere and two dragoons turned right. Varrier, Lausard and Rocheteau set off in the other direction, pushing open doors as they went. At the end of the corridor stood a pair of double doors. Varrier held up a hand for the other men to wait as he gently turned the handle, somewhat surprised to find it unlocked. He pushed and the doors swung back on their hinges.

The Duke of Enghien looked up as the men entered the room, his face registering little emotion. He was dressed in a shooting jacket and held a glass of brandy in one hand. The thirty-two-year-old nobleman regarded the intruders with little more than curiosity for a moment but then he took a step forward. There was a small table at the bottom of the bed and on it Lausard could see two pairs of pistols and a shotgun. He prepared to draw his sword as the duke drew nearer the array of weapons but the aristocrat merely smiled and stood his ground.

'Louis Antoine Henri de Bourbon-Conde, Duke of Enghien,' Varrier said flatly. 'I have orders to arrest you. I urge you not to resist.'

Enghien smiled.

'I could blow out your brains,' he mused, 'but you are too fine a fellow for that. I will come with you.'

The words had barely left his lips when Ordener and the other men entered the room.

'It is done,' Varrier remarked. 'In the name of France and the First Consul.'

'If you have no objections, I will inform my wife of our predicament,' Enghien murmured and turned towards another door behind him.

'Do not try to escape,' Ordener told him. 'There is nowhere to run. The château is surrounded.'

'I have no intention of running.' He walked calmly to the door and opened it. Lausard saw him standing at the threshold speaking softly to whoever was inside. A moment later a young woman emerged. She was barefoot, wearing only a fine silk gown and a shawl. Her dark hair cascaded over her shoulders and Lausard was struck by her delicate beauty. Princess Charlotte de Rohan-Rochefort regarded the dragoons indifferently for a second then stepped forward and kissed her husband lightly on the cheek.

'May we be permitted to dress?' she asked, her tone matching her air of serenity.

Ordener nodded.

Varrier stepped towards the table that bore the weapons and looked first at the general then at Enghien.

'I will take these,' the gendarme said, reaching for the guns.

'There is no need,' Enghien murmured. 'We will not resist and I have no desire to end my own life.'

Ordener put out an arm and beckoned to the gendarme to leave.

'We will be waiting downstairs,' he informed the two aristocrats.

The troops left the room.

The coach moved slowly along the driveway from the château towards the road, cavalrymen on all sides of it. From his own position in the column, Lausard could see inside the vehicle and, every now and then, he would catch a glimpse of the Duke of Enghien or his wife sitting almost regally within the coach. Neither of them looked out of the windows and it seemed to Lausard that this was because they had no wish to see the men who had captured them. No desire to look upon those whom they viewed as inferior, he mused. Two coachmen guided the vehicle that was pulled by four large grey horses, the animals pulling their burden with ease despite its size. Behind it came a second coach containing half a dozen maids, valets and the remainder of the aristocrats' most valued staff.

'I expected trouble,' Rocheteau said, glancing in the direction of the first coach.

'Why?' Lausard wanted to know. 'Enghien had no idea we were coming. And even if he had, it would have done him no good to fight.'

'We still have to get him back across the border,' the

corporal persisted. 'Those Bavarian troops may not be too accommodating if we run up against them.'

'They have no need to fight,' Lausard said. 'They would be fools to die defending a man who meant so little to them.'

'His wife is a fine looking woman,' Giresse observed, leaning forward slightly in the saddle to catch a glimpse of Princess Charlotte.

'Shortly to be a fine looking *widow*, I'll wager,' Lausard remarked. 'Remember, we were sent here to arrest an enemy of France and of Bonaparte. Our First Consul does not usually treat his opponents with leniency.'

'What is his crime?' Giresse wanted to know.

'What does it matter? The bastard is an aristocrat,' Delacor interjected. 'He deserves to die.'

'And he is a Bourbon,' Rocheteau added. 'I thought we had seen the last of them back in '93.'

'They ran from France like rats from a sinking ship,' Delacor hissed. 'Desperate to save their skins. But they bred like rats, too. There are still many hiding around Europe. Cowering in the darkness like hunted animals until they dare emerge again. If they ever do.'

Lausard glanced at his companion, then at the coach carrying the duke and his wife. He didn't speak. There was no point. There was nothing he could say.

'If they have any sense,' Giresse mused, 'they will stay silent as long as Bonaparte rules France.' He looked again in the direction of the princess and smiled. 'That one would not remain silent for long in *my* company. She would be singing my praises when she felt the touch of these hands.' He flexed his fingers and some of the men nearby laughed.

'To her you are scum,' Delacor snapped. 'We *all* are.

You would never get close to her.'

'Then she is to be pitied, for she will never know the true exultation of spending time with me.'

Again some of the men laughed.

Captain Milliere looked angrily back over his shoulder and the men fell silent again.

'Where are we taking them anyway?' Rocheteau wanted to know.

'To Strasbourg, I heard,' Lausard told him. 'A day's march from here.'

'And then?' Rocheteau asked.

His words hung unanswered in the air.

The column moved on with surprising speed and Lausard thought that General Ordener seemed less concerned about detection now that their prisoner was in custody. Perhaps now that they had completed the main objective of their mission the commanding officer was content to fight his way out of neutral territory if the need arose. Certainly Lausard and the other dragoons were more than capable of coping with such an eventuality. Even so, it came as little surprise to the sergeant when Tigana and Karim were again sent ahead of the column to scout for Bavarian troops.

'Why the hell didn't Bonaparte just order us to kill this Bourbon?' Delacor wanted to know. 'It would have been easier. At least that way we wouldn't have had to play wet nurse to him and his precious wife.'

'Bonaparte wants him for a reason,' Lausard said flatly. 'If Enghien *is* plotting against our Corsican then he will want to make an example of him. This isn't merely a kidnapping. It's a declaration of intent.'

'Do you think that Moreau and Pichegru are involved in this plot?' Bonet offered. 'Is it of such magnitude that it reaches beyond the frontiers of France herself?'

Lausard could only shrug.

'Time will tell,' he mused. '*That* is not our concern. Getting Enghien safely to Strasbourg *is*.'

Thirteen

'Seven days in this place now,' said Rocheteau wearily as he used the currycomb expertly on his horse. 'We wait here for orders like kitchen help.'

The stables smelled of damp straw and dung. The men had been billeted in an old school that stood across a square from the stables where they now tended their mounts.

Dressed in the green surtouts and grey overalls usually donned for such work, they fed and watered their mounts then washed and brushed them. Since their arrival in Strasbourg, it seemed they had been doing little else. Lausard inspected the hooves of his chestnut. The animal had lost a couple of nails from one rear shoe and he made a mental note to replace them from the spares he carried in his portmanteau. At first he had thought the horse was going lame but it was obviously merely slipping on that one loose shoe.

'And what orders would you have us receive?' the sergeant enquired.

'We were instructed to arrest the Duke of Enghien and

return him to France, were we not?' Rocheteau reminded his colleague. 'Why are we still here when our mission was completed a week ago?'

'I agree,' Delacor interjected. 'If Bonaparte was so anxious to have Enghien in his grasp then why make us wait here with that accursed Bourbon? Why not take him back and get this matter over with?'

'And once it is over. What then?' Lausard said, challengingly. 'We will be ordered back to Boulogne to prepare for the invasion of England.'

'In that case, I hope we stay here,' Sonnier offered, to the amusement of some of the other men.

'It isn't so bad here,' Bonet interjected. 'The locals have been very kind to us.'

'There is plenty of food,' Joubert added.

'And the women are beautiful,' Giresse chuckled. 'Or perhaps, Delacor, you would prefer to be surrounded by those ugly dog-faces who accompanied us on the first part of our march into Bavaria.'

More laughter greeted the remark.

'We are soldiers, not spies and kidnappers,' Delacor snapped. 'We have done our duty. If Bonaparte wanted this Bourbon arrested why did he not send some of Fouché's secret police? They specialise in that kind of operation.'

'He has a point, Alain,' Rostov said.

'Don't look to me for answers,' Lausard said. 'Do you expect me to know the inner workings of Bonaparte's mind? I am as clueless as you about our future. As frustrated as you that we cannot rejoin our regiment, but there is nothing we can do but wait until we are ordered to do otherwise.'

'Perhaps our officers want to keep this Duke here for

their own amusement,' Delacor hissed. 'They dine with him every night.'

'And what would you have them do, Delacor?' snapped Lausard. 'Throw him and his wife into some rat-infested cell? Push food under the door for them periodically? These are political prisoners we are talking about. Not common thieves.'

'Like we were?' Rocheteau grinned.

Lausard nodded, forcing a smile.

'Sergeant Lausard is right.'

The men turned towards the sound of the voice and saw Lieutenant Royere standing in the doorway of the stable. The officer waited a moment then entered.

'What news of our prisoner, Lieutenant?' Lausard wanted to know.

'The Duke is to be escorted this very night to the Château de Vincennes where he will be tried by military court for his part in the conspiracy against Bonaparte.'

'So he *was* in league with Moreau and Pichegru?' the sergeant murmured.

'Captain Milliere said there was no evidence to support that assumption but papers were found back at Ettenheim that proved he was in the pay of England. Apparently, he was to lead an invasion of Alsace. His crime is not that he was part of a conspiracy but that he was an émigré being paid by a foreign power to invade France.'

'And now?' Lausard wanted to know.

'General Ordener, Captain Varrier of the Gendarmes and a dozen men will take him to meet his judges at Vincennes,' the officer informed him. 'I came to ask you to select six of your own men to form part of the detail.'

'And what of the rest of us, Lieutenant?' Delacor

demanded. 'Are we to return to our regiment? Or rot here until the summer?'

'You are to return to Paris,' the officer replied. 'The whole squadron. We are being given leave of one month as a reward for the successful completion of our mission.'

A cheer echoed around the stable as the men voiced their delight.

'A month of good food,' Joubert smiled.

'A month of peace,' Sonnier echoed.

'And of good company,' Giresse chuckled, blowing a kiss into the air. 'Here's to the women of Paris. May God speed me back to them.'

Moreau crossed himself.

Only Lausard held the officer's gaze, apparently unmoved by his proclamation.

'What time do we leave for Vincennes?' he asked, never taking his eyes from Royere.

'In one hour.'

Lausard nodded and returned to brushing his horse, the excited chattering of his companions filling his ears.

Night fell like a shroud over the land and brought with it the threat of rain from the thick banks of cloud scudding across the heavens. As the small detail made its way across country, Lausard waited for the first drops that would signal a downpour. His horse was skittish, another sign that the possibility of a storm was none too distant. The irony was not lost on the sergeant. The elements seemed to be aligning themselves against France as surely as the rest of Europe was. He glanced at the the coach that carried the Duke of Enghien and wondered what thoughts must be going through the man's mind. He had said tearful farewells to his retainers and his wife back in Strasbourg and now he was alone. The coach was little more than a mobile cell for the captive aristocrat. Dragoons rode on either side, as well as at the front and behind. Every now and then Captain Varrier would guide his horse alongside and glance in at the duke, as if to reassure himself his captive was still inside. On more than one occasion, Lausard caught the eye of the gendarme and the two men looked at each other silently.

'You don't like him do you, Alain?' Rocheteau said quietly, seeing the sergeant's expression darken every time he caught sight of Varrier.

'Is it that obvious?' Lausard murmured. 'He seems to be enjoying his work a little too much. Perhaps he wants to be the one to pull the trigger when the time comes.'

'What do you mean?'

'Isn't it obvious? We are not escorting Enghien to his trial. We are sentries overseeing his execution.'

'He conspired against Bonaparte, against France. What would *you* have done with him, Alain?'

'I am not defending him, Rocheteau. What I find distasteful is the pretence that he is to be tried for his crime. There will be no trial. It will be a pronouncement of guilt. The verdict was decided before we even took him captive. I would sooner our orders had been to find him and kill him where he stood than go through with this kind of charade. We have gone to great lengths to ensure no harm comes to this man when we all know we are transporting him to certain death. What did it matter *where* he died? It would be just as easy for us to pull him out of that coach now and put a bullet in his brain.'

They rode in silence for some way, the only sounds the jingling of the horse harnesses and steady rumble of the coach. Despite the fact that their mission had been accomplished, that no one had been injured in its completion and the men could now look forward to the promise of a month in Paris, there was a peculiarly inexplicable solemnity about the escort, personified, it seemed, by Lausard himself. More than once, Rocheteau looked at his companion and saw that his face was set in hard lines. It was a long time before he spoke to the sergeant again.

'What will we do when we reach Paris?' Rocheteau mused.

Lausard merely shrugged.

'We could visit the places we used to live,' he said dismissively. 'See how many thieves, rapists and murderers now frequent the same sewers we once did.'

'I want to visit the grave of my wife,' Rocheteau said quietly.

'I didn't know she had a grave,' Lausard murmured, his tone softening. 'She died of smallpox, didn't she? Wasn't she buried with the other victims of the epidemic?'

Rocheteau nodded.

'That is true,' he said quietly. 'But after the hole had been filled in, I went back that night and removed her body. I didn't want her sharing her final resting place with hundreds of others I didn't even know. I took her to a place on the banks of the Seine, close to Notre Dame, and I laid her beneath one of the trees there. Not a day passes that I don't think of her. Do you think me foolish for that, Alain?'

'I would think you a lesser man if you had buried her memory with her. You should never forget those who have been close to you. To do so is an insult. Besides, what does a man have if he abandons his memories?'

'We have the future to look to.'

'A future that will bring war and possibly death. Living in the past would seem a preferable option for most men.'

'But not for you?'

Lausard shook his head.

'The army is all I have now,' he said. 'The thing I do best in life is fight. But for four years now, I, like the rest of the army, have been without purpose. A soldier without a war is as useless as a musket without powder.'

'I have heard rumours that war is close. Not just against the English but against Russia and Austria, too. Some say the fate of that man,' he nodded towards the coach carrying the Duke of Enghien, 'could help to trigger this war.'

'If that is the case then so be it. I will be ready when the time comes. We all will. We will fight and, if necessary, we will die for France. At least now we have that choice. Ten years ago we didn't.'

Rocheteau nodded almost imperceptibly.

'Wasn't that the purpose of the revolution?' he mused. 'To give all men equal choice?'

'I think that many who supported the revolution, either for military or political reasons, have lost sight of exactly what that purpose *was*,' the sergeant offered.

'What about us, Alain? Do you think we have lost sight of *our* purpose?'

'And what was that? We *had* no purpose until the army became so short of men it began emptying prisons to find new recruits. Would any of us have volunteered to fight? No. We would have been content to survive as thieves. If not for the revolution we would all be dead now. Executed by the very country we fight for. Just as this Duke will now be sentenced by those he would once have ruled.'

Lausard felt the first spots of rain as they rode on but he paid them little heed. Rain had been threatening for hours and, as yet, was little more than a shower. It was one, perhaps, that presaged more violent climactic change, but for now the elements withheld their full ferocity as the fateful procession continued its journey. On more than one occasion the sergeant saw the Duke of Enghien peer out of the carriage window but, when he did, he seemed to be looking past the dragoons escorting him. It was as if to acknowledge them would be a sign of defeat. Or perhaps, Lausard reasoned, there was resignation in that disdainful glance. Surely this aristocrat must know what fate awaited him. He had dared to plot against Bonaparte, to undermine the stability of France herself. From his demeanour, he either foolishly expected to receive a fair trial or had already reconciled himself to the inevitable. It was the same kind of look Lausard had seen on the faces of those who had been brought to meet the guillotine in the Place de la Revolution during the blood-drenched years of The Terror. For in that look was also a disdainful resentment of those who held him prisoner. Despite his apparent charm during his captivity, Lausard was sure that Enghien still found his presence among so many of the lower classes unpalatable. Men whom he would have treated with contempt ten years earlier were now transporting him to almost certain death and it was that knowledge that made his predicament even more intolerable. Lausard knew what those feelings were like. He understood the workings of Enghien's mind in the same way he empathised with any of the troopers in his regiment. Years of living a double life had allowed him the ability to view most situations from both sides. It was not always something he embraced, rather something he had learned to cope with. To progress in any sphere of life, the sergeant had found, a man had to be adaptable. In Lausard's case, progress had not been the prerequisite. It had been a matter of survival. And, despite the feelings of self-hatred he still nursed, he had accomplished that transition with an ease he could hardly have imagined, so much so that it had troubled him to begin with. He wondered if Enghien would have done the same if he had been given the opportunity. Would he have been prepared to forsake his birthright and his heritage in order to save his life, as Lausard had done? Would he have been so willing to turn his back on his class in order to remain alive? Could he have learned to live, and grow strong, in surroundings normally so abhorrent to him? Lausard doubted it. But then, when self-preservation was at stake there seemed no limit to man's ingenuity. Lausard was the living embodiment of that.

His thoughts were interrupted by the sound of Rocheteau's voice.

'Alain, look,' he said quietly, jabbing a finger ahead towards a towering black edifice that loomed out of the night as if it was part of the umbra itself.

The Château of Vincennes lay on the outskirts of Paris. It was surrounded by thick woods that seemed to be doing their best to hide the gaunt building from sight. A single road, barely wide enough to accommodate the coach or three horsemen riding abreast, led towards its main entrance. As the procession drew nearer, Lausard wondered if there was even anyone present at the château. He could see no lights burning either inside or outside the forbidding structure. As they drew nearer to the château, the column seemed to speed up, the men eager to bring this part of their mission to an end and be away from the place. The leading horsemen, then the carriage itself and the remainder of the detail rumbled over the wooden gangway that spanned the dry moat. The inner courtyard of the château was well lit and, as the men brought their mounts to a halt, Lausard saw several ranks of infantrymen drawn up on three sides of the cobbled yard. All had their bayonets fixed, muskets held at the 'Present' position. The coach was driven into the centre of the waiting foot soldiers and Lausard watched as Captain Varrier and General Ordener both saluted the officer commanding the infantry, the man having approached the vehicle that held Enghien. Varrier opened the door and gestured to the duke to climb out, which he duly did, pausing only briefly to look around him at the troops and the inner courtyard of the château. As the dragoons looked on, he was escorted towards one of the doorways leading off from the yard which was lit on both sides by blazing torches. The door was slammed behind him, reverberating through the night like a gunshot.

'We have orders to wait here until otherwise instructed,' Captain Milliere announced, walking his horse across the cobbles to the waiting dragoons.

'What more is there for us to do, Captain?' Lausard wanted to know. 'Are we to be his executioners as well as his escort?'

Milliere exhaled wearily.

'There is food inside for us and also for our horses,' the officer continued. 'I suggest we avail ourselves of it.'

'And what of Enghien?' Lausard wanted to know.

'That is no longer our concern, Sergeant. We have completed our mission as instructed. What happens now is neither of consequence nor concern to us.'

'That isn't what you said before we took him prisoner,

Captain. You know as well as I what will become of the man.'

'A traitor, Sergeant, what would *you* have us do with him?'

'Does it matter, Captain?'

Lausard's words hung in the air.

The room smelled of charred wood and smoke. The fire that had been lit in the grate had virtually gone out, despite the efforts of the dragoons to keep it alive. It was a high-ceilinged vestibule barely large enough to accommodate the horsemen. They stood or sat around, some crouching to avoid contact with the freezing stone floor, huddling around the remnants of the fire in an effort to glean some warmth from its embers. They had found bread, broth and several bottles of wine awaiting them inside and had accepted the offering gratefully. It had gone some small way to assuaging the hunger they felt. None of them had eaten a decent meal since they'd left Strasbourg two days earlier. Joubert mopped his bowl with a piece of bread which he pushed into his cavernous mouth. Around him, the other men were silent. Karim puffed away at his pipe. Rostov drank from a bottle of wine then handed it to Carbonne. Rocheteau and several of the other dragoons stood around the dying fire, watching the last of the feeble flames as if entranced by them. Lausard stood alone in one corner of the room, head lowered in thought.

'We should be in Paris by sunrise,' Captain Milliere intoned, pouring himself some wine. He offered some to Lieutenant Royere who accepted gratefully, holding the metal cup in his hand, allowing his superior to fill it.

'In time for the celebrations?' Lausard remarked sardonically. 'The removal of another of Bonaparte's enemies and a Bourbon at that. Surely there will be a day of national rejoicing.'

'You have a strange way of showing your patriotism, my friend,' Lieutenant Royere offered. 'I thought that you, like the rest of us, would have rejoiced in the arrest of Enghien.'

'He is one man, Lieutenant. One of many who oppose our First Consul. Do you think he will be the last to challenge Bonaparte? Only next time, France will face not a group of opportunistic conspirators but entire nations.'

'I fear I must agree with the sergeant,' Milliere echoed. 'War does seem to be the only outcome in these circumstances.'

'We would have fought the English anyway,' Rocheteau offered. 'If the Austrians and the Russians choose to oppose us then we must crush them too.'

'Enemies at her borders,' rasped Lausard. 'Enemies within. We fought countless battles and lost thousands of men and for what? So it could all begin again at the whim of Bonaparte.'

'Do you blame the First Consul for war?' Royere wanted to know. 'He is merely doing his duty as leader of our country. If we are threatened we must respond.'

'Had Enghien been allowed to remain where he was then war would have been a more remote possibility,' Lausard said.

'And his continued existence would have prompted others to try to undermine and destabilise France,' Royere retorted.

'Lieutenant, France is the most powerful nation in Europe,' the sergeant snapped. 'In us, his army, Bonaparte has the most feared and efficient fighting force seen on this continent since that of Gustavus Adolphus. As long as he controls the army, no one can hope to challenge him. These plots and conspiracies are meaningless. Bonaparte has used them as propaganda to manipulate the people, to unite them behind him and it has worked magnificently; but do not, for an instant, think that *anyone* could erode or destroy what it has taken Bonaparte eight years to build. How many voted him Consul for life? Three million? He holds supreme power already. As I said to you once before, Lieutenant, he is a king in all but name.'

Royere shot the sergeant an angry glance.

'He would, I am sure, question your choice of title, Sergeant,' said the officer. 'Bonaparte would not betray the spirit of the revolution he so fervently believes in for the sake of a position that died with Louis XVI. This country is a democracy now, thanks to Bonaparte. He would not allow that to change.'

'I hope you are right, Lieutenant,' the sergeant said flatly. He held the officer's gaze for a moment longer then took a step towards the door.

The rain that had threatened had still not begun to fall, other than in sporadic light showers. Lausard looked up at the banks of scudding cloud smeared across the blackened heavens then wandered out into the courtyard. Most of the troops who had been present when the dragoons arrived with their prisoner were still in position. More than three hours had passed since Lausard had first laid eyes on the blue-jacketed grenadiers, their tall bearskins ruffled by the breeze. They stood stiffly, the cold enveloping them. Only their gaze followed the dragoon sergeant as he passed before them, heading towards the main gate of the château. There were two sentries there and, as he approached, they lowered their muskets, pointing the fifteen-inch bayonets in his direction. Lausard was unimpressed by the glinting steel held inches from his stomach. He merely regarded each of the sentries in turn.

'No one is to leave the confines of the château without permission,' said the first of the sentries, a tall man with a bushy moustache and long sideburns.

'Whose permission?' the dragoon wanted to know.

'Those were our orders,' the other sentry told him. 'Given to us directly by Captain Varrier of the Gendarmes.'

'What is happening outside the château that makes it so imperative no one leaves?' the sergeant enquired.

The two sentries looked at him quizzically for a moment then the first raised his Charleville, resting the weapon on his shoulder. His companion waited a second then mimicked his actions.

'When did Captain Varrier give you the order?' Lausard persisted.

'Less than an hour ago,' the first man told him.

'And if I try to pass, what will you do? Shoot me? I will answer to Varrier. I have been in his company for too long anyway.'

'Were you with him when he arrested the Duke of Enghien?'

Lausard nodded.

'It must have been some battle, getting him out of Bavaria,' the second sentry said. 'Varrier said he was a dangerous man.'

'He came willingly. At no time were we in any danger. His guards were kitchen maids and cooks. I fear Captain Varrier's imagination is better than his memory.'

Again he looked at the two men.

'Will you let me pass?' he wanted to know.

'Are you so anxious to see the end of the traitor?' the first sentry asked.

For fleeting seconds, Lausard looked puzzled then the realisation spread swiftly through his mind.

'The firing squad is already assembled,' the sentry continued. 'Enghien himself was escorted out less than ten minutes ago.'

Lausard took a step forward but neither of the men made a move to stop him. He walked briskly out on to the wooden gangway that stretched over the dry moat and saw that, indeed, twelve grenadiers were gathered there, muskets at the ready. Less than ten feet from them, clad only in shirt and breeches, stood the Duke of Enghien. His hands were bound behind his back. Lausard also saw General Ordener and Captain Varrier standing close by. It was the gendarme who gave the order. Two drummers began hammering away as the grenadiers raised the muskets to their shoulders, fixing the duke in their sights. He gazed indifferently at them, apparently unmoved by his fate. Lausard heard commands being bellowed but it was difficult to distinguish them over the drummers' frenzied beating. He saw the members of the firing squad draw the butts of their muskets tight into their shoulders, preparing to receive the recoil. He watched Varrier raise his arm into the air, then bring it sweeping down. All twelve muskets were discharged at once, the barrels flaming, the dry moat momentarily filling with choking, sulphurous smoke. The sound of gunfire reverberated through the darkness, then there was nothing but silence. The drummers, too, had stopped. The Duke of Enghien lay on his back, his shirt stained crimson. Varrier took a step towards the body, leaned close, then moved away again.

Lausard stood watching for a moment longer then turned and headed back inside the Château of Vincennes.

Fourteen

The carriage that transported Napoleon Bonaparte through the streets of Paris was escorted by fifty elite mounted chausseurs. The light horsemen all rode magnificent grey or black horses. Resplendent in their green jackets and breeches, scarlet dolmans slung over one shoulder and black fur colpacks with red bag and plumes of the same colour, they guided their mounts over the cobbles, aware of the admiring glances from those civilians who stopped to stare at the impressive procession. Small children and some women waved at the First Consul's personal bodyguards. Some men even stopped and saluted the magnificent horsemen. The occasional shout of '*Vive Bonaparte!*' could be heard amidst the loud clattering of hooves. Inside the coach, Bonaparte himself sat back on the red velvet seat gazing out of the window. Opposite him, Talleyrand brushed fluff from his breeches and regarded the Corsican evenly. He was aware of the fire blazing in the First Consul's eyes and knew it presaged the kind of furious outburst he had come to know only too well during his years of service to the Corsican. The piece of paper Bonaparte held in his hand was the main source of his fury.

'Torn from the wall of a house in Montmartre,' the Corsican finally snarled, holding up the piece of paper accusingly. 'One of thousands plastered upon walls all over the city.' He glared at it.

'I have read it,' Talleyrand told him quietly.

'You and most of Paris,' rasped the First Consul.

'*"Je vécus très longtemps de l'emprunt et l'aumône,"*'

he read aloud.

'*"De Barras, vil flatteur, J'épousai le catin;*
J'étranglai Pichegru, J'assassinai Enghien,
Et pour tant de forfaits, J'obtins une couronne."' *

The Corsican balled up the piece of paper and hurled it from the carriage. 'A song,' he snorted dismissively. 'My enemies' only retort against me now is a song. Word has it the Marquis de Nadaillac is responsible for this childishness. He has been quoted as saying the execution of Enghien has caused universal revulsion throughout Europe and throughout France herself. How dare he presume to do such a thing? France is united behind me just as she always has been. This business with Enghien was unavoidable and, besides, what is the life of one man?'

'If songs are the only weapons your enemies choose to

---

* 'I lived very long on borrowing and charity,
Of Barras, vile flatterer, I married the whore,
I strangled Pichegru, assassinated Enghien,
And for such noble efforts obtained me a crown.'

use against you then your triumph would appear to be complete,' Talleyrand observed, smiling.

'Enghien is dead. Pichegru was found dead in his cell and Moreau is banished. If there is still opposition to my rule then it has not shown itself since the death of that Bourbon princeling. I stand by my decision to have him executed.'

'And the country respects your actions but there are other problems that must be resolved. The matter of your successor is still one of great concern. Even the Senate is now in favour of some kind of hereditary rule. You must take up the position of Emperor and establish a new aristocracy. But one founded on achievement and loyalty, not on outdated royalist principles.'

Bonaparte stroked his chin thoughtfully.

'I agree, Talleyrand,' he murmured. 'A new dynasty with myself at its head. Emperor Napoleon the First of France. I have already begun to formulate plans to create several strata of this new order. When the time is right, I will introduce a Marshalate. Promote the worthiest of my commanders to the rank of Marshal of France.'

'Have you considered the roles and positions of your own family in this new order?' the Foreign Minister asked.

Bonaparte sighed.

'As much as I love them, they seem drunk with the riches and positions they have acquired since my own power increased,' he said wearily. 'They are overladen with honours and they show little gratitude. As you know, I myself would be perfectly willing to name my brother Louis's son, Charles, as my heir but my other brothers refuse to renounce their rights in his favour. They squabble like children. Lucien's marriage to Madame Jouberthou is unlikely to enhance any imperial dignity I strive for. The woman, after all, is the widow of a bankrupt speculator. Jerome is bound for the Antilles. Joseph and Louis seem content to argue amongst themselves over a title they will never hold.'

'What of your sisters? How do they view this new order?'

'Pauline has married Prince Borghese without even affording me the opportunity to pass judgement on such a union. Caroline is happy with Murat but both she and Elisa, married to that hopeless Corsican Bacciochi, seem more enraged that I did not create them Princesses. And, behind them all, my beloved mother plots and schemes. They are united in but one thing. Their hatred of my wife. Of the woman who will become their Empress.'

'You are willing to risk the fury of your family?'

'Josephine is my wife. Who else would you have rule alongside me? I love the woman with my very soul. I am devoted to my family, but Josephine has my heart. She always will.' As he spoke, the Corsican gazed out of one window, momentarily lost in thought. The ensuing silence was broken by Talleyrand.

'Are you prepared to base your new position solely on a mandate from the people?' the Foreign Minister wanted to know.

'Do you doubt they will support me?'

'I have no such misgivings but I feel consecration by the Pope will dignify and legitimise further what you are now considering. You need his blessing, if only to show the rest of Europe that your position as Emperor is not a counterfeit one. But, be warned, Pius will not be overanxious to cooperate. The execution of Enghien has made him nervous. He may well see his acknowledgement of your title as a direct affront to some of the other leading

European states. He may be a man of God but he is also a statesman when necessary.'

'In that case he may be bargained with,' Bonaparte said flatly. 'If he feels he is to gain by blessing my appointment as Emperor then I suspect his concern for my enemies will wane. Since the Concordat, his power has been limited in the churches of France. Persuade him that I am willing to reappraise that power.'

'He seeks to obtain modification of the Organic Articles and possibly the restoration of the Legations.'

'Then dangle that particular carrot before him, Talleyrand. Send for his representative, Caprara. Have him brought to Paris. Persuade him there is more to be gained than lost by Pius supporting France and her Emperor. Cardinal Consalvi and Cardinal Fesch will conduct negotiations in the Vatican. Between you, you must persuade him that his support is both necessary and desirable for both sides.'

'And if he refuses?'

'He will not.'

'You sound very sure of that.'

'Before the year is out I will wear the crown of Emperor, even if I have to place it upon my own head.'

Over the years, both in and out of the army, Alain Lausard had found that time had a propensity merely to evaporate. At least that was how it seemed to the dragoon sergeant. Like water in a desert, time seemed transient and just as likely to disappear, to be lost as surely as some prized possession. On campaign, the daily drudgery of marches, bivouacs and drill was occasionally punctuated by the monstrous hell that was battle. In peace-time, the monotony of life could sometimes be tedious in the extreme. Rather than welcoming a respite from conflict, Lausard found the months or years of non-aggression ate away at him like some incurable disease. Battle was the only place he could hope to find salvation. War was the only hope for him. While the other men in his regiment and, he assumed, most men in the remainder of the army, were delighted with the chance to experience a hard-won peace, for his own part he longed for the day when the order would come for the men to prepare themselves for the meeting with a new enemy. Intervals of leave had been punctuated by seemingly endless periods of drill and manoeuvre. Lausard knew, and accepted, the purpose of this endless training but it could not satisfy his impatience and frustration. He walked slowly along the tree-lined road that led towards the Rue Saint Jacques, glancing up occasionally at the late November sky, watching the swelling rain clouds gathering ominously over Paris.

'We shouldn't be here, we should be on the coast,' said Rocheteau. 'Preparing to invade England.'

'You should be used to our position by now,' Lausard told him. 'We've been in Paris for almost nine months.'

'I never thought I could become bored with the most beautiful city in the world,' Carbonne murmured.

'Troops come and go every day but we remain here,' Rocheteau said. 'Why is that? Is Bonaparte planning something else for us?'

'The capture of another traitor perhaps,' Delacor offered and the men laughed.

'There are no traitors left are there?' Lausard said dismissively. 'No opposition to our new Emperor.'

'He isn't truly an Emperor until he is crowned,' Bonet interjected.

'He's been an Emperor since the Senate declared him

so in May,' Lausard said flatly. 'In his own mind he has probably occupied that position for much longer.'

'He was approved by the people, Alain,' Bonet said. 'The plebiscite showed more than three and a half million in favour of him assuming that position and less than three *thousand* against.'

'I don't dispute his right to rule and I can understand the need for a line of succession in the event of his death. But is it not a fact that over half a million votes confirming his position were recorded as having come from the army and navy in the last plebiscite?'

Bonet nodded.

'At any time were *we* asked to vote?' Lausard continued. 'Do you know any man in any regiment who was given that opportunity?'

The former schoolmaster merely shook his head.

'Are you suggesting the vote was not a true one, Alain?' Rocheteau asked.

Lausard shook his head.

'Not for one moment,' the sergeant told him. 'If we had been asked I have no doubt we would all have offered our support anyway. I am sure that every man in the army would. I am merely making the point that, to some, it would appear that the very men who put him where he is are not deemed worthy of an opinion.'

The men walked a little further in silence, the others considering Lausard's words.

'And tomorrow we are to escort his coach to Notre Dame where he will be crowned by the Pope, watched by his Marshals, worshipped by his people,' the sergeant continued.

'It is a great honour for us to be chosen as part of his escort,' Carbonne said proudly.

Lausard nodded.

'I wonder if his Marshals will stop bickering among themselves long enough to pay homage to him,' Rocheteau chuckled. 'They seem more concerned with amassing fortunes for themselves than showing loyalty to Bonaparte. I hear that many of them are still unsatisfied with their promotion. Others are jealous of their brothers who have also been given batons.'

'I was speaking to a sergeant in the horse artillery and he said that General Marmont was furious he had been overlooked,' Bonet said.

'He was the only Corps commander not to be created a Marshal,' Lausard mused. 'It appears Bonaparte has forgotten his part in the Battle of Marengo. No reward for commanding the last five guns we had. I can understand his annoyance, especially when you look at some of the others who were awarded the title.'

'Four were honourary appointments, were they not?' Bonet offered. 'Kellermann, Lefebvre, Pérignon and Serurier. The remainder were all active, serving Corps commanders.'

'I cannot understand why Bonaparte created Brune a Marshal,' Delacor said dismissively. 'The man is an incompetent ass. And why Davout? And what has Mortier ever done?'

'Each of them has served the cause of the revolution and the army in some way,' Lausard told him. 'Perhaps it was because so many of them embodied the *ethics* of the revolution. Look at their backgrounds. Berthier was the son of an engineer. Murat of an innkeeper. Jourdan's father was a doctor. Bessiéres is the son of a surgeon. Augereau's father is a mason. Bernadotte, Soult, Brune and Moncey were all the offspring of lawyers. Davout's father was an officer. Massena's a tanner and soap maker. Ney, Lannes and Mortier came from truly humble stock. Ney's father was a cooper, Lannes' a peasant farmer and Mortier's also a farmer. All of them are good officers but they also symbolise everything the revolution stood for. No matter what a man's background, he may still reach an exalted position if he has the will and the ability. Look at Bonaparte himself. His family were lesser Corsican nobility and now their son is preparing to accept the mantle of Emperor of the French. Perhaps Aristotle was right.'

'Who is Aristotle?' Delacor wanted to know. 'Is he that corporal in the third squadron?'

Bonet laughed.

'He was a Greek philosopher,' the former schoolmaster said, looking slyly at Lausard. 'Regarding man's ability to achieve greatness, he once said that if a man rose so high so quickly then we must think he was misplaced in his origins. That *is* what you meant, isn't it, Alain?'

Lausard smiled and nodded.

'And what the hell does *that* mean?' Delacor demanded.

'That these men Bonaparte created Marshals have been rewarded as much for their backgrounds as their abilities,' Bonet explained.

'You speak a foreign language most of the time, schoolmaster,' Delacor snapped.

'I speak the same language as you. I cannot help it if your limited intellect prevents you from understanding me.'

The other men laughed.

As they crossed the bridge, the magnificent edifice of Notre Dame confronted them, rising up into the sky like some kind of stone sentinel. The bells inside the cathedral were already ringing as they had been for several days. In their barracks just off the Rue de Vaugirard, the dragoons were able to hear the bells that had hardly been still as they signalled the rejoicing to come, an unending chorus of exultation Bonaparte expected to sweep through the whole of France when confirmation of his position as Emperor was final.

'And what do you think of all this, Karim?' Lausard said, glancing around at the Circassian who was looking up at the imposing splendour of the cathedral.

'Bonaparte is as much my Emperor as yours,' he replied. 'When I joined your ranks, I became as you. A servant of France.'

'Is Notre Dame not the most magnificent of sights?' Moreau offered. 'A fitting testament to God.' He crossed himself.

'To *your* God,' Karim corrected him. 'Allah, all praise to Him, does not alway need such monuments to prove His greatness. The prayers offered to Him are heard with as much clarity whether they are said in a mosque or in a hovel in the desert.'

'And do you think He listens?' Lausard wanted to know.

'He hears all,' Karim assured the sergeant.

'There is only one true God,' Moreau said angrily. 'The God of the Bible, not of some heathen Arab.'

'There is room for all our beliefs in this world,' the Circassian said. 'Do not insult my God because He is different to yours, Moreau.'

'Everyone in Paris, apart from Moreau, will be looking at Bonaparte tomorrow,' Lausard offered. 'You will be watching for the Pope, won't you?'

'Of course,' Moreau said defensively. 'All good Christians will.'

'Didn't the revolution outlaw the worship of God?' Rocheteau asked. 'That was why you were imprisoned wasn't it, Moreau?'

'No man can supersede God. I would not give up my beliefs because of the threats of a few lawyers and "pekinese".'

'It is Bonaparte's word that is preached from pulpits throughout the country now, not God's,' said Lausard. 'The Pope is here only as his puppet. Present because he was summoned.'

'He is our only link with God here on earth. No man can command him. Not even Bonaparte.'

'So you believe,' Lausard said dismissively. 'I feel that even your God will have some competition tomorrow in the shape of our Emperor. If there were a crown he could wear to make himself a deity, I am sure it would be under construction as we speak. From Emperor to God is a small step for our Corsican.' A number of the other men chuckled. Moreau crossed himself again.

'Throughout history, more men have died in the service of God than of any Emperor,' Bonet interjected.

Lausard nodded almost imperceptibly.

'Come tomorrow,' he murmured, 'that may well change.'

Barnabas Luigi Gregorio Chiaramonti sipped at the red wine then moved towards the fire that had recently been stoked by a servant. The suite of private apartments he had been given within the Tuileries Palace was cold and the sixty-four-year-old man was inclined to feel the chill more acutely than those who served him. He had scarcely been warm since his arrival in Paris two days earlier. The man better known as Pope Pius VII placed the fine crystal goblet upon the mantelpiece and warmed his gnarled hands before the dancing flames. There were liver spots on his skin and the wrinkles around his eyes and across his forehead were deep. His eye-glasses, perched on the bridge of his large nose, were thick, a testament to his failing eyesight. The pontiff moved slowly, almost ponderously, as if wishing to conserve a measure of energy. But for all the outward appearance of a weary old man, he possessed a quickness and alertness in his stare that belied his physical state. For what seemed like an eternity, he stood looking into the fire, tracing shapes in the flames, until a knock on his apartment door shook him from his reverie.

Napoleon Bonaparte entered without waiting for an invitation.

He drew his heels together and bowed curtly in the direction of Pius who remained where he was beside the fire.

'I trust I am not disturbing you, Your Holiness,' Bonaparte said, crossing to the table and pouring himself a glass of burgundy. 'I wanted to speak with you before you retired for the night.'

'Of what do you wish to speak, my son?' Pius wanted to know.

'I merely sought to ensure you were comfortable and had everything you needed. I trust you are being cared for adequately?'

'Your hospitality is overwhelming and I have been blessed with many visitors since my arrival here. Your Foreign Minister, Monsieur Talleyrand, called on me this very afternoon. As did Cardinal Maury and, indeed, your own wife.'

Bonaparte looked somewhat surprised at the mention of the last caller.

'She is nervous regarding the ceremony tomorrow,' he replied. 'I suspect she sought your reassurance.'

'On the contrary. She seems more concerned with her marital state than with the events that are to embrace us all so soon.'

'What concerns does she have?'

'She is *your* wife, my son; surely you have discussed this matter?'

Bonaparte's eyes narrowed slightly.

'She informed me that your marriage was only a civil one, conducted before a registrar,' Pius told the Corsican. 'You were not married in the house of God. Before Him, your union is unblessed.'

'Meaning what?' Bonaparte demanded.

'I cannot carry out your coronation tomorrow until this situation is rectified.'

'For the sake of a few words said by a priest you would try to deny me my rightful title?' rasped the Corsican. 'You are merely God's representative, not God Himself, to make such judgements. Do not presume to deprive the people of France of their Emperor because of such a trifling matter.'

'A small matter in your eyes, my son, but an important one.'

Bonaparte paced the floor agitatedly for a moment or two then turned his attention back to the pontiff.

'Would you oppose me on this?' he demanded.

'I am merely informing you of the Church's moral position.'

'So, what solution would you offer?'

'I will marry you now, here in this very room, if that is what you so command.'

'I do not seek to *command* you, Holy Father. You came

to Paris out of choice, not because I brought you here. You are not my prisoner.'

'And if I had chosen to remain in the Eternal City? What would you have done? Sent soldiers to bring me here? Forced me to place the crown upon your head?'

'Is that what you think?'

'I know that you are a very ambitious man and that you would not allow anything to prevent you from achieving your aims. Even the opposition of a Pope. Cardinal Fesch made that very clear to me during our meetings.'

'My uncle is a very direct man and he speaks the truth. I intend to wear the crown tomorrow, whether or not you choose to place it upon my head. By this time tomorrow night, France will have an Emperor and at my side will be the Empress Josephine. But, if it will ease your conscience, then you may perform the ceremony you speak of. I will summon my wife.'

'It is not my conscience I seek to satisfy. I desire only to follow the laws of God. If I were to crown you and your wife tomorrow, I would be breaking one of those laws.'

'Then marry us, Holy Father,' Bonaparte said flatly. 'Now.'

Fifteen

The sound of cheering was deafening. Lausard marvelled at the sheer volume of noise coming from the crowds that thronged every street. As the imperial procession passed along the Champs Élysées, he allowed himself a glance to his right and left and saw a sea of delighted faces held back by the ranks of infantry, all standing with their muskets at the 'Present' position. The foot soldiers, as with all troops on duty that day, were dressed in full ceremonial uniform. The plumes on their headgear waved in the slight breeze. Their officers, gold epaulettes gleaming, stood with their swords drawn, the polished leather peaks of their shakos also glinting. Gold and silver cords hung from them like jewels. The triumphal procession moved on towards the Place de la Revolution, even the sound of so many horses' hooves eclipsed by the fervent crowds. There were representatives of every branch of the cavalry present. The dragoons themselves were clad in full dress uniform: green jackets and red lapels, turnbacks, collar, cuffs and flaps. Thirty-three highly polished pewter buttons, embossed with the regimental number, ornamented each habit. Seven small buttons were placed on each lapel, one on each shoulder and three on each cuff flap. Three larger ones were at the top of the right-hand skirt, two more in the small of the back and one each in the angle of the two trefoil pockets on the skirt. Beneath the habit, the dragoons wore white waistcoats, bleached to almost blinding brilliance and adorned with another single row of gleaming pewter buttons. Like his companions, Lausard had spent most of the previous night bleaching his breeches and polishing his knee-length black boots and, upon his head was the crowning glory of the uniform. The copper helmet they usually wore was now encircled by a fur turban with a heavily embossed copper crest supporting a thick black horse-hair mane that reached to the middle of their backs. The chin straps were copper scales attached by a rosace. Just forward of the left-hand chin strap they sported huge red plumes. Officers wore magnificent leopard-skin turbans around their copper casques. Lausard caught a glimpse of Gaston looking particularly resplendent in his scarlet tunic and a white horse-hair mane trailing from the crest of his helmet. Even the horses seemed to be basking in the adulation of the crowd, stepping high over the cobbles, their coats combed until they seemed to glow.

Lausard saw the other cavalry units. The swarm of hussars in dazzling combinations of colours. Light-blue pelisses and yellow dolmans, bristling with white and gold braid. Huge plumes of all colours nodding in the breeze. Chasseurs in their magnificent green uniforms, black colpacks sporting gold and silver cords and red-tipped green plumes, their officers' saddles covered by leopard-skin shabraques. Cuirassiers, their body armour shining, huge horses carrying these powerful men along and stepping as spryly as the ponies of the light cavalry. Mounted Grenadiers of the Imperial Guard, their towering bearskins and red plumes making them seem like giants as their lace-trimmed blue shabraques flapped in the wind and their trumpeters, dazzling in white bearskins and light-blue tunics, all mounted on magnificent black Breton horses, completed the bodyguard on the most awesome part of the procession. The imperial coach, drawn by twelve superb black horses, trundled along, driven by coachmen attired in long blue, gold-trimmed coats and bicorns that carried ostrich feather plumes. Within that coach, Lausard knew Bonaparte sat. Already dressed in his robes of state, he was less than ten minutes from his destiny. The twin towers of Notre Dame drew closer by the second and Lausard was sure the cheering of the crowd grew even louder.

They passed the Tuileries and the Palais Royal then turned right to cross the bridge that would take them directly to the front of the cathedral. As they began the last part of their journey, Lausard could see a mass of white-clad men standing on the steps of the cathedral and he realised they were priests. Dozens of them, it seemed. They looked to the sergeant like a flock of geese standing patiently. On either side of the stone steps that led to the entrance to Notre Dame, Bonaparte's marshal's waited. They were all dressed in their ceremonial uniforms of blue jackets and white breeches, many of the high-ranking men decorated with the Legion of Honour. He recognised Ney, his shock of red hair visible from a distance. Beside him stood Lannes and Berthier. On the other side of the steps, Lausard had no difficulty picking out the stunning figure of Marshal Joachim Murat. He wore a gold-trimmed shako topped with several massive ostrich feathers, a white dolman and pelisse, both weighed down with gold braid, red Hungarian breeches and white boots. A sabre hung from his gold-trimmed belt, sheathed in its jewel-encrusted scabbard. Looking positively conservative next to him was the familiar bald pate of Davout. At his side, the imposing figure of Bernadotte. At the foot of the stairs, in ranks three deep, stood the imposing figures of Bonaparte's personal bodyguard. Grenadiers of the Imperial Guard, dressed in blue jackets with red epaulettes and massive bearskins adorned by brass front plates, yellow cords and red plumes, all waited for the arrival of the man they would soon hail as Emperor.

The procession came to a halt and footmen hurried to open the doors of the imperial coach. The accompanying cavalry escort brought their mounts to a halt and Lausard patted his chestnut lightly on the neck to calm it. The animal pawed the ground, as impatient, it seemed, as its rider to see the emergence of the Corsican from within. The level of noise which Lausard had already found surprising rose to unbelievable levels as Bonaparte stepped into view. He was wearing purple and scarlet robes trimmed with ermine and gold. Even Lausard could not fail to be impressed by the Corsican's appearance and he watched as he made his way up the stone steps, to be greeted by the gaggle of priests and marshals. Close behind him came Josephine, her train supported by half a dozen maids-in-waiting. The two of them disappeared inside the stunning edifice of Notre Dame but the cheering continued. Lausard shifted position slightly in his saddle, wondering how long he and his colleagues were going to remain seated outside the cathedral. He looked across at Lieutenant Royere who managed a smile. The first chants of '*Vive l'Empereur*!' began to fill the air.

Candles, burning by the thousand inside the cathedral of Notre Dame, cast deep shadows and their yellow flame gave a burnished appearance to the sea of gold that Bonaparte saw before him as he stood at the altar. Gold on uniforms, on scabbards, on robes and on the mitre of Pope Pius VII. He saw it too on the imperial sword of state carried slowly up the main aisle, on its cushion, by Marshal Lefebvre. He was accompanied by Marshal Kellermann who had been entrusted with the imperial crown itself and by Berthier, who guarded the sceptre and orb. Bonaparte watched as the three men made their way along the nave, past the north and south transepts, towards the high altar where he and Josephine waited. The Corsican was aware that all eyes were upon him and he welcomed their gaze. He knew that so many emotions were contained within those probing looks. Envy. Admiration. Anger. Relief. Even love. But, to him, none of those emotions mattered. None could prevent him from attaining that which was rightfully his. That which he had *made* his. The crown of Emperor. As Lefebvre, Berthier and Kellermann drew nearer, past the chancel, Bonaparte was aware of movement behind him then he saw Pius move to his side, preparing to accept the crown that Kellermann carried on its gold cushion. He looked at the faces of his marshals, of his family, of the clergy gathered around in their white robes like feathers from a torn pillow. All gazing at *him*, kneeling on his red velvet cushion, waiting for the Pope to take the crown and place it upon his head. When Kellermann was no more than two feet away, Bonaparte rose to his feet and stepped forward. He was vaguely aware of a sound that Pius made deep in his wrinkled throat, a sound of disbelief. Of anger perhaps. But, to the Corsican, it was immaterial. He took the crown from its cushion and raised it above his head, allowing his gaze to take in every detail of the gold laurels. For what seemed like an eternity he remained motionless; then, before the eyes of the assembled masses, he lowered the crown on to his head and turned to look at Pius who took a step back towards the golden chair from which he had risen.

'You see before you a new Emperor,' called Bonaparte. 'Crowned not by God's hand but by the hand of a soldier. By my own hand.'

Bonaparte then took the imperial sword, raised that into the air for a second and kissed the blade and hilt before placing it back on the cushion. He did the same with the sceptre and the orb.

'These are not the instruments of power,' he said, his voice a hoarse whisper. 'They are the *accessories* of power. True power lies in the hands of the man who wields them.'

Holding the crown in one hand, he took a step towards Josephine and held the glittering headdress over her bowed head.

'I proclaim you Empress Josephine of France,' he said and touched the circlet lightly to the top of her head.

Beyond her he caught the eye of his older brother, Joseph, and a slight smile creased his lips.

'If only our father could see us now,' he whispered.

Then, once more, he turned to face the sea of faces gathered before him.

'Behold,' he called, his voice rising, filling every part of the cathedral. 'Emperor Napoleon the First of France.'

He extended his arms in a cruciform position, his gaze darting around the inside of Notre Dame like those of a predator searching out prey.

The first shout came from somewhere to his left but he could not be sure where. From one of his own marshals perhaps.

'*Vive l'Empereur!*'

The cry was taken up by other voices.

The sound grew until it was a deafening cacophony, reverberating off the ancient walls until it seemed it would shatter them, such was its intensity.

'*Vive l'Empereur! Vive l'Empereur!*'

Bonaparte moved towards the golden throne set on the high altar and took his seat between Josephine and Pius, who cast him an angry glance.

'God had no part in my achievements,' the Corsican said curtly. 'Why should He be concerned with my coronation? The people chose me. Not God.'

Pius did not answer.

There was nothing to say.

Inside Notre Dame the cheers continued.

Lausard had no idea how long he and his companions had been sitting outside the cathedral. All he knew was that his horse was growing restless, as were a number of the other mounts gathered before the building. Cavalrymen, trained for years in the saddle, adjusted and readjusted their positions on their mounts with barely discernible movements. When Bonaparte had entered the cathedral the order had been given for the units accompanying the procession to stand down. The cavalry were permitted to sheath their swords and rest, as best they could, in the saddle until given further orders. The infantry, for their part, were kept at the ready, partly to prevent the enthusiastic crowd from spilling into the square that fronted Notre Dame. Lausard glanced around and thought that every single person in Paris must be present somewhere within the crowd. Indeed at times during the procession to the cathedral he had wondered if every citizen of France herself was in the capital on this auspicious day. He saw Gaston looking around, mesmerised by the sights that met his eyes. Rocheteau was patting the neck of his horse gently. So too was Tigana. Karim remained bolt upright in his saddle, his eyes never leaving the main doors of the cathedral. The smell of horse dung was strong in the air but it was an odour the men were more than familiar with and it certainly didn't bother them. Somewhere in the crowd, a group of the waiting populace had begun singing the old revolutionary song '*Ah Ça Ira*', and Lausard felt a peculiarly melancholy feeling descend upon him. He had heard it many times during the last ten or fifteen years. It had been particularly popular with the mobs gathered around the guillotine in the Place de la Revolution. Choruses of it could be heard being sung exultantly as the never ending parade of aristocrats and political enemies were laid beneath the bloodied blade.

It had been sung the day his own family had been executed. The song, and the image of his family climbing the steps to their deaths, still remained as painfully imprinted upon his mind now as it had when he had first witnessed it. By another peculiar coincidence, he mused, it had been at a market outside Notre Dame that he and Rocheteau had been arrested for stealing bread, the theft that had seen them imprisoned and condemned. In other circumstances, Lausard might well have found the irony of the situation amusing. Back in those days he had been a thief; now he formed part of the ceremonial guard for the Emperor of France, a man who had himself at that time been a lowly gunner in the artillery. How time changed men, Lausard thought. The revolution had first taken his family then given him back his freedom. It had given Bonaparte a crown.

He glanced at the coachmen tending to the horses that drew the imperial coach, then his gaze moved towards the great doors of the cathedral and he was one of the first to make out the unmistakable figure of the Corsican as he emerged, surrounded by his marshals, the sceptre and orb clutched in his hands. Rocheteau too saw the Emperor and looked in Lausard's direction. The sergeant nodded almost imperceptibly. Gradually, more and more of the troops facing the cathedral saw the Corsican and his entourage and now the crowd too had become aware of the presence of their new Emperor. The cheering became even more frenzied, even when Bonaparte raised his hands as if to silence them; but finally he merely smiled and lifted the orb and sceptre into plain view. It was a gesture met by an almost palpable explosion of noise from both the crowd and the watching troops. Again the chants began, like a ceaseless litany.

'*Vive L'Empereur!*'

Emperor Napoleon the First of France stood for a moment longer at the top of the steps, Josephine close beside him, then he descended slowly and clambered into the imperial coach. Hands were thrust in his direction and the Grenadiers of the Imperial Guard strained every muscle to keep the adoring populace back behind the human cordon they had formed. Orders were shouted, by Captain Milliere among others, barely audible above the crowd. But Lausard and the other cavalrymen knew what was expected of them. They shouldered their swords and, with the precision only superbly trained men are capable of, they moved off at a walk behind the coach, seemingly oblivious to the pandemonium around them. The shrieks and roars of adulation echoed in their ears.

Bonet held up the copy of *Le Moniteur* and read aloud;

'"His Imperial Highness, the Emperor Napoleon the First of France, has granted three days of national celebration to commemorate his coronation and to reflect the will of the French people. *Vive l'Empereur*."'

'What do we call him now?' Tigana wanted to know. 'Your Highness? My Lord?'

'We may as well call him king,' Delacor said bitterly. 'You were right, Alain. He is now king in all but name. He has betrayed the spirit of the revolution.'

'Since when has the spirit of the revolution concerned *you*?' Rocheteau wanted to know.

'I overheard Lieutenant Royere and Captain Milliere talking about it,' Delacor explained as the other men around him laughed.

'I don't know what *you're* going to call him, Tigana,' Bonet continued, 'but the paper says that the English government are already calling him "The Usurper".' He tapped the periodical with an index finger. 'Some are calling him "the successor to Robespierre".'

'What he did was necessary for the stability of France,' Carbonne offered.

'You mean for the advancement of Bonaparte himself,' Delacor snapped.

'"Henceforth, in matters of state, he is to be known as the Emperor Napoleon",' Bonet read.

'Does this mean he will no longer command the army?'

Giresse wanted to know. 'Are we to be left at the mercy of men like Soult, Davout and Brune?'

'He will not relinquish control of the army,' Lausard said with a measure of certainty. 'He is still a soldier at heart. Beneath the robes of state he wears a uniform. He built this army. He will not entrust it to others.'

Lausard sat on his bed listening to the conversation around him, watching the rain as it coursed down the windows of the barracks. Three days had passed since the coronation of Napoleon and the city had been in ferment ever since. The manifestation of undiluted joy and adoration that Lausard had witnessed outside Notre Dame that day had most certainly continued. The near-hysteria had been sustained by almost ceaseless parades in Napoleon's honour, a number of which the dragoons themselves had taken part in. To Lausard, it seemed as if the new Emperor was barely concerned with the fact that he was still deeply embroiled in an economic conflict with England that, at any day, could escalate into open war. The fact that rumours of Russian and Austrian coalitions against France had been rife even *before* the coronation served to keep Lausard's personal feelings about the current situation in check.

'And what of us?' Roussard asked. 'What do we do now?'

'What we always did before,' Lausard told him. 'We wait until our Emperor chooses his course of action and then we follow whatever orders he may issue.'

'Do you think he will invade England?' Giresse wondered.

Lausard shrugged.

'Over a hundred and fifty thousand men still wait along the coast for such an order,' he offered. 'But, as before,

159

the situation seems to be dependent upon control of the seas.'

'I'm tired of waiting,' Delacor snapped. 'Parading around like some toy soldier for the amusement of the people of Paris.'

'Our Emperor would have us parade again this very afternoon in the Champ-de-Mars,' Lausard said flatly. 'We are to be presented with our new standards, our eagles. Every regiment in the French army will receive one.'

'And after that?' Rocheteau wanted to know.

Lausard had no answer for him. He was still gazing out of the window, watching the rain as it pelted down.

As morning became afternoon, the rain increased in ferocity. Lausard sat astride his horse, water dripping from the oilskin cover on his helmet. It also poured from his green cape. The breath of men and horses clouded the air. Rain water filled the gutters to overflowing and formed pools in the Champ-de-Mars where so many troops were gathered. Men representing every regiment in the French army were crammed into the cobbled area. Horsemen, foot soldiers, gunners – all stood miserably beneath the driving rain watching the figure striding back and forth before them on a specially constructed wooden dias. Napoleon was wearing the dark blue overcoat of a grenadier. Rain was dripping from his battered black bicorn but he strode the platform seemingly oblivious of the foul weather. Before him, two ranks of the Imperial Guard stood to attention. Behind them, Lausard could see several high-ranking officers, wearing capes against the elements. He noticed Marshal Ney. Close by him Davout, Lannes, Murat and Augereau. General Rapp, one of Napoleon's most senior ADCs, glanced alternately between his Emperor and the masses of soaking men before him. Also on the dias stood another rank of grenadiers, their bearskins sodden by the rain. Each was holding a long staff from which hung a piece of cloth that Lausard could not yet make out. At a signal from Bonaparte, each man unfurled the cloth and the red, white and blue flag so familiar to French troops everywhere fluttered into view. But these were different. Atop the staff was an eagle of gilded bronze, twenty centimetres high, its metal wings spread wide as if it was about to take flight. The flag itself was of oiled silk, eighty-one centimetres square. It had a central white lozenge on one side of which, Lausard could quite clearly see, in gold letters, L'EMPEREUR DES FRANÇAIS AU 23 RÉGIMENT and, on the other, VALEUR ET DISCIPLINE, plus the number of the battalion or squadron. The triangles at the corners of the flags were alternately red and blue, beginning with a blue triangle at the top of the flag, nearest the staff and the imposing eagle. In each of the triangles was the number of the regiment surrounded by a laurel wreath, both in gold. As a strong breeze whipped across the vast open area, he saw one of the eagles flutter more strongly than the rest and it opened out to reveal that it was a swallow-tailed guidon with rounded ends. The number he saw upon it was that of his own regiment. The swell of pride he felt took him by surprise somewhat and he afforded himself a smile as he saw the eagle of his regiment.

'Soldiers, here are your colours,' roared Napoleon, gesturing towards the eagles. 'These eagles will always be your rallying point. They will fly wherever your Emperor deems necessary for the defence of the throne and his people. Do you swear to lay down your lives in their defence and, by your courage, to keep them ever on the road to victory?'

The eruption of noise that greeted his words was breathtaking.

'We swear!' bellowed the assembled throng of troops and Lausard found his own voice joining the mass, growing louder as the eagles were raised aloft. They fluttered in the wind like beacons, the eagles glinting despite the downpour.

The torrential rain did nothing to affect the paroxysm of patriotic fervour precipitated by the appearance of these new standards. Through his own furious yelling, Lausard wondered what effect their awesome appearance would have on a battlefield.

Even the assembled marshals were howling their delight, clenched fists punching the air in triumph as the first men marched forward to receive their eagles amidst the tumultuous sound that enveloped them. Ney was waving his marshal's baton around as if it were some kind of ornate club. Lausard had never felt such unbridled pride away from a battlefield before and, like many cavalrymen around him, he rose in his stirrups to yell his approval, drawn, almost against his will, into the tumult.

'*Vive l'Empereur!*' shouted someone close by and, within moments, the entire mass of troops had joined in the chant. Lausard among them. He felt the hairs on the back of his neck rise and the rivulets of rain coursing down his cheeks were like tears of exultation.

On the dias, Napoleon took off his bicorn and waved it above his head. The look on his face was one of pure triumph. He pulled one of the eagles towards him and kissed the majestic bird that topped the staff. It brought an even more rapturous response from the watching men.

Lausard, like the other troops, continued to cheer wildly.

Sixteen

Captain Milliere stood in the doorway of the barracks, looking around at the dragoons, waiting for the questions he knew would come. The news he had brought had been greeted by a chorus of mournful groans and resigned grunts. Joubert had slumped back on his bunk, the structure creaking ominously for a moment beneath his weight. Sonnier had sighed wearily, as had a number of the other troopers. The officer had caught the eye of Lausard and found only indifference in the sergeant's gaze.

'Back to Boulogne within a week,' murmured Giresse.

'I received the orders this very morning,' Milliere told him.

'So, is the Emperor going ahead with his plan to invade England?' Lausard wanted to know.

'It would appear so,' the officer told him.

'And what of Nelson and the English fleet?' Bonet interjected. 'Have they been defeated? Is the Channel clear for our crossing?'

Milliere could only shrug.

'You know as much as I,' he said flatly. 'I received

these orders, I am relaying them to you. You have two days' leave before we depart for the coast. At least take advantage of *that*.'

'Back to Moulin-Hubert,' snorted Delacor. 'To more drilling. More of Marshal Soult's torture.'

'Two days' leave is better than nothing,' Giresse remarked cheerfully. 'It gives me time to say farewell to some of the women who have been fortunate enough to make my acquaintance while we have been here in Paris.'

Some of the other men laughed.

'Time for a few more good meals,' Joubert said, rubbing his large belly.

Lausard looked on with little apparent regard for what was happening around him.

'What will you do with *your* two days, Sergeant?' Milliere asked.

Lausard shrugged.

'Prepare myself, Captain,' he said quietly. 'For whatever our Emperor wishes of me.'

Milliere could not help but detect a note of scorn in the NCO's words.

'You told me, after we kidnapped the Duke of Enghien, that I would have the war I wanted. I am still waiting.'

'Be thankful for this peace. It will not remain indefinitely. For nearly five years now we have lived without war. I fear we will see its face before the end of this coming autumn. Rumours already circulate about an alliance signed between England and Russia. English gold has bought the allegiance of the Tsar. It seems only a matter of time before Austria joins them, possibly Prussia, too. God help France if she is to face four nations simultaneously.'

'If Enghien had been allowed to remain where he was then France might not be in this position.'

'Come now, Sergeant, there is more to it than that. The execution of one man could not precipitate a war involving most of Europe. You attach too much importance to this dead Bourbon.'

'We shall see,' Lausard said. When Milliere left the barracks, the NCO followed. 'How much importance should I attach to the crowning of our new Emperor, Captain?'

'What do you mean?'

'Would France still be in this position were our "little corporal" still a First Consul and not the first of a new dynasty? His appointment as Emperor has been greeted with anger throughout Europe. I suspect he anticipated that.'

'Well-established monarchies are never keen to accept an interloper,' Milliere observed, smiling.

'He has done everything he can to provoke them,' Lausard said. 'First he took the title of Emperor then he crowned himself King of Italy in Milan. The very heart of territory once possessed by Austria.'

'Territory that French soldiers fought and died for in 1796 and again in 1800,' Milliere reminded him. 'I should have no need to remind *you* of all people, Sergeant. You and this regiment suffered as acutely as any in the army during the Italian campaigns.'

Lausard nodded.

'And yet our opponent is to be England?' he mused. 'With Russia and Austria prepared to fight him, our Emperor's face is turned towards the Channel. Perhaps he should think about protecting his back.'

Lausard headed off towards the stables.

Milliere waited a moment then strode on to the next barrack room to repeat his orders to more of his men.

Lausard found the stables empty but for the horses of his squadron. The animals had recently been fed and watered and, due to the amount of drilling the troops had undergone during their stay in the capital, were in spectacularly good condition. The sergeant approached the stall where his chestnut mare waited, nuzzling the fresh straw around its hooves. He patted the animal's neck in greeting then began to fasten the black leather harnesses on the horse. He was in the process of tightening the girth strap when he heard footsteps entering the stable. Lausard turned to see Rocheteau approaching him. The corporal smiled, watching as Lausard threw the green shabraque over the horse's back, fastened it in place then lifted the saddle on to it before securing it.

'Karim and myself were also considering giving our horses some exercise,' Rocheteau said.

The Circassian appeared silently beside the corporal, the ever-present pipe stuck between his lips.

'It was something more than exercise I had in mind,' Lausard told his companions, adjusting his stirrups. 'Before we leave for Boulogne there is something I must do.'

'May we join you in this venture, whatever it may be?' Karim asked.

Lausard smiled and patted the Circassian's shoulder.

'No, my friend,' he said reluctantly. 'But I thank you for your offer.'

Rocheteau opened his mouth to speak but Lausard shook his head, the gesture enough to silence the corporal.

'Take care, Sergeant,' Karim said. 'May Allah, all praise to Him, protect you.'

'Who do you seek, Alain?' Rocheteau wanted to know.

'If you are intent on putting yourself in danger then let us share that danger with you.'

'I said nothing of danger, Rocheteau,' Lausard smiled. 'I will be back within a day. If anyone asks where I am, tell them not to concern themselves.'

Rocheteau nodded.

'You are sure you want no company?' he asked.

Lausard shook his head.

'What I must do, I must do alone.'

Alain Lausard rode south, through the Faubourg Saint Jacques district of Paris. Eventually, he turned along an easterly route, practically following the path of the Seine all the way beyond the confines of the capital. Buildings began to thin out and the metropolis gave way to sprawling countryside. Here and there, wheat waved in yellow masses beneath a watery sun as he guided his horse along. He saw farmers working in their fields. As he passed a windmill, he noticed sacks of flour being loaded by two young men who waved happily to him as he passed. After an hour he paused at a stream, filled his canteen then allowed his horse to drink. He picked a handful of blackberries from a nearby bush and ate them, enjoying their succulent taste. When the horse had drunk its fill, he remounted and continued his journey. There was no urgency about his progress and, for the most part, he barely coaxed the chestnut beyond a steady canter. Like a nobleman surveying his lands, he rode sedately, drinking in the sights around him, listening to birds singing in the trees, glancing up occasionally to see that the sun had finally forced its way out from behind the scudding clouds. It cast deep shadows behind him and, as noon passed, the temperature began to rise.

Ahead of him the narrow road forked. To the right lay the village of Brieneville, a farming community of less than five hundred people. Lausard took the left-hand fork. He rode beneath a canopy of trees that blotted out the sun and cooled the sweat on his face and neck. Where rays of light managed to penetrate the natural umbrella, the ground was mottled light and dark. The smell of earth was strong in his nostrils. He guided the horse on, towards an open area free of the rustling trees. When he emerged the heat of the sun was more powerful than he'd imagined but, despite the warmth, the hairs at the back of his neck rose and he tugged on the reins to bring the horse to a halt.

The iron gates before him were rusted. One was barely attached to the perimeter wall by its hinges and the stonework around it was discoloured like the flesh around an untreated wound. Parts of the stone wall were damaged, but Lausard knew that this was caused by more than the ravages of time. He slowly swung himself out of the saddle and walked up to the gates, holding his horse by its reins. Beyond the gates lay a wide pathway, now overgrown and neglected. Grass grew to his boot top. The pathway led towards what had once been an imposing house but, like the perimeter wall, it too had suffered from exposure to the elements as well as something more malevolent. Even from such a distant vantage point, Lausard could see that the roof was holed in several places. Some of the windows had been boarded up. Others were smashed, some had even lost their frames. There were several small outbuildings, all but one of which had been burned down. Pieces of blackened timber and broken beams, protruding from the wreckage, looked like discoloured bones. Lausard fastened his horse's reins loosely to a

nearby tree stump, patting the animal's muzzle. Then
he took hold of the rusted iron gates and pushed. The
hinges shrieked in protest but the gates opened a couple
of feet. Lausard pushed a little harder and opened the
gate wide enough to allow himself and his horse to pass
through. Then he swung himself back into the saddle and
walked the animal up the overgrown pathway towards the
deserted house.

The silence was almost palpable, broken only by the low
breathing of Lausard's mount and the sound of its hooves
on the ground. The high grass whispered as the animal
made its way towards the house. The sergeant barely
took his eyes from the building, taking in every detail,
every crack in the paintwork, every blemish on the stone.
Ten yards from the front door he dismounted, tethered
the horse to a small bush and made his way towards the
entrance. The wood was rotten and he was able to pick
pieces of it away with ease. High above him he could
hear the buzzing of wasps and Lausard surmised that
the insects had built a nest in the shattered roof. Birds
also looked down upon him from their high vantage
points. Some of them had also taken advantage of the
ramshackle state of the house to construct nests there.
A crow gave voice to its strident song then flapped away,
a black arrowhead against the sky. Lausard pushed hard
against the rotting door. It stood firm. He pushed harder,
surprised that the partition still resisted him. Finally he
kicked hard against it and the entire structure swung back
on its rusted hinges. Clouds of dust billowed into the air
and Lausard waved his hand before his face as the motes
clogged in his eyes and nostrils. He paused at the threshold
for a second before stepping inside.

Despite the warmth of the day, it was cold within the

building. Lausard took a step inside, his boots stirring up more dust that lay inches thick on the hall floor. Immediately before him was a staircase shaped like an inverted fan. It led to a high gallery-like landing. To the right and left of him on the ground floor there were doors, all firmly shut. He moved to the first and pushed it open. The windows were boarded up so that it was gloomy inside the room. There wasn't a stick of furniture left. In the far corner he saw a dark shape and moved towards it but closer inspection revealed it to be nothing more than a dead rat. Lausard moved back out into the hall and then investigated each of the rooms individually. Every one showed the same signs of decay and neglect. All were devoid of furnishings. Some were in worse repair than others. Each room he entered was smothered with dust and on more than one occasion Lausard had to cover his mouth and nose with his hand. But he looked around every room before finally returning to the hall once more. Then, placing one hand on the balustrade of the staircase, he began slowly to climb. The stairs creaked protestingly beneath his weight and his sword clanked against each step as he walked. He reached the landing then paused again before moving towards the first of the bedrooms.

The doors upstairs were all open and Lausard walked straight into the nearest room. As with the ground floor, the rooms were empty. It looked as if a plague of locusts had descended and devoured everything. All that remained in this room was a broken vase lying close to where a bed had once been. Lausard knelt and picked up a piece of the shattered china, turning it over in his hand. He crossed to the window and looked out on to what had been the garden. Topiaried hedges, so carefully cared for in years gone by, had degenerated into shapeless masses of privet. Flower beds had become clogged with weeds. An ornamental fountain had been smashed into a dozen pieces and moss now grew on the cracked stone like gangrene in a wound. As he looked out, the sun momentarily disappeared behind a bank of cloud and a shadow fell across the garden. It was as if nature herself wished to draw a veil over the devastation. Lausard turned away from the window and, as he did so, he heard a sound from below.

Footsteps.

Someone else was inside the house.

Lausard stood motionless for a moment then he heard the stairs groaning as the intruder began to climb.

With incredible stealth, Lausard eased his sword from its scabbard and gripped it in his fist.

The footsteps had reached the landing now.

Close to the room where he waited.

When they had reached the outside of the room he stepped out on to the landing, levelling the sword.

The man standing before him was in his fifties. He looked first at the point of the sword, only inches from his throat, then at Lausard. He raised his hands as if in surrender, his gaze finally settling on the sergeant's face.

'I should gut you like a fish,' Lausard told him. 'What are you doing in here?'

'*Vive l'Empereur,*' the man said softly, running his eyes appraisingly over Lausard's uniform.

'Don't try to save yourself with your empty tributes,' snapped the dragoon. 'Why are you here?'

'I saw you ride up to the house,' the man told him, sweat beading his forehead.

'Do you always spy on people who come here?'

'No one comes here anymore. That is why I was curious. Even more curious when I saw that you were a soldier. Are there more troops with you?'

'What business is that of yours?' he rasped, pressing the point of the sword against the flesh of the older man's neck. 'Have you already tried to steal my horse and my equipment? Are your accomplices waiting to ambush me downstairs?'

'I am alone. I was tending my sheep on the hills overlooking the road. That is when I saw you. I meant no harm.'

Lausard was aware that the man had barely taken his eyes from him in the last couple of minutes. He seemed mesmerised by the sergeant.

'I feel that I know you from somewhere,' the man told him quietly.

'How could you know *me*? All soldiers look the same to civilians, don't they?'

'Did you live in Brieneville at some time? Your face reminds me of someone I once knew. Did you know the family who lived here?'

Lausard didn't speak; he merely lowered his sword slowly. The older man rubbed at his neck where the tip of the blade had been pressed.

'What do *you* know of that family?' the dragoon enquired.

'They were named Lausard. As well as the mother and father, there were three children. A daughter and two sons. They were good people.'

'They were aristocrats,' Lausard retorted, forcing the requisite amount of feigned indignation into his tone.

'They were human beings. They were not like the others carried to the guillotine. Some said they were Girondins, enemies of Robespierre. That stinking butcher. They did not deserve their fate.'

'And what do you know of that fate?'

'A group of men came here one morning and arrested them. Word has it that they were taken to Paris and executed.'

'Do you not believe in the spirit of the revolution? All the rich had to die. Why do you feel pity for this particular family?'

'I worked for them in their stables for more than twenty years. Like my father before me. I was here the morning they were taken.'

'Their deaths gave you your freedom.'

'They never treated me like a servant. They treated all those who cared for them like friends. From the humblest kitchen maid upwards.'

Again Lausard was aware of the older man's intense gaze upon him.

'Were they all executed?' he enquired.

'The parents, the youngest son and the daughter were. I am not sure what fate befell the elder son. He was a fine man. His name was Alain.'

'He is dead,' said the dragoon flatly. 'At least, the man *you* knew is dead.'

'Did you know him?'

'I knew him once, many years ago. The man I knew is no more. The man who lived here has ceased to exist.'

Lausard headed for the stairs, the older man scurrying after him.

'You look like him,' the man said. 'You look like the eldest son, like the man I knew.'

Lausard kept walking. He reached the hallway and

strode on out into the sunlight once more where he untethered his horse.

'Then keep that memory,' Lausard said. He extended his right hand and the older man, suddenly bewildered, shook it warmly. 'Remember him as he was. You will not see him again.' The dragoon swung himself into the saddle. 'Farewell, François Auteil.'

Lausard turned his horse.

'How do you know my name?' the older man called, running a few yards after Lausard's mount. 'Tell me. How do you know?'

He stopped running, his breath coming in gasps.

'Tell me,' he called again, a note of desperation in his voice.

Lausard put spurs to his horse and rode swiftly away from the house.

Auteil watched him go.

Not once did Lausard look back.

Seventeen

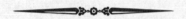

The smell of food inside the hut was mouth-watering but Napoleon seemed distinctly uninterested in the repast before him. The same could not be said of his staff. Several of the other men present gazed longingly at the chicken, pork, potatoes and carrots laid out on the long table. Goblets of burgundy also awaited them, should their Emperor ever deign to tear himself away from the window. Napoleon was gazing out into the gloom, apparently tracing the path of raindrops that coursed down the glass. Beyond lay the camp of Boulogne. Smoke rose from many of the makeshift chimneys as his troops enjoyed their own meals. But food, it seemed, was the last thing on the Corsican's mind.

'Is this information you gave me correct, Berthier?' he said, finally turning to face the assorted generals who either sat at the dinner table or loitered within the hut awaiting orders.

The Chief of Staff nodded.

'There is no reason to think otherwise, sire,' Berthier told his superior. 'As we always suspected, it was only a matter of time before Austria joined with England and Russia against us. They further anticipate the support of the German and Baltic states and Naples.'

'Naturally,' Napoleon sneered. 'Naples has always been a Bourbon stronghold.'

'At present,' Berthier continued, 'the only support we can count on comes from Bavaria, Württemberg and the areas of Northern Italy, Holland and Switzerland that we control.'

'What of Prussia?'

Berthier could only shrug.

'So far they have made no committment one way or the other,' he explained. 'Despite the pro-Russian feelings of his Queen, King Frederick William is content to remain unimpressed by either side.'

'The close proximity of Marshal Bernadotte's corps to Prussian territory may well have gone some way to helping him decide,' remarked General Jean Rapp with a grin.

'It is a formidable coalition that we face nonetheless,' offered Armand Augustin Louis Caulaincourt. The Master of the Horse looked around as if for support from some of the other high-ranking men present.

'And it is a formidable force that our *enemies* face,' Napoleon said, a slight smile on his face. 'I am confident that any regiment in this army is more than equal to whichever English, Russian or Austrian unit dares to oppose it.' He crossed to another table on the other side of the room where maps were laid out. Some of those still seated resignedly rose and joined their Emperor as he studied the documents before him.

'What do we know of their troop dispositions so far?' Napoleon wanted to know.

'As much as we know of their motives, sire.' Berthier grinned. 'Intelligence reports indicate that the forces allied against us are intent upon restoring Europe to the territorial balance of 1789.'

'Am I to assume they are not happy with France's expansion during the past ten years?' Napoleon chuckled.

'Quite so,' the Chief of Staff added.

'How many men are currently arrayed against us?' Napoleon wanted to know. 'And, more to the point, where are they positioned?'

The officers gathered more closely around the maps, watching as Berthier marked each enemy formation with a pin.

'As far as our intelligence is aware,' the Chief of Staff began, 'there are to be four main, connected offensives against us. Fifteen thousand British troops are to be landed at Cuxhaven. They are to be supported by twelve thousand Swedish troops and twenty thousand Russians, massing at Stralsund. A further fifty thousand Russians, under General Bennigsen, are to join them from Puklawi on the Vistula. There are also reports of another force being organised at Riga by Buxhowden and Michelson.'

'Presumably, the presence of so many Russian troops is intended to sway the opinion of the Prussian King and bring him into their fold?' Napoleon mused.

'Yes, sire,' Berthier nodded. 'If Frederick William *does* decide to join them then we could be facing up to two hundred thousand Prussians as well.'

'We will deal with that problem when and *if* it happens,' Napoleon mused. 'What of the other planned allied offensives?'

'Bavaria is to be occupied by ninety thousand Austrians,

commanded by General Mack and the Archduke Ferdinand,' Berthier continued. 'They will be joined, eventually, by General Kutusov at the head of eighty-five thousand Russians. Command will then be passed to the Emperor Francis. Together, these armies intend to advance on the Rhine from the direction of Ulm, sweeping through the Black Forest, Swabia and Franconia towards Strasbourg.'

'The Tsar has promised that Kutusov will be on Bavarian soil by 20 October,' added General Rapp, scratching at one of his bushy sideburns.

Napoleon shrugged.

'Have they not taken into account the dates?' he mused. 'The twentieth of October in Russia comes *before* 20 October in Austria.'

The other officers looked puzzled.

'The Russians still operate on the Julian calendar,' the Corsican said gleefully. 'The Austrians on the Gregorian. The Gregorian is ten days ahead of the Julian system. It will be impossible for them to coordinate their troop movements using two different timetables. Their *first* mistake.'

Berthier nodded then returned to the maps.

'The South German front is to be linked with Northern Italy by twenty-five thousand Austrians under the command of Archduke John,' continued the Chief of Staff. 'These men will occupy the Tyrol and the neighbouring Alpine passes. This will enable them to operate northwards towards Ulm or south into Italy. It is Italy where the Austrians expect our main counterattack to come. The Aulic Council has already allocated ninety-five thousand men, under Archduke Charles, to cross the river Adige. His initial objectives are Mantua, Peschiera and Milan.'

'They are basing their entire strategy upon the assumption that I will strike in Italy once again,' Napoleon said. 'Their *second* mistake.'

'The Aulic Council have not forgotten the campaigns of 1796 and 1800,' Berthier offered. 'They are also determined to force Viceroy Beauharnais out of Lombardy. Once that is done, they will invade the South of France.'

'Eugene will stand firm,' Napoleon said unflinchingly. 'He may be my stepson but I love him as if he were my own blood and I have no reason to doubt his ability, his devotion or his courage. They will find him a formidable adversary.'

'A further force of seventeen thousand, made up of British, Russian and Albanian troops, are to be joined by thirty-six thousand Bourbon troops from Sicily with the intention of reconquering Naples. They will then join with the men commanded by Archduke Charles,' General Rapp interjected. 'There is also strong evidence that more Russian troops are preparing to advance from Odessa into Moldavia and Wallachia.'

'Britain has also promised to raise an amphibious force to mount raids against the coasts of France and Holland,' Berthier remarked. 'They are also keen to encourage a new *chouan* revolt in Brittany and La Vendée, on behalf of the Bourbons.'

'Is there anywhere they *don't* intend to attack us?' Napoleon smiled.

The other officers in the room laughed, watching as the Emperor placed both hands on the largest map before him and ran his expert eye over it.

'We are severely understrength to deal with such an onslaught, sire,' Caulaincourt intoned.

'Where is your faith, my friend?' Napoleon chided.

'By a combination of our own abilities and our enemies' failings we shall prevail. All these grandiose plans of the allies appear daunting on paper but actually coordinating them is another matter. They have already made two crucial errors and I see many more. For instance, the Austrian army in the Tyrol is far too large for what amounts to little more than a liaison role. It is a waste of good troops. They would have been better employed making diversionary attacks against Switzerland. But who am I to interrupt an enemy when he is busy making a mistake?' The Corsican grinned. 'Furthermore, the allied chains of high command are defective in the extreme. The Tsar instructs Kutusov to obey orders issued by the Austrian Emperor or the Archdukes. But not by *any* other Austrian General. The Austrians themselves have a dual system of command in Germany. Archduke Ferdinand is the commander in chief but only until he relinquishes control to the Emperor Francis. Who himself has greater faith in the abilities of General Mack and has ordered Ferdinand to obey his own Chief of Staff. It can lead only to discontent and that discontent can lead our enemies to destruction as much of their own making as of ours.'

'That does not alter the fact that our forward resources are widely separated in Hanover, Swabia, Piedmont and Naples,' Caulaincourt insisted. 'Our only ally, Bavaria, can call upon barely twenty thousand men to protect herself. Bernadotte, Marmont, Saint Cyr and Jourdan have barely one hundred thousand men to protect the frontiers of France against over four hundred thousand allied troops. And all we can do is sit here, on the coast, over seven hundred miles from our only ally and wait to be attacked.'

'How many men have we at our disposal within France herself?' Napoleon asked, looking at Berthier.

'Over two hundred and fifty thousand trained troops and a further one hundred and fifty thousand conscripts,' answered the Chief of Staff. 'But, as Caulaincourt rightly suggests, many of those now reside in the coastal camps.'

'It has, as you know, gentlemen, never been my habit to wait for the enemy to make the first movement,' Napoleon declared. 'And, in these circumstances, to allow that would be both foolish and also possibly suicidal. We will strike first.' He regarded the faces of his men one by one then continued, that familiar fire in his eyes. 'Berthier spoke of the allies attacking from four possible directions. Let us consider those more closely. Two of those attacks can be dismissed immediately. Any onslaught against Hanover from Pomerania would have little effect upon the major issues of the war. In fact, it could, should it come to fruition, be a very foolish manoeuvre indeed. It may well induce Prussia to throw her might behind France. Similarly, an allied attack on Naples would also be so far away from the main theatre of war as to be inconsequential. That leaves two lines of attack we must consider. Both viable and both potentially more serious.'

The officers looked on as if mesmerised.

Napoleon jabbed fingers at the maps, removed pins and replaced them in different positions with dizzying speed. His concentration was total, his enthusiasm exhausting. But it was also inspiring the men who looked on, gripped by the fever of amazement and awe the Corsican never failed to ignite in those around him, be they common soldiers or marshals of the Empire.

'Archduke Charles is a very able man,' the Emperor

continued. 'Should he manage, somehow, to defeat Eugene, he would be able to dominate Northern Italy and even invade Southern France. But most serious of all is here.' He jabbed a pin into the area on the map that marked the river Rhine. 'If the Russians are allowed to join Austrian forces already deployed in *this* area then there would be very real danger to France. Those are the two areas in which we must concentrate our efforts.'

'Do you intend to ignore the threats to Naples and Hanover, sire?' General Rapp wanted to know.

'Most certainly not. But, as I said, those two areas are sufficiently distant from the main theatre of war. I will not waste troops in arenas where they will be unused when they could be better employed under my direct command in more important areas.'

'So, how do we counter these proposed offensives, sire?' Rapp continued.

'We strike first,' he said flatly. 'We gain the initiative on the Danube. There we will destroy the Austrians of Ferdinand and Mack before the Russians have time to arrive in support. When the Tsar's men reach their objective, they will find themselves without allies and we will destroy *them* too. It is imperative that the armies of Austria and Russia are not allowed to combine too early. The men currently occupying the coastal camps will move towards the Danube by the fastest and most direct routes possible. During the march they will be joined by twenty-five thousand Bavarian troops. Once that has taken place, they will swing southward from the Rhine and envelop Mack's army.'

'What if the Austrians do not maintain their advance into the Black Forest?' Caulaincourt wanted to know.

'They will,' Napoleon told his companion with unswerving certainty. 'Marshal Murat will provoke the advance by a feint attack in that region. Once the Austrians have been dealt with, we will turn our attention to Russia and inflict upon them so crushing a defeat that no amount of Pitt's gold will wipe the lesson of their humiliation from their minds.' He spoke the last few words with undisguised venom. 'Our main offensive in Germany will be supported by Marshal Massena who will be detailed to occupy the fifty thousand troops under the command of Archduke Charles in Italy. General Gouvion St Cyr will march on Naples with twenty thousand men to cover the eventuality of allied interference there. General Brune will remain here at Boulogne with thirty thousand troops to guard against any British interference.'

'You propose to move over two hundred thousand men from this coast to the Danube?'

The question came from General Geraud Christophe Michel Duroc, a tall slim man with dark hair and slightly protuberant eyes. As Grand Marshal of the Palace, he was in a position both of great trust and responsibility. When he spoke, his voice was calm and unhurried and he stood close to Napoleon looking down at the maps, stroking one side of his acquiline nose contemplatively.

'What else would you have me do, my friend?' Napoleon wanted to know. 'Leave them to rot here while our enemies overrun France?'

'If they are to reach the Danube before the end of September they would have to march thirty miles a day,' Duroc insisted.

'You have been with me long enough to know that France's greatest triumphs have rested on the stamina of my troops, on their abilities to cover large distances rapidly. This is no different to what we achieved in Italy and Egypt.'

'With all due respect, sire, the troop movements you speak of were indeed carried out swiftly, but with infinitely smaller numbers of men. You are now proposing the movement of two hundred and twenty-six battalions of infantry, two hundred and thirty-three squadrons of cavalry, one hundred and sixty-one artillery and sapper companies and three hundred and ninety-six cannon. Not to mention a general staff of over one thousand. Nothing on this scale has ever been attempted before.'

'Where would man be if he never took chances, Duroc?' Napoleon said, patting his companion on the shoulder. 'Where would *I* be now if I had never dared to gamble? But this is not a gamble. The distances are great, I do not deny that. So are the demands to be made upon the troops. But the men of this army are the finest ever to wear its uniform. Better trained, better equipped and better led than any army before it. They are more than equal to the task. I am surprised you doubt them.'

'I do not doubt them, sire, just as I do not doubt, for one instant, your strategy. I was simply voicing my opinion. In the seventeenth century, Marshal Turenne suggested that strategic movements could be undertaken by armies of up to fifty thousand men.'

'You are right. And in 1704 the English Duke of Marlborough marched forty thousand men from Holland to the Danube.'

'But you are proposing to move five times that number of troops, sire. The logistical considerations are immeasurable,' Duroc continued. 'You are preparing to send not regiments, brigades or divisions but seven *corps*, perhaps numbering twenty or thirty thousand men in *each*, on such a march.'

'And it will succeed,' Napoleon told him, a tone of utter conviction in his voice. 'For the first time, France has one single army, *La Grande Armée*, to carry out my commands. No longer will there be an Army of England or an Army of the Interior, or of Italy. From this point, the main force is to be known by that title and it is this new formation that will destroy our enemies. This fighting force that has been honed as finely as steel during the past five years.' Again he began stabbing pins into the maps before him. 'The left wing will move from Hanover and Utrecht to rendezvous in Württemberg. The centre and right, made up of the men from the Channel ports, will mass along the Middle Rhine at Mannheim, Spire, Lauterbourg and Strasbourg. Once there, they will advance over the river. While Marshal Murat continues to distract Mack and his Austrians with a diversionary attack, seven army corps will sweep through Germany towards a general rendezvous on the Danube.' He slid his hand across the map in the direction the advance was to take. 'Once this concentration has been achieved we will cross the river and seize Augsburg, which I will use as a new centre of operations. That will cut Mack's lines of communication and supply and leave him isolated.'

'What of the area between the Rhine and Upper Danube?' asked Caulaincourt.

'Marshal Augereau's Seventh Corps will advance from Brest and secure it,' Napoleon said flatly. 'It is a simple enough plan, gentlemen.'

The officers looked at the maps, at each other and at their Emperor.

'The problem of supplies can be solved by routing each

of the seven corps along an independent line of march,' Napoleon continued. 'As well as ensuring that only one single formation at a time will have to live off the land, it will also avoid congestion on the roads. Having said that, I want each corps no more than one or two days' march from the other. They must be within supporting distance of each other should the need arise. Also, each corps must contain a division of light cavalry to screen its movements. It is imperative that the size of our force is not revealed to the enemy until the very last moment. The supply trains will be issued with four days' ration of bread and biscuits to be distributed only if a major action is imminent. Everything must be done to ensure maximum mobility.'

He looked around at his subordinates. 'Are there any questions?'

The men looked on blankly.

Napoleon smiled.

'We stand on the threshold of a great victory, gentlemen,' he said. 'By the end of the year, no nation in Europe will be capable of standing against us.'

Eighteen

Lausard heard a high-pitched whinny then a loud crash as the horse fell forward. It was the leading offside animal in the team of four. As it slumped to the ground it pulled the traces with it, causing the other animals dragging the bridging wagon to stumble too. Lausard looked and saw the team driver reaching, for one insane moment, for his whip; but then, realising that no amount of beating would rouse the animal, the grey-clad corporal leapt down and strolled across to the stricken horse. He cut the traces with a knife and stood back as the animal floundered on the ground. Lausard and the other dragoons walked their horses past the stranded wagon, keeping to the furthest edges of the road. The sergeant looked back and saw that other vehicles in the column were already coming to a halt, their passage blocked by the bridging wagon. Men were already trying to guide the vehicle off the road but the ground on either side of the road sloped away sharply, particularly on one side where it led down to a shallow stream.

'It would be a kindness to shoot that horse,' Lausard observed.

'Little wonder the poor beast is exhausted,' Tigana mused, looking back at the fallen horse. It was lying on its side, lifting its head occasionally as if soliciting help from those around it.

'More than twenty days on the march,' Delacor muttered, 'with barely a decent rest for man or horse. It seems that Bonaparte is trying to kill us before the Austrians do.'

'Or the Russians,' Tabor added. 'There are Russians ahead of us too, aren't there?'

'Does it matter from which country the bullet comes that kills you?' Sonnier grunted.

'There *are* Russians, aren't there?' Tabor persisted.

'Yes, my friend, there are,' Bonet told him gently.

'If they shot it we could eat it,' Joubert interjected. 'When was the last time we had any food? I'm dying of hunger.'

'We should eat *you*, fat man,' Delacor said. 'There's enough meat on you to feed the entire squadron.'

Some of the others laughed.

Lausard patted the neck of his own horse and the animal tossed its head. Like the others of the squadron and, indeed, every animal in the army, it was tired and badly in need of food. But, the sergeant reasoned, so too were the *men* of *La Grande Armée*. The march from Boulogne had been accomplished in remarkably good order, something he would have expected from such highly trained troops. But the distance they had been forced to cover had taken its toll on even the hardiest campaigner. Many of the men in the army, like himself, had been used to long marches before – in the blistering heat of Egypt and the numbing snowstorms of the Alps – but never before had any of them marched seven hundred miles in such a short space of time. Had Lausard not been so exhausted, he might well have taken the time to marvel at the sheer magnitude of the achievement. From the Channel to the Rhine in less than a month. It was an incredible feat. The one saving grace of the incredible manoeuvre had been that the autumn weather had remained fine. Most of the journey had been completed in moderate temperatures and with very little rain. Just as well, Lausard had thought. With over three and a half thousand wagons carrying everything from supplies to bridging equipment, as well as the additional bulk provided by artillery caissons and the guns themselves, the last thing the French needed was bad weather. Had the rain fallen and turned the roads into quagmires, the sergeant had no doubt that the march would have taken three times as long.

'There's only one good thing about being part of the advance guard,' Joubert muttered. 'At least we reach any supplies before the rest of the army.'

'We also reach the *enemy* before the rest of the army,' Roussard reminded him.

'And why the hell is it always us?' Delacor demanded. 'Three squadrons in our regiment and which one is picked to be part of the advance guard? Us. As usual.'

'You know why that is,' Lausard told him. 'At least you should by now. It is because we are expendable.'

'After all these years they still will not let us forget who we were,' Rocheteau grunted. 'They still punish us for what we were over ten years ago. Haven't we done enough to prove ourselves by now?'

'Personally, I'd rather be ahead of the rest,' Lausard commented. 'The sooner we reach the enemy the better.'

'I agree,' Delacor added. 'And it keeps us away from those complaining dog-faces too.'

'And the stinking Imperial Guard,' Giresse grunted. 'They are given privileges far above their worth. The best supplies. The best billets. The best pay.'

'They are Bonaparte's personal bodyguard,' Lausard reminded him. 'What do you expect?'

'Are they any better than us, Alain?' Rocheteau wanted to know.

The sergeant shook his head.

'I would back our squadron against any troops in the army,' he said, smiling. 'Guard or otherwise.'

A number of the men nearby cheered. The sound was met with a furious scowl from Captain Milliere who was riding slightly ahead of them.

'Word is that the Emperor has been forced to call up eighty thousand conscripts one year early to boost the strength of the army,' Bonet offered.

'Then it's a pity he didn't put some of *them* in the advance guard instead of us,' Roussard grunted.

'It hasn't been popular with the public,' the former schoolmaster continued.

'Does it matter?' Lausard said. 'What difference does one year make? Some will die at nineteen instead of twenty. That is all.'

'I can remember *my* nineteenth birthday,' Giresse said. 'I stole some money and spent the entire day and night in a brothel just off the Rue Saint Denis.' He smiled wistfully.

'How close do you think we are to the Austrians, Alain?' Rocheteau wanted to know.

'We'll be closer once we've crossed the Rhine,' Lausard said. 'If we can *get* across. They may already have the bridges defended, fortified or mined. It will not be easy. The Austrians are good troops.'

'What about the Russians?' Charvet asked.

'If they are all like Rostov here then they will pose a far greater threat.' Lausard smiled, looking at his companion and nodding in his direction. 'Are all your people like you, my friend?'

'They are not my people anymore,' the Russian told him. 'The Tsars let my family and me starve. I owe them nothing but hatred.'

'Just remember whose side you're on when the fighting starts,' Lausard said and some of the other men laughed.

Karim patted the Russian gently on the shoulder and smiled.

The trees on either side of them began to thicken and the ground began to slope upwards more sharply until it levelled out on a wide plateau that gave a good view in all directions for at least ten miles. The column rode on at a trot until Captain Milliere raised an arm and slowed it to a walk. The road dipped before them, widening as it led up to a wide bridge. The areas around the bridge were unguarded and afforded the French a clear view of the countryside on both sides of it. Lausard looked at the murky water that flowed swiftly beneath the structure.

'The Rhine,' he murmured.

'And what awaits us on the other side?' Roussard wanted to know.

Lausard didn't answer. He merely coaxed his horse on towards the crossing point. The column continued to move forward.

Napoleon Bonaparte stood gazing into the flames of the camp fire, his hands clasped behind his back. Despite the chill of the night he wore no overcoat over his blue grenadier's uniform, unlike the chausseurs who walked their horses back and forth around his tent and who were dressed, to a man, in long green capes. The grenadiers of the Old Guard, huge men with bristling moustaches and immaculately clean uniforms who guarded the entrance to the imperial tent, also wore long blue coats to protect them from the cold. Napoleon seemed oblivious to the elements. He continued watching the dancing flames, as if hypnotised by them, then finally turned to face the gaggle of officers gathered near the entrance to the tent.

'The fox has taken the bait.' He smiled. 'General Mack has advanced west, beyond Munich towards Ulm as I anticipated. He is walking into the trap I set. All that remains for us is to spring that trap when the time is right.'

'Have our leading units reached their first objective yet, sire?' Duroc wanted to know.

Napoleon nodded.

'Freudenstadt was taken without a fight,' the Corsican revealed. 'Mack moved more men in that direction as I intended. The Austrians are in the Black Forest defiles. God will it that they stay there. My only fear is that we shall scare them too much. The next fortnight will see many things happen.'

'Is Mack still unaware of the size of the army facing him?' Duroc enquired.

'Of its size *and* of its intention,' Napoleon told the Grand Marshal. 'A combination of the Black Forest itself, the Jura mountains and Murat's cavalry screen has served to mask both our strength and our intent from him. It is going well for us, my friends.'

'What news of the Russians?' Duroc enquired.

It was Berthier who spoke.

'Still more than ten days' march from their ally,' said the Chief of Staff. 'General Mack can expect no support from Kutusov or Bennigsen. He is already close to being isolated.

'The advance guard will continue to proceed between Stuttgart and Ansbach. Lannes and d'Hilliers will press on through Pforzheim to join Ney's Sixth Corps. They will create the flank around which the more northerly formations will pivot as they move towards the Danube. We have opened a door and invited General Mack and his Austrians through. All that remains for us to do is to slam it shut behind him.'

The outbuildings of the farm were visible through the trees. Lausard could make out a barn, stables and a small hut that he guessed housed pigs. The undergrowth inside the woods was sparse and he found it easy, as did the dragoons behind him, to walk his mount over the mossy carpet beneath the canopy of leaves. To his right, Captain Milliere held up a hand to slow the progress of the horsemen. One or two of the mounts snorted impatiently but were silenced by reassuring pats from their riders. As Lausard watched, Milliere dismounted, pulling his carbine from the boot on his saddle. The firing mechanism was bound with oilskin which the officer quickly stripped off. He also fitted the fifteen-inch bayonet, then advanced through the trees in an effort to get closer to the farm. Lausard waited a moment then imitated his actions, signalling to Karim, Delacor, Sonnier and Charvet to follow him. Other troopers took the bridles of their dismounted colleagues, watching as the men moved swiftly and silently through the trees. The five dragoons spread out in a line, each man no more than five feet from his companion, using what little cover the woods offered as they drew nearer the collection of buildings. The ground sloped down sharply and Lausard almost lost his footing. Charvet shot out a large hand to aid the sergeant and he remained upright as the men continued their advance.

Twenty feet from the nearest outbuilding the woods ceased abruptly and there was nothing but open ground between the dragoons and their objective. A narrow stream coursed through the gulley and Lausard could hear it rushing over the stones, swollen as it had been by recent rainfall. He was not the only one to notice something steaming close to the opposite bank of the stream. He was also not alone in realising that the pile was horse dung.

'It's fresh,' whispered Karim.

'Someone got here before us,' Milliere murmured.

The Circassian suddenly broke free of the cover of the woods and scuttled down to the bank of the stream. Bent low to the ground he moved with incredible speed, occasionally dropping to the earth to inspect the many indentations there. Then he hurried back to the cover of the trees.

'There are dozens of hoofprints,' he said. 'All of them on the far side of the stream.'

'They could be *our* light cavalry?' Milliere offered.

Karim shook his head.

'If they belonged to French horses they would be on *this* side of the stream,' he said, jabbing a finger at the ground beneath him. 'The only tracks are on the far side. The stream was approached from the opposite direction to that which we take.'

'It must be an Austrian patrol,' Milliere offered.

Before the officer could say another word, Lausard broke cover and, followed by Sonnier, Delacor and Charvet, ran headlong across the open ground towards the rear of the barn. As the men reached the stream, they gathered themselves and leapt over it, landing with unexpected grace on the other bank, barely breaking stride as they hurried up the incline towards the cover of the building. Once there, all four pressed themselves against the wooden wall. Lausard raised a hand in Milliere's direction and the officer nodded.

Sonnier and Delacor moved one way, Lausard and Charvet the other. The dragoons on the other bank watched intently.

As Lausard crept slowly to the end of the barn wall he heard the sound of horses.

It was difficult to tell how many but now he also heard voices and the occasional laugh. The language they spoke was German. He stood up and peered cautiously around the edge of the barn into the farmyard itself.

He counted fifteen Austrian hussars.

Some were mounted, others wandered about in the muddy yard searching for provisions. He could see that two of the men were carrying sacks they'd taken from the barn. One of the sacks had a large hole in it and potatoes were dropping from it. A hussar called to his companion who was leaving a trail of the vegetables across the yard and the other men laughed. They were clad in light-blue uniforms, their pelisses, trimmed with black and yellow lace, fastened to keep them warm. Their green shakos were covered by oilskins to protect them from the inclement weather. They all wore the familiar black and yellow barrel sashes and red sabertaches, edged red and black. Even on campaign, these spectacular troops retained an air of visual brilliance. It also made them easy targets. Lausard could see that, in addition to the sacks of vegetables they had already collected, the Austrians had slaughtered several pigs and bundled their carcasses into a wagon. Three or four other animals now nuzzled around in the yard, some chewing on the fallen potatoes.

Lausard stood up, his back pressed against the wall of the barn, and lifted his carbine across his chest with careful exaggeration; then he slowly and again with great deliberation loaded it. Watching from the other side of the stream, hidden by the trees, Milliere understood. When Lausard lifted the carbine above his head and waved it first towards the dragoons then back towards the farm, the officer hurried back to his waiting men and climbed into the saddle.

Charvet, Sonnier and Delacor had also loaded their carbines by now and they crouched behind the barn waiting for Lausard's order. He looked again at the hussars, then back towards the dragoons who were advancing at a walk in a broken line, swords still sheathed but carbines at the ready.

The jingling of harnesses began to fill the air and Lausard saw one of the Austrian troopers turn his head in the direction of the stream. He barked a couple of words in his own language and the other men stopped dead, listening intently. Lausard felt his heart beating more swiftly. The blood seemed to be coursing through his veins with increased speed. It was a feeling he had not known for a long time. And it was one he had missed. He swung the carbine up to his shoulder and fired.

The recoil slammed the Charleville back against his shoulder and a cloud of sulphurous smoke filled the air. The ball struck the Austrian in the chest and he fell backwards from his saddle. Immediately, Sonnier also fired. Another hussar hit the ground, blood pouring from the wound in his stomach. The advancing dragoons suddenly quickened their pace and the first half a dozen drove their horses up the incline and into the farmyard. They fired from the saddle at the surprised Austrians who were momentarily thrown into confusion, not knowing whether to fight back or run, unsure of how large a force of Frenchmen confronted them. As more spilled into the farmyard, they could see their situation was serious.

Delacor fired his carbine then ran at the nearest hussar and swung the weapon like a club, grinning maniacally as the butt shattered his nose. He slammed it down repeatedly on the back of the man's head before running the bayonet into the motionless hussar.

Rocheteau shot an Austrian sergeant in the arm then pulled his pistol from its holster, pressing the barrel against the man's cheek as he fired. The lead ball punched in most of the left side of the man's face.

The Austrians on foot had no chance.

Giresse rode one down and shot another in the back, sliding his carbine back into its boot in order to draw his sword. He pulled the three-foot-long steel free in time to parry a sabre blow from one of the mounted hussars. Sparks flew from the point of contact and Giresse ducked over the pommel of his saddle to avoid the second slash. He turned in the saddle and thrust his straight blade into the Austrian's side, driving it between ribs until it burst from the other side of the man's body. He tore it free and stabbed again, this time into the chest. The hussar slumped forward over the neck of his horse, blood streaming down the flank of the animal. It reared, hurling his body into the mud.

Lausard stuck his bayonet into the thigh of another Austrian, driving so deep that the wickedly sharp point momentarily pinned the man to his saddle. He shrieked and struck out at the sergeant with his sabre but Lausard ducked beneath the swing, wrenched the bayonet out and drove it upwards into his opponent's stomach, pushing on the weapon until he unseated the hussar who fell to the ground and rolled over once before the sergeant stabbed him again to finish the job.

Any remaining hussars now bolted, hurtling away into the enveloping safety of the trees.

Rocheteau rode up, holding the reins of Lausard's horse, keeping the animal steady while the sergeant swung himself into the saddle.

Lieutenant Royere led a dozen dragoons in pursuit of the fleeing Austrians, many of whom fired after their foes. Royere himself shot another from the saddle; the man toppled sideways, slamming into a tree with a savage impact that broke his neck. One foot remained in the stirrup and he was dragged through the woods as his terrified horse careered on.

Lausard looked around at the bodies of the dead Austrians. Several of the dragoons, Delacor and Rocheteau among them, were rifling the pockets of the corpses, comparing finds. Rocheteau grinned as he came upon a gold crucifix around the neck of one man. He tore it free and dropped it into the pocket of his tunic. Delacor seemed happy with an engraved snuff box he took from the same trooper. Elsewhere, men were gathering potatoes and carrots and stuffing them into their portmanteaus. Food was treasure of a different kind for the dragoons. Tabor, Rostov and Gaston were already carving the dead pigs into more manageable portions with their swords.

Tigana was inspecting the horses the Austrians had left behind.

'Are they of any use to us?' Milliere wanted to know.

'Two need reshoeing, Captain,' he called. 'But they're in good enough condition. They'll do for remounts.'

The officer nodded and rode across to join Lausard who was wiping blood from his face. He looked around at the eight or nine dead Austrians lying in the yard. The corpses were still being looted by Rocheteau and several other dragoons. Each fresh find, be it a watch or a plug of tobacco, was greeted with a cheer.

'Is this the war you promised me, Captain?' Lausard asked.

Nineteen

Napoleon Bonaparte sipped at his wine and nodded appreciatively.

'Whoever used to live in this house had admirable taste,' he mused, helping himself from the bottle. Over a dozen had been found in the cellar of the house in Augsburg and the Corsican had already consumed two of them during his protracted stay in the building.

Marshal Berthier smiled wanly and dipped his quill into the ink as if anxious for the Emperor to issue his orders. The Chief of Staff ran a hand through his frizzy hair and coughed theatrically, as if the gesture might galvanise Napoleon. Still the Corsican pored over his maps and reports, digesting every piece of information carefully until he was satisfied. Outside he heard the sound of falling rain. The weather had been bad for the last week or so. Heavy showers, punctuated by freezing temperatures, had made life almost intolerable for his troops. But Napoleon knew that the men of his *Grande Armée* would suffer any hardship in his name and, once he gave them the victory he anticipated, they would follow him to the ends of the earth.

Again Berthier coughed but this time he put down the quill and began nibbling at the nail of his right index finger.

'Send the following orders,' Napoleon said suddenly.

The Chief of Staff snatched up his pen.

'Each corps commander will act accordingly and in respect of the orders I will now give you,' said the Corsican. 'Each order to be carried out to the letter.'

'Sire, I feel it only right to inform you that Marshal Bernadotte has already violated neutral Prussian territory by marching through Ansbach,' Berthier offered. 'The news has not been well received by King Frederick William in Berlin.'

Napoleon waved a hand in the air dismissively.

'He acted in the interests of speed, did he not?' the Corsican said. 'It was a necessary violation. Speed is of the essence in this campaign. You know that, Berthier. The entire army is now in position to trap General Mack and his Austrians. Have there been no counter measures taken by them?'

'Mack must be aware of the movements against him by now but our advance guard report only one major skirmish so far, at Wertingen. Two thousand prisoners were taken by Marshal Murat and Marshal Lannes.'

'It would appear that the rabbit is hypnotised by the snake,' Napoleon chuckled. 'They could have launched offensives against one of our southernmost columns, tried to slow the rate of our advance. At the very least they could have taken steps to defend the crossings over the Danube, the Lech, the Isar and the Inn. Instead, all they have done is concentrate their forces in and around Ulm.

'General Vandamme has already seized the Donau crossings and Marshal Murat has taken possession of

Munster. He then sent a division across the Danube to take the bridge over the Lech at Rain.

'Half of the army has cut Mack's communications and will turn his flank from the north. The other half has denied the Austrians use of the Lech bridges. There is nowhere for him to go but eastwards. Straight on to our bayonets. My intention, when we meet the foe, is to envelop him on all sides.'

'If that is to be done then any possible escape routes must be closed, sire. Mack may realise his only hope of survival is to launch a counterattack of his own. He still commands close to forty thousand men.'

'He may also attempt to retire into the Tyrol but, by doing so, he will be forced to abandon his mission to cover the approaching Russian armies. Have we any information on their current position?'

Berthier shook his head.

'No, sire,' the Chief of Staff said. 'But they must be at least one hundred miles distant and in no position to offer support to Mack in time to save him.'

'I feel sure he will not attempt to retreat along the north bank of the Danube for fear of exposing the road to Vienna and also isolating himself and his men from his southern depots. The Aulic Council would hang him. What news of our other corps?'

'Marshal Soult is making good progress towards Landsberg. Marshal Davout has already reached Dachau and Marshal Bernadotte is now within six miles of Munich.'

'An order to Marshal Murat,' Napoleon snapped, pointing at his Chief of Staff. '"The enemy, harassed as he is, will fight. It is therefore imperative that your reserve and the corps of Ney and Lannes, which together make some fifty to sixty thousand men, should march as closely together as possible, so as to be able to reunite within the space of six hours in order to crush the enemy."'

Berthier's quill scratched frantically across the paper.

'As far as I see it, Berthier,' Napoleon mused, 'a battle will be fought near the river Iller. Let our troops continue to converge on that point. If it is to be as decisive as I hope then we will need all our troops in that vicinity by the fourteenth. The Austrians are to be eliminated. Not one is to escape.'

The horse sank up to its fetlocks into the glutinous mud and it was all Lausard could do to keep his mount moving. The animal whinnied protestingly and struggled to pull itself free while the sergeant tapped its flanks with his spurs to urge it on. All around him, his companions were in similar difficulties. Karim had dismounted and was trying to lead his horse along by the reins but the Circassian himself was sinking in the mud and found it hard to move. A number of the dragoons had forsaken the saddle for their own struggle through the ooze and they were making tortuous progress. Behind them, infantry hauled themselves along, their uniforms drenched, the bottoms of their greatcoats hanging in the discolouring mud. Up ahead, a battery of four-pounders was stuck firmly in ground that resembled little more than a swamp. It was a mire of sucking mud and liquefied horse dung and the stench was appalling. The gunners grunted and strained to shift the artillery pieces while drivers lashed savagely at the horses but the animals, like their crews, were powerless to shift the guns. At the side of the road, strewn about like the abandoned toys of some huge child, were dead horses and equipment of all kinds. Lausard saw shabraques, saddles, muskets, swords, packs, headgear and even boots – some, he reasoned, sucked from the feet of their owners by the mud. There was even an artillery caisson, complete with its load of ammunition, overturned by the roadside. As the dragoons struggled on, every few yards they would see men slumped at the roadside simply unable to muster the strength, or indeed the will, necessary to take another step. Lausard and his companions had seen this kind of thing before, but in the searing heat of Egypt, not the freezing, rain-soaked plains of Swabia.

Delacor dug his spurs into the flanks of his mount, furious that the animal could not make progress. Lausard grabbed its bridle angrily, noticing that several gashes has appeared where the spikes had cut deeply.

'Stop that, you fool,' he hissed. 'Get off and walk.'

Delacor held the sergeant's gaze for a moment then swung himself out of the saddle and did as he was told.

Just ahead, Lieutenant Royere was also leading his mount, his own feet sinking deep into the filth. His cape, like those of the other troops, was discoloured and sodden by the rain that was still falling. The downpour they had experienced earlier that morning had eased but an icy drizzle continued to fall and Lausard, on more than one occasion, had wondered if it would turn to snow before the day was over. He looked up at the swollen clouds and struggled on.

'Was this one of the glories you foresaw under your Emperor, Lieutenant?' Lausard mused.

'It almost makes one long for the camp of Boulogne, doesn't it?' Royere grunted. 'Hours of drill or this. I know which I would prefer.' He slipped in the ooze and only managed to remain upright by grabbing on to his saddle.

'If the navy could have secured the Channel we would have been in England now,' rasped Delacor. 'Not up to our arses in mud in the middle of nowhere.'

Gaston, his red trumpeter's tunic covered by a film of muck, slipped and fell into the rut left by a wagon. Reeking water sprayed up all around him, spattering the men close by. He gripped the corner of his shabraque and hauled himself upright again.

'If the Austrians attack us now, we're finished,' Sonnier groaned, looking around him at the rain-soaked land on either side of the road.

'It's a wonder we haven't been detailed to carry the members of the Imperial Guard along this road,' grunted Rocheteau. 'After all, the Emperor wouldn't want his precious toy soldiers getting *their* feet wet, would he?'

'A commander is never popular when his men are suffering discomfort, is he?' Royere observed.

'It wouldn't be the first time our Emperor has subjected us to discomfort would it, Lieutenant?' Lausard answered. 'And I doubt if it will be the last. Sand. Snow. Now mud. Perhaps we should be thankful for the variety our commander has offered us over the years.'

Some of the men laughed in spite of their predicament.

'I have a copy of the latest army bulletin here,' Bonet offered, almost overbalancing in the slimy ooze.

'Read it,' Lausard told him. 'We are all anxious to know our commander's thoughts.'

Royere looked at the sergeant and saw him raise his eyebrows.

'It says "The enemy advanced into the passes of the Black Forest",' Bonet read aloud, '"where he planned to position himself and hold up our penetration. He hastily fortified the Iller, Memmingen and Ulm. However, our patrols, which are scouring the countryside . . ."'

'Or would be if they could move,' Lausard interjected.

The remark was greeted by more laughter.

'". . . assure me that he has abandoned his plans",' Bonet continued, '"and that he appears to be gravely worried by our moves which are as unexpected as they are novel."'

'Very novel,' Lausard offered. 'Sinking up to our backsides on roads that are virtually impassable.'

Again Bonet continued: '"This great and vast movement has carried us in only a few days into Bavaria, avoiding the mountains of the Black Forest, the line of parallel rivers running into the Danube valley and the inconvenience of a system of operations always threatened from the flank by the passes of the Tyrol; furthermore, it has placed us several days' march in the rear of the enemy who has no time to lose if he is to avoid a complete disaster."' The former schoolmaster folded the piece of paper and stuck it back inside his tunic. 'The words of our Emperor,' he said.

'We covered thirty miles a day when we first set out from Boulogne,' Lausard grunted, struggling through the muck. 'On roads like these we are lucky to do five.'

'Where are the Austrians?' Tabor wanted to know.

'Waiting for us, you half-wit,' Delacor snapped. 'Probably waiting to ambush us.' He stumbled in the sucking ooze and dropped to his knees, reeking mud spewing up over his cape. He dragged himself upright and ploughed on.

'According to Bonaparte *we* are behind *them*,' Bonet said. 'There is no danger of an ambush.'

'Surely the roads can't be this bad everywhere,' Carbonne

mused. 'The Emperor will have to halt the advance if things get much worse.'

Lausard stood still for a moment and peered ahead, wiping mud and rain from his face. The road widened before them as it began to climb a range of low hills.

'We are in the estuaries of the Danube itself,' the sergeant said. 'Many of them have flooded due to the rain. The roads should be better when we reach the higher ground on the other side of the river.' He jabbed a finger in the direction they were heading.

'There's a town beyond those hills,' Lieutenant Royere offered. 'We might have a chance to dry our boots there, in Elchingen.'

As the rain continued to fall, the column struggled on.

Night brought with it some respite from the rain but, to the dragoons' dismay, the cold winds carried the first flecks of snow. As afternoon had become dusk, the order had been given to bivouac for the night but, due to the appalling state of the ground, the men found that even the simple act of pitching a tent was all but impossible. Lausard was not the only one to realise that the swollen waters of the estuaries had broken their banks in places. The meadows where the French troops now found themselves were little more than marshland. He was also convinced that the water level was rising. Some trees had been felled, the trunks split and placed on the sodden ground in an effort to protect the men from the worst of the conditions, but it was an impossible task. Other pieces of timber had been placed beneath the wheels of the cannons and caissons to enable them to move more easily over the almost liquescent terrain. The horses suffered as badly. All they could do was stand immobile, up to their fetlocks in reeking water, as hungry and cold as their riders. Every time one of them pawed at the earth it sent up geysers of freezing water. Lausard and a number of the other men had left just the shabraques over their mounts in an effort to keep the animals warm and also to prevent the green saddle cloths from becoming more soaked than they already were. Saddles were stacked on felled logs to keep them dry, the whole lot covered by tarpaulin. Men huddled in foetal positions in an attempt to snatch some precious sleep but in the appalling conditions even the hardiest found it impossible. The lighting of fires had been forbidden in case the enemy should spot the smoke and the French positions be given away.

'How the hell are they going to see us?' snapped Delacor. 'They're all supposed to be trapped inside Ulm, aren't they? Why don't we just press on and finish the job? Then perhaps we could all find some food and warmth.'

'Especially some food,' Joubert intoned, rubbing his mountainous belly and chewing on a potato.

Karim sat cross-legged on a piece of timber sharpening his scimitar with a flat stone he'd dredged from the ever-rising water.

Sonnier was wrapping his carbine in strips of cloth he'd cut from a discarded infantryman's jacket earlier in the day. The firing mechanism had been carefully protected by oilskin for much of the campaign already. All the troops, both infantry and cavalry, had received such an order.

Roussard and Tabor were sharpening their bayonets.

Rostov was cleaning his sword, ensuring that he did not return it to its scabbard damp. Should rust eat into the steel, the three-foot-long weapon would be useless.

'I thought Egypt was bad,' grunted Giresse. 'I think this place is worse.'

'It's not much of a choice, is it?' Bonet offered. 'Up to our necks in water, or choking on sand. When we were *there* we wanted to be here. Now we're *here*, we want to be *there*.'

Some of the men managed a forlorn laugh.

Lausard, who had been crouched on one of the struts of wood listening to the grumblings of the men, stood up.

'Delacor and Giresse. In five minutes, you two relieve Charvet and Moreau on sentry duty.' He stepped off the platform of wood and sank up to his calves in muddy water.

'Do you want some company, Alain?' Rocheteau asked.

Lausard nodded and the two men set off into the gloom, passing through countless huddles of troops camped in the meadow. The sergeant saw that some of the artillerymen were attempting to sleep by lying on their limbers and caissons. They were precarious perches but they offered some respite from the rising water and soaking ground. One gunner was actually lying across the carriage of a four-pounder. Sleep was impossible but at least it kept him out of the stinking water.

'The Emperor doesn't need soldiers to fight this war,' Rocheteau mused. 'He needs ducks.'

Lausard didn't answer, he merely strode on as best he could through the waterlogged meadow, occasionally slowing his pace when his boots sank too far into the glutinous mud beneath the surface. The two dragoons made their way towards their horses and saw Tigana moving from mount to mount, patting, comforting and reassuring the horses as best he could. Gaston was with him. Both men were swathed in their cloaks and looked like gigantic bats in the darkness.

'The horses need food, Alain,' Tigana said. 'Many of them won't last more than a couple of days. They've barely the strength to carry their *own* weight, let alone ours.'

'Then call upon Bonaparte and tell him our predicament,' Lausard said flatly. 'Perhaps with his new-found power and position as Emperor he will be able to conjure up some hay for the horses or put a stop to this rain.'

Rocheteau chuckled.

'I mean what I say, Alain,' Tigana repeated. 'In two days we will be searching for remounts.'

'We will take them from Austrians, my friend. If we ever find any,' the sergeant assured him.

Lausard and Rocheteau moved on, past more soaking wet freezing troops, past infantry who were attempting to keep their muskets dry but who had already lost what was an unwinnable battle. The sergeant saw one man lift his Charleville by the barrel and upend it. Water cascaded from the muzzle; all around him others were doing the same. The guns would be useless unless the men had the chance to dry them out. It wasn't so difficult to keep cartridges dry, due to the fact that they were kept in the soldiers' cartouches as well as being wrapped in greased paper. But, if the muskets were left for too long without being adequately dried, then irreperable damage would be done to them.

The best way might be for the infantry to discharge a few rounds the following morning but, Lausard reasoned, if too many of the weapons were still damp an orgy of meaningless fire could easily reach the ears of a vigilant enemy, the *exact* whereabouts of whom was at that moment still something of a mystery.

'Would the Austrians really have withdrawn all their forces into Ulm?' Rocheteau asked, as if reading Lausard's thoughts.

Lausard could only shrug.

'It's possible,' he answered. 'They seem to have no idea of the size of our army. Perhaps if they knew its condition they would be more willing to fight. While *they* remain trapped within a stronghold, at least they have food and shelter. Should they try to break out they may find the task easier than they imagined.'

'And once the Austrians are disposed of, we must face the warriors of Holy Russia.'

Lausard smiled as he picked his way through the flooded meadow.

'I hope Rostov remembers whose side he is on when the time comes.'

Both men managed to laugh, the sound attracting the attention of two sentries nearby. Both were light infantrymen, both soaked to the skin. They lowered their muskets in the direction of the dragoons, the fifteen-inch bayonets aimed at their chests. Lausard saluted and the men returned to their tired wanderings back and forth.

'Have you heard?' one of them said, coughing harshly. 'We are to be joined by more troops tomorrow.' His voice trailed off into another coughing fit. He hawked and spat. 'The Fifth and Sixth Corps under Marshals Lannes and Ney are to meet us at Elchingen.'

'How do you know?' Lausard enquired.

'Some of my companions overheard orders being given to our commanding officer earlier today by one of the

Emperor's aides. Even Napoleon himself is nearby.' The man was again shaken by a bout of prolonged coughing. He spat into the water.

'And yet we are all to be under the command of that "peacock" Murat,' said the other man, a note of disgust in his voice.

'He is a very brave man,' Lausard interjected.

'He knows nothing of *real* fighting,' the first sentry countered, again coughing harshly. 'He has only gained his position because he is married to the Emperor's sister. I wonder if he rides *her* as well as he rides his pretty horses.'

'Why do you doubt his ability?' Lausard wanted to know.

'He has spent his life in the saddle,' the first sentry rasped. 'He knows nothing of the hardships we infantry go through. Why should we take orders from him? All you high horsemen are the same.'

'We have saved your dog-face skins often enough in the past,' Rocheteau rasped.

'All of France's greatest victories have been won by the infantry.'

'Were you at Marengo?' Rocheteau asked. 'Who charged the Austrians there?'

'Who took the bridge at Lodi? The infantry.'

'You have your uses,' Lausard said dismissively. 'Although I seem to recall it was we who secured the victory at Rivoli in that same campaign. Perhaps we should speak again when *this* campaign is over.' He and Rocheteau walked away, the sound of the infantryman's hacking cough floating on the air behind them.

Lausard shook his head.

'An army united behind an Emperor,' he mused. 'What

do we need with the Austrians or Russians when we can fight amongst ourselves?'

'Could it be true that the Emperor himself is close?'

'If it is, why would he hand over command to Murat? He may not be far but he must be far *enough* if he is willing to allow his brother-in-law to take command.'

'So you think they could be right about the arrival of Lannes and Ney?'

'If they are, then the battle we have all waited for is closer than any of us could have imagined.'

Twenty

Even in the most comfortable surroundings, Alain Lausard did not usually sleep well. In the freezing, waterlogged meadow where the dragoons were camped, he felt as if he had spent the entire night awake. Only two or three times did he drift off to sleep, propped against the wheel of a mobile forge, a piece of roughly hewn wood beneath him. Even when those precious intervals of oblivion enveloped him, he experienced only light sleep. He had been easily woken on several occasions by the grunts and groans of his companions, the neighing of stricken horses or by the wind whipping around him, jabbing icy fingers of cold into every exposed part of his body. Despite being wrapped in his cloak and a blanket, the cold found its way in with the ease of a thief into an unlocked house. The sound that woke him early in the morning, however, was unmistakable.

The rolling volleys of musket fire seemed as if they were right next to his ear.

They were followed, sometimes eclipsed, by the thunder of cannon fire.

Lausard scrambled to his feet and saw that men all over the rain-soaked meadow were doing the same.

A number of infantry were already scrambling towards the road leading to Elchingen, their officers roaring orders at them. NCOs physically dragged men to their feet, shoving them after their companions.

The horse artillery were limbering up their guns, drivers whipping the horses on to greater efforts as they struggled to pull the four-pounders free of the mud they'd been encased in all night.

And, all around him, urged on by Captain Milliere and Lieutenant Royere, his own companions were saddling their horses, an operation Lausard hastily mimicked. The procedure was carried out with astonishing precision and speed. Men swung themselves on to their mounts and, within minutes, the first of the dragoons, led by Lausard himself, were dragging themselves towards the road.

Beyond the range of low hills the sounds of gunfire seemed to be intensifying. Smoke was rising into the grey sky.

Lausard looked at his watch and saw that it was approaching eight a.m.

He saw Captain Milliere call Karim to him and, moments later, the Circassian guided his horse along the rutted, slippery thoroughfare at a speed that didn't seem possible. He disappeared in the direction of Elchingen while the remainder of the dragoons formed a column behind their officers, then moved off at a walk.

The horse artillery were also on the move and Lausard marvelled at how men and animals, on the same road that had virtually brought them to a standstill the previous day, were now moving reasonably freely through the sticky mud. The cold they had suffered during the night may well have gone some way to hardening the surface and therefore making it more easily passable, he reasoned.

The sounds from beyond the low hills were now unambiguous.

Volleys of musket fire and cannon shot. They could even hear the shouts of men. Above it all, the noxious smoke was beginning to grow thicker, whirling like a sulphurous cloud at the whim of the brisk breeze.

Lausard saw Karim galloping back towards the column, hunched low over the saddle, his horse straining every muscle as he drove it on. The Circassian brought the animal to a halt close to Milliere.

'There are nine thousand Austrians defending the Elchingen bridge and the high ground beyond it, Captain,' he said breathlessly. 'The position was given to me by one of Marshal Ney's own aides.'

'How many of our own men?' the officer wanted to know.

'I have no idea,' Karim told him.

Milliere rose in his stirrups and signalled with one hand, then he turned to Gaston and the trumpeter sounded the notes instructing the dragoons to increase their pace to a trot.

Mud sprayed up from the churning hooves as the squadron advanced, picking up speed despite the clinging muck. The jingling of harnesses grew louder but still not loud enough to eclipse the now continuous cacophony of musket and cannon fire.

As the dragoons emerged from the veil of trees on to the top of the low ridge, Lausard could see the position for himself.

In the dismal early morning, he saw ranks of blue-clad French troops advancing towards a partially demolished bridge. On the far side, white-clad Austrians poured volleys of musket fire into them and already many bodies were strewn across the muddied ground. All along the bank, batteries of four- and eight-pounders were blasting away at the Austrians while their own gunners replied. Lausard saw barrels flame. He saw the clouds of smoke drifting across the fields and he saw geysers of water and mud erupting each time one of the solid roundshot ploughed into the earth. Occasionally, one of the cannons would spew out canister and men would be swept away as if by some massive broom, whole ranks of them transformed into bloody piles of butchered humanity by the ferocity of the fusillades. He could see detachments of horsemen dashing backwards and forwards on both sides of the river, seemingly with no discernible purpose. Every now and then, a choking bank of smoke would obscure the entire battle but through it all was the ever-present roar of weapons.

The main French advance, though, was centred on the bridge and it was towards that bridge that Milliere now led the dragoons.

The ground sloped upwards gently at first but then inclined more sharply. Lausard urged his mount onwards and the animal, as if infected with the same fury as its rider, responded.

There was a thunderous blast behind Lausard and he heard several screams as a mortar shell exploded. Men and horses crashed to the ground, some of those following toppling over the debris. More than one of the wounded dragoons were ridden over by their companions.

A tree close to the road was hit by a roundshot from one of the Austrian six-pounder batteries on the far bank of the river, its trunk obliterated by the solid ball.

Lausard saw a column of the 6th Line regiment advancing towards the bridge, its eagle flying proudly in the reeking air. Then, for the first time, he caught sight of a familiar figure. Clad in full dress uniform, sword in hand, his red hair visible for all to see, Marshal Ney rode his horse into the water, stood in his stirrups and urged the column on. A blast of canister took two dozen men, some of the four-and-a-half-ounce balls ploughing into the earth. One missed Ney by inches as it tore into the bank of the river. Lausard could see other men around Ney as he held his horse steady in the churning water. Grey-jacketed troops were struggling to repair the damaged parts of the bridge. Lausard saw several go down under the concentrated fire of the Austrians and already the water beneath the parapet was turning red. Not once did Ney move his horse or attempt to hide himself. Instead, he divided his time bellowing encouragement at the bridging unit and the advancing infantry.

The dragoons were now within two hundred yards of the bank.

Another volley of roundshot cut through them and a trooper close by was cut in half by the projectiles. Blood exploded into the air, drenching those nearby, Lausard included. Further down the line, a horse was decapitated by the deadly load, its rider falling forwards over what was left of its neck. He snatched at the reins of a riderless mount and pulled himself into the saddle.

'Fight on foot,' bellowed Captain Milliere and the dragoons leapt to the ground, seeking cover anywhere along the bank.

Lausard pulled his carbine from the boot on his saddle

and hastily pulled off the oilskin from the firing mechanism, then he dragged a cartridge from his cartouche and began loading the Charleville. All along the bank, his companions were doing the same.

Sonnier picked out an officer of artillery and shot him down before hastily reloading.

Lausard and Rocheteau both brought their carbines to bear on a gunner with a portfire who was about to light the fuse of another six-pounder. Both lead balls hit him and he collapsed over the barrel, blood pouring from his wounds. But one of his companions snatched up the portfire and jammed it into the firing hole. The cannon flamed and a withering blast of canister raked the far bank. One of the balls tore the cuff from the knee of Delacor's boot. Another killed the man beside him, tearing through his chest and erupting from his back. The river bank was ploughed up and, almost immediately, another fusillade of roundshot tore into the French.

Lausard saw the eagle of the sixth topple as its carrier was decapitated but another man snatched up the prized standard and the advance continued.

'Bring your fire to bear on the far end of the bridge,' Milliere shouted, trying to make himself heard over the incessant roar of guns. Those dragoons who had heard him obeyed. Infantry, cavalry and artillery were all concentrating their fire on the Austrian-held bank now, particularly the narrow strip of ground around the bridge itself.

In the bloodied water, the bridging crews worked like demons to secure the crossing for the troops who would swarm across when the time came. If that time came.

Lausard ducked as another battery opened fire, shot scything through the French.

A roundshot passed so close he actually heard it part the air close to his left ear.

Sonnier shot another Austrian down and reloaded with breathtaking speed.

Already the men were deafened by the continuous gunfire and Lausard found he had to bellow into the ears of his companions to make himself heard. He scrambled along the bank of the river, ducking behind fallen trees every time the cannon on the opposite bank opened up. He snatched a cartouche from a dead infantryman and found it was still full of cartridges.

'Help me,' he shouted, nudging Rocheteau.

Lausard bit the end off the cartridge, spat the ball out then poured the powder into the cartouche. He did that with a dozen more of the cartridges until his mouth was dry and grains of the coarse black powder stained his teeth, gums and lips. He coughed and spat, even scooping some of the bloodied muddy river water into his hand to wash his mouth out. He swilled the foul-tasting liquid around for a second then spat that out too. Rocheteau followed his example, tearing off the ends of the cartridges, pouring the powder into a cartouche he himself had taken from a dying dragoon.

'What the hell are we doing?' he asked, his own mouth dry.

Lausard finally closed the cartouche then jammed one more cartridge into it.

'We light them,' he bellowed back at the corporal. 'When I give the word, throw them at the far end of the bridge.'

'You're insane.'

The voice came from close to Lausard and he turned to see that more than a dozen voltigeurs, distinguishable by their hunting horn turnback badges, had joined the dragoons on the river bank. The sharpshooters kept up a steady fire, most of them trying to pick off officers or NCOs from the white-clad Austrian ranks across the bridge.

'You cover us while we prove we're not,' Lausard snapped.

The voltigeur nodded and called several of his companions to him, watching as Lausard and Rocheteau scrambled to their feet and scuttled closer to the bridge. The water was not too deep – Lausard could tell by the way it only reached the belly of Marshal Ney's horse. He and Rocheteau waded out into the river, holding their carbines and their makeshift bombs over their heads to keep them dry.

Bullets struck the water around them and one cracked against the sergeant's helmet and sang off the brass but he remained upright.

'Ready,' he roared and Rocheteau nodded.

They both fired their carbines close to the one cartridge that protruded from each cartouche like a fuse. The flame from the pan ignited them and both dragoons hurled the ammunition boxes with all their strength towards the far end of the bridge.

Two large explosions erupted almost immediately and dense clouds of smoke billowed upwards and also across the river bank.

The two men ducked under the bridge, sheltering from the savage fusillade of fire that suddenly exploded from both banks simultaneously. Musket balls and cannon shot tore into both sets of troops as infantry and artillery seemed to redouble their efforts but the French seemed possessed of a spirit of desperation not shared by their enemy and it was that which seemed to be turning the battle.

Lausard and Rocheteau struggled from the water within feet of Ney's horse.

'Good men,' he shouted. 'You are a fine example to others.'

At last he guided his horse up the bank and Lausard saw him waving the sixth infantry regiment on.

They had stopped halfway across the bridge and were drawn up in three ranks, firing almost constantly into the Austrians barring their way. With robotic skill they kept up their fusillades. When a man fell, another stepped forward to take his place. The entire bridge was shrouded in choking smoke. Lausard's eyes stung, his mouth was hanging open and his ears were ringing but he struggled back to the bank where the other dragoons and voltigeurs were also pouring fire into the gun crews and infantry opposite them.

'I was right,' said the voltigeur as they passed him. 'You *are* insane.' He grinned and slapped Lausard on the shoulder before squeezing off another round.

'Advance.'

The order was roared by a jubilant Marshal Ney and, turning to squint through the smoke, Lausard saw that the Austrians guarding the far end of the bridge had finally broken and were falling back towards the higher ground behind them.

'Mount up,' bellowed Captain Milliere and the dragoons hurried towards their waiting horses as Gaston blasted out the notes of command.

Already, Lausard could feel the ground shaking and, as he watched, he saw a swiftly moving column of French hussars hurtle across the bridge, sabres already drawn.

They crashed into the closest Austrians like a battering ram and simply rode them down. However, several other batteries of six-pounders had been assembled higher up the steeply rising ground and they opened up immediately.

Ranks of the hussars crashed to the ground. Men were sent spinning from their saddles. Others died with their feet still in the stirrups, their bodies punched through by canister shot or simply obliterated by roundshot. The screams of dying men and horses rose to join the ceaseless cacophony of fire.

'Draw swords,' roared Milliere, his horse rearing wildly at the head of the dragoon column. For an instant, all Lausard heard was the deafening metallic hiss as hundreds of steel blades were pulled from their scabbards. Ahead of him he saw the swallow-tailed guidon of the squadron fluttering in the breeze, gripped tightly in the fist of Sergeant Delpierre. It filled Lausard with the same swelling pride now as it had when he had first glimpsed it on the Champ-de-Mars over a year earlier. He roared his defiance, sword held high above his head. Gaston blasted out the climbing notes of the advance and the dragoons moved off at a canter.

As they thundered across the bridge, a volley of fire from the fleeing Austrians caught them and Lausard saw one man topple from the saddle into the water below but the column swept on. They reached the far bank and, through the drifting smoke, Lausard saw the extent of their task.

The ground sloped upwards so sharply that, in places, it was barely possible for the horses to gain a foothold. The hamlets of Oberelchingen and Unterelchingen formed the town itself and the conglomeration of buildings was perched high on a steep ridge already swarming with white-uniformed Austrians. Dominating the skyline, Lausard saw an abbey. Around it, the cannon of the Austrians rained canister and roundshot down on to the advancing French, careless as to whether or not they struck their own troops, so desperate were they to keep their attackers at bay.

Several loud explosions rocked the ground and geysers of fire shot skyward. Pieces of shrapnel flew in all directions and one sliced through the ear of Lausard's horse. The animal reared but the sergeant retained control of it. Another piece of the flying metal slammed into the scabbard of Charvet's sword and buckled it. Smoke rolled across the battlefield, cutting visibility to less than ten yards in places. It was as if part of the sky had fallen, as if the very clouds themselves had descended from the heavens to obscure the views of Frenchman and Austrian alike. Lausard's eyes were streaming and tiny black particles floated in the air like a swarm of minute insects, the cinders from so many burnt cartridge papers and of incinerated wood. Yet still he forced his horse on, sword at the ready, his drenched uniform drying off in the heat generated by so many explosions and so much exertion. Steam, as well as smoke, was rising from the battlefield as men found their uniforms drying on them. They appeared to be on fire. It was difficult to take a breath so clogged was the air. All around, the air was filled with the sound of clashing blades, gunfire and the shrieks and bellows of men as they fought and died.

A volley of musket fire struck the dragoons and Lausard saw two men close to him fall. Captain Milliere hissed in pain as a ball cut through the upper part of his arm, ripping away part of one epaulette. Joubert's horse was hit in the neck and slumped forward, catapulting the big man from the saddle. He rolled twice then, with agility remarkable for his size, leapt back to seek cover behind the dead animal as several more bullets tore into the carcass. Karim caught the reins of a riderless mount and spurred towards him. He held the horse still long enough for Joubert to haul himself into the saddle. The two men exchanged a glance. Joubert nodded his thanks.

Slapping angrily at the wound in his arm, Captain Milliere formed the dragoons into two lines as a strong breeze swept away a rolling bank of smoke to reveal the source of the gunfire. A regiment of Austrian infantry had formed a square less than one hundred yards away. From behind the kneeling front rank, two more files were preparing to unleash another volley into the French cavalry. Dozens of French hussars were whirling uselessly around the tight-packed formation, occasionally swinging their sabres at the white-uniformed infantry, but the bristling hedge of bayonets kept them at bay. As the dragoons waited, Milliere cantered from one end of their lines to the other roaring at the top of his voice and gesturing towards the square.

'Front rank, fire from the saddle,' he bellowed. 'When I give the word, draw swords and we'll finish the bastards then.'

As one, the leading horsemen sheathed their swords and pulled their carbines free. They advanced at a walk, the Charlevilles propped against their thighs in readiness. Lausard could see the Austrian infantry pulling their muskets hard into their shoulders, ready to fire off another fusillade. Close to him, Moreau crossed himself. He could also see Karim's lips moving silently as he whispered a prayer to his own God.

The French hussars were still milling around the square, many of them wounded, all of them exhausted. Riderless horses were dashing around in all directions. Lausard saw one hurtle past with the pommel blasted off its saddle. The seat was drenched with blood and the rest of the harness was missing. There was a single boot wedged into the right-hand stirrup. As he watched the wretched animal he heard an all too familiar sound.

The ground began to shake and the rumble of hundreds of heavy horses joined with the cacophony of other sounds already rending his eardrums.

'Jesus, look,' snapped Rocheteau, nodding to their right.

In their familiar enamelled black breastplates and tall helmets, several ranks of Austrian cuirassiers, swords drawn and brandished in the air, were hurtling towards the hussars. The speed of their charge was aided by the fact they were moving down the precipitous slope. Big men on big horses, they looked like a black and white tide threatening to sweep the hussars away. But, as Lausard watched, the French light cavalry hastily formed a column and, under the exhortations of their officer, suddenly swung to the right, away from both the square and the onrushing cuirassiers. Lausard could only marvel at the speed and efficiency of the manoeuvre. It took the Austrians by surprise and, already having charged more than four hundred yards, the heavy cavalry began to slow down, their horses blown.

'Fire,' roared Milliere.

The leading line of dragoons opened up with a withering salvo. The noise was incredible and another vast cloud of sulphurous smoke was discharged, joining the choking smog already shrouding the battlefield.

Wearing only breastplates, the cuirassiers with their backs to the dragoons were helpless. Lausard saw many hit in the back with bullets, the whites of their jackets flowering red where they were shot. A standard bearer was struck in the face and toppled from his horse, the flag trampled beneath the hooves of the terrified horses. Bodies tumbled from their saddles as the sergeant and his companions hurried to reload. With consummate skill, the mounted troops half-cocked their carbines, tore the tops from fresh cartridges with their teeth, poured powder down the barrels then spat the balls after them. Their mouths filled with the coarse black grains, they reached for their ramrods and drove the remainder of the wadding, and the ball, down hard into the barrel. Then, rapidly replacing their ramrods, they swung the weapons back up to their shoulders, preparing to fire again. Before Milliere could shout the order, the column of French hussars suddenly smashed into the disorientated cuirassiers, sabres churning the air. Normally, light cavalry wouldn't even have engaged heavy horsemen but, with the Austrian cuirassiers struggling to regain their formation, the hussars drove in among them.

Rocheteau and a number of the other dragoons grinned as they saw the heavy cavalry suddenly turn and ride off with some of the hussars in pursuit.

'The square,' shouted Lausard and the men suddenly returned their attention to the obstacle before them.

'Fire,' roared Milliere again and this time the salvo of shot tore into its intended target.

Lausard saw dozens of Austrian infantrymen fall, gaps yawning in the previously impenetrable formation.

'Second rank, charge,' Milliere roared and, led by Lieutenant Royere, the other line of dragoons hurtled towards the square, driving their horses towards any gaps in the tight-packed ranks of infantry. Some closed up in time and a number of men and horses were impaled on the long bayonets but elsewhere the Austrians hesitated under the onslaught. Lausard pulled his own sword from its scabbard and dashed towards one of the gaps. He struck savagely to his right and left. The three-foot blade sliced a part of a corporal's face off; then, bringing his sword down again with devastating force, Lausard sheared through the shako of a private and split the black felt headgear in two before cleaving his skull. Alongside him, Karim swung his scimitar and decapitated an onrushing infantryman. Another stroke hacked off a hand with ease. Delacor, the reins gripped in his teeth, drove down with both his sword and the axe he always carried. He buried the axe in one man's head, tore it free then skewered another infantryman through the throat.

Tigana simply rode his horse into the Austrians, allowing the animal to trample them.

Tabor did likewise, yanking on the reins to avoid a bayonet thrust. He felt the point jab into his boot top but then he struck at his attacker and cut the man across the face, almost hacking his nose off with the powerful cut.

The square was breached.

More and more dragoons forced their way through the gaps and, as Lausard looked around, he saw that a number of the infantry were beginning to waver. The wounded, dragged back into the centre of the square, could only lay helpless as the French rode over them in their eagerness to reach the backs of the men forming the far walls of the formation.

Lausard began slashing madly at the unprotected men

and, within minutes, panic had spread through the white-uniformed mass. Royere led a dozen more dragoons into another gap on the left-hand side of the square, driving his sword into the chest of a mounted officer who came at him. The square began to crack. First small gaps then much larger ones appeared; men began to drop their weapons. Some tried to surrender. Giresse cut down two who raised their hands. Others merely began to run. Many hurled their muskets aside to lighten the load, anxious only to be free of these maniacal horsemen who were now slamming into them from every direction.

Lausard, his face and uniform drenched with blood, continued to hack at everything around him but his attention was focused on a standard bearer who wasn't sure whether to flee or stand his ground. Lausard felled the man with one devastating blow and snatched the captured flag from the Austrian's hand, raising it high above his head for all to see. Roars of delight greeted his feat.

The men were sweating, barely able to breathe from a combination of the noxious air and their own exertions. Lausard's horse was lathered and, like its rider, seemed to be running on adrenalin. The smell of blood and excrement began to mingle with that of sulphur and gunpowder. It was a smell they had all come to know well during the last ten years. It was the smell of battle. And Lausard revelled in it. He tugged hard on his reins to halt his horse, seeing that the remains of the square were fleeing up the incline towards the abbey that dominated the high ridge above Elchingen. Indeed, through the swirling smoke, he could see large columns of Austrian troops retreating towards the higher ground, some of them harrassed by French hussars, others pursued by blue-clad infantry. He saw Marshal Ney gallop past, his uniform spattered with mud and blood, his bicorn gripped in his hand, its brilliant white feathers fluttering in the air, the star of the Legion of Honour blazing on his chest. A column of infantry followed him, racing up the incline like hounds in pursuit of a fox.

The sergeant suddenly felt a hand on his shoulder and saw Captain Milliere grinning at him.

'Now you have your war,' roared the officer.

Lausard brandished the captured standard, his face a bloody mask, his eyes blazing triumphantly.

Twenty-One

Napoleon gazed raptly at the citadel of Ulm as he walked slowly back and forth in front of the massive bonfire, his hands clasped behind his back. From his position at the top of the steep incline overlooking the city he could see everything. The spires and rooftops beyond the walls, the countryside surrounding the fortified stronghold and, all around him, drawn up in a vast semi-circle, the men of his *Grande Armée*. The gates of the city were open and, as Napoleon watched, the first of the white-clad Austrian troops began to emerge. They marched with their muskets at the slope, their cartridge boxes slung over their packs, never wavering from the regulation seventy-five paces a minute. The leading column moved seamlessly from the city, closely followed by another. The mounted officers guided their horses ahead of the marching men but Napoleon heard no orders being shouted. He finally stopped pacing and concentrated his full attention on the steadily growing numbers of enemy troops in the plain before him. Behind him, the vast campfire continued to blaze, pieces of wood crackling and burning.

'What will history say of them, Berthier?' the Emperor mused, turning to his Chief of Staff. 'Will the Austrians be ridiculed as fools or will *we* be praised for our strategy?'

'I feel history will be more concerned with *your* triumph rather than *their* predicament, sire,' Berthier told him.

The first of the Austrian columns had paused at the foot of the Michelsburg Heights. They stood perfectly still until orders rang out, echoing across the curiously silent countryside.

As one, the infantry threw their '*Alt Sühler*' muskets to the ground swiftly followed by their cartridge boxes. As each file passed and repeated the action, the pile of equipment began to grow. Now unarmed, the leading column marched towards Napoleon who began wandering towards the foot of the hill. Berthier, Rapp, Ney and Lannes followed, all clad in their full dress uniforms.

'You see what English gold has brought you?' shouted Napoleon as the defeated Austrians traipsed mournfully past. 'Only defeat and humiliation. Pitt promised your leaders a great victory. A victory that would crush France. He bought your Emperor's allegiance with gold, tempted him with riches and promises of triumph. And what has he to show for his greed? Ignominious defeat. All over Germany your comrades have suffered similar humiliations and all because of your Emperor's misguided loyalty to England. A loyalty bought with the coins of Judas. It is *you* who are betrayed. You honest soldiers. Your Emperor will keep his gold. He has lost nothing. You have lost your honour. That is not something which can be bought, even with gold. England wanted victory and they were willing to pay for it but to pay for others to suffer in their place. You were those chosen to bear this humiliation. Remember that. You owe your current position to England and the greed of your Emperor.'

The weary Austrians continued to troop past, their faces pale and wan. One or two glanced at the Emperor, who continued with his tirade, but most were anxious just to be free of the city that had been a prison, not a refuge, for the past five days.

Alain Lausard watched as the mountain of discarded weapons grew steadily higher. The dragoons sat at ease, their squadron drawn up in three ranks, watching, like the rest of the army, as their enemies continued to pour out of Ulm. The pile of muskets was huge. Swords, axes, pistols and carbines also joined the infantry weapons at the foot of the Heights, no longer needed by men who were utterly beaten.

'I didn't expect them to surrender without a fight,' Rocheteau mused, watching the columns that still marched out of the city with depressing regularity.

'What choice did they have?' Lausard commented. 'They were surrounded. They couldn't break out. They had no chance of reinforcements. They did the right thing.'

'Cowards,' Delacor snorted dismissively.

'And would you rather they had resisted?' Lausard snapped. 'Would you have preferred a siege? Or the storming of a fortified city protected by twenty-five thousand men? What cost in lives would we have had to bear to capture such a stronghold?'

Delacor didn't answer.

'According to the latest army bulletin over four thousand Austrians have been killed since the start of the campaign,' Bonet said. 'Twenty-five thousand men, sixty guns and forty standards have fallen into our hands here at Ulm alone. Almost sixty thousand prisoners of war have been taken. All that in less than thirty days. At the cost of just two thousand of our own men.'

'Our Emperor is a genius,' Charvet offered. 'He has invented a new way of making war. He makes it more with our legs than with our swords.'

A ripple of laughter greeted the remark.

'Perhaps you should tell the men who died at Elchingen, Haslach and Wertingen,' Roussard grunted.

'We should thank God,' Moreau added, crossing himself.

'And Allah, all praise to Him,' Karim murmured.

'Thank who you like,' Giresse said. 'It was Napoleon's strategy that gave us victory, not God.'

Some of the other men laughed.

'And now what?' Rocheteau wanted to know, his eyes never leaving the dismal columns. 'Where do we go next?'

'Wherever Bonaparte orders us to go.' Lausard told him.

'I heard rumours it would be Vienna,' Bonet offered. 'There are thought to be Austrian *and* Russian armies waiting there.'

'More fighting,' groaned Sonnier.

'Perhaps the Russians too will surrender before we have to engage them in battle, Alain,' Roussard offered.

Lausard didn't answer.

His eyes were firmly fixed on the ceaseless stream of Austrians still pouring out of Ulm.

At the foot of the Michelsburg Heights, the stack of equipment was now as tall as a man.

The columns continued on their weary route.

*　　*　　*

The group of men who approached Napoleon was led by a tall man with grey hair and the Corsican could tell from his uniform that he occupied a high rank. He wore a bicorn with wide gold edging and the imperial cypher FII in gold. From this headgear a dark green feather plume drooped. The officer was dressed in a long skirted white coat, trimmed with a red collar and liberally decorated with gold lace. A red, gold-edged waistcoat, red breeches, cuffed boots and a gold and black silk waist sash made his rank unmistakable. Napoleon took a step forward, watching as the Austrian general drew his sword, turned the hilt towards the Corsican and lowered his head in supplication. The officers around him did likewise.

'I am General Mack of the Imperial Austrian Army,' said the tall man. 'I offer you my sword as a token of my surrender.'

'Keep your sword,' Napoleon told him.

Mack stepped back slightly and sheathed the blade.

The Emperor gestured to the officers around him who mimicked his action.

'Perhaps you would have been better served following the theories put forward in your own book, General,' mused the Corsican. 'You wrote a book back in 1794, did you not? *Instructions for Generals*, if I recall.'

The Austrian nodded.

'In which you stressed the importance of the offensive in campaigning. True?' Napoleon smiled.

The defeated Austrian nodded and, for the first time, Napoleon became aware of an almost bewildered look on his opponent's face. Mack was running his gaze over the Emperor, apparently dismayed at the fact that his greatcoat and uniform were soaking wet and spattered with mud.

'Does something about my appearance trouble you, General?' asked the Corsican. 'It is a legacy of more than a month in the field. Your master has tried to make me remember that I was a soldier. I hope he will acknowledge that the throne and the imperial purple have not made me forget my original profession.'

'Are we to be held as your prisoners?' Mack wanted to know, his face set in hard lines.

'I have no desire to retain captives of any rank. But how can I be certain that I will not again face these same men who have surrendered here today? If I send them back to Austria, the Aulic Council will have them rearmed and ready to fight again within a month.'

'You have my word that will not happen,' Mack said.

'And you expect me to accept the word of an enemy?'

'I can offer you nothing more, General.'

Napoleon glared at Mack.

'You see before you much more than a general,' he snapped. 'You see an Emperor. As worthy as your own Emperor Francis or Alexander of Russia. But, unlike them, I *earned* my majesty. It was not a gift of birth or the product of some archaic system of primogeniture. The blood that flows through *my* veins is that of ambition and ability. Not of privilege. And these men—' he gestured to the officers around him '—they are not the sons of aristocrats and dukes but of working men. To those you serve it will appear that your army of privilege has been destroyed by a force of peasants. How will the Aulic Council look upon that? How will your Emperor look upon it? Or your allies? Any disdain they feel will be returned to them ten-fold when I send my men against them in the next stage of this campaign.' The Corsican turned his back briefly. 'Now go, rejoin your men. My business *here* is finished. I have other matters to attend to.'

Accompanied by his officers, Napoleon made his way slowly back up the hill towards the blazing bonfire. Its flames leapt high into the sky, as if threatening to engulf the heavens themselves.

Lausard pulled up the collar of his cape as another icy gust of wind swept across the road. It carried with it flecks of snow that felt like frozen needles as they struck the sergeant's face. He narrowed his eyes and tugged the scarf he wore more tightly around his mouth and nose. The dragoons moved at a respectable pace, the roads having become more easily passable with the onset of the colder weather. In some ways, Lausard reasoned, the cold was to be welcomed over torrential rain. Nevertheless, the conditions only served to make the plight of the French more acute. He himself had not eaten for more than a day. The horses had been fed a meagre meal of oats at a farm the dragoons had come across a day or two earlier. The ribs of many mounts were clearly visible, pressing against their thin flesh. For the most part, the light cavalry, still pressing on ahead of the advance guard, had stripped the countryside as clean as if it had been visited by a plague of locusts.

'Those peacock bastards,' grunted Delacor, his breath clouding in the air. 'They get all the food before we have a chance to lay our hands on it.'

'We'd do the same in their position,' Rocheteau told him, ducking his head slightly and closing his eyes as a particularly violent blast of wind rocked the horsemen. Several of the weaker horses almost overbalanced.

'Where the hell are we anyway?' Rostov wanted to know.

'Ten miles north of Vienna,' Lausard told him. 'We should be there before nightfall.' The sky was already slate grey, pregnant with swollen cloud.

'What more does Napoleon want from us?' gasped Roussard. 'We have been marching over twenty miles a day for more than ten days now. We've lost more men to hunger and the weather since we left Ulm than we have to the Austrians or the Russians.'

'We haven't even *seen* the Russians,' Rocheteau reminded him.

'And all the time we're stuck on these accursed roads,' Roussard continued, 'while our Emperor is travelling along in his comfortable coach, sheltered from the worst of the weather and with plenty of food to keep him happy.'

'There will be food in Vienna won't there, Alain?' Gaston asked.

'If Murat's men or the Guard haven't got there before us,' Lausard told the young trumpeter.

'Vienna has no strategic value,' Bonet said, coughing harshly. 'Surely Marshal Murat would be better employed engaging the Russians.'

'How can he fight them when they seem intent on running?' Carbonne wanted to know. 'I heard that they are already half way into Bohemia.'

'Good,' Roussard mused. 'Let them keep running all the way back to their Motherland. I'll be happy if the only Russian I ever see is Rostov here.' He slapped the Russian on the shoulder. Some of the other men laughed.

'The time will come soon enough,' Lausard said. 'The

Russians won't run forever. And when they do turn and fight we might all wish they hadn't.'

An icy blast of wind screamed across the road. It sounded to Lausard like a wail of pain.

Twenty-Two

The spires of St Stephen's Cathedral jabbed upwards towards the swollen clouds like accusatory fingers. Lausard stood looking up at the magnificent edifice, its doors, windows and towers adorned with countless carvings. Gargoyles leered down into the huge open square that surrounded the cathedral. To the sergeant and the men with him it seemed as if the stone demons were watching them, perhaps wondering who these hungry, exhausted, mud-spattered, filthy troops in reeking uniforms were and what exactly their business was in Vienna.

'They look as if they're laughing at us,' Tabor observed, shielding his eyes from the falling snow as he glanced up.

'Perhaps they know something we don't,' Lausard murmured, his breath forming clouds as he spoke. 'Perhaps *they* know where the Austrian armies have run to or why the Emperor Francis has abandoned his own capital city.'

'Someone said that Vienna had been declared an open city,' Tabor interjected. 'What does that mean?'

'It means the Austrians gave it up without a fight, you half-wit,' snapped Delacor.

'They also gave up five hundred cannon, a hundred thousand muskets and much ammunition,' Bonet said.

'It's a pity they didn't give up some food too,' Joubert intoned.

'There must be food in the city,' Rocheteau said. 'It's just a matter of finding it.'

'You can be sure the Guard will have found it *and* eaten it by now,' Delacor rasped. 'And I'll wager our Emperor has no shortage of food at Schönbrunn. He resides in that Austrian palace like a king.'

'What do you expect him to do?' Lausard wanted to know. 'Share our billets? Camp in one of the royal parks?' He looked disdainfully at his companion then walked on, still glancing up occasionally at the staggering vision that was St Stephen's.

'I think I will go inside and pray,' Moreau said.

'For what?' Joubert asked.

'I wish to thank God for delivering us safely into the city.'

'While you're in there, ask Him if He knows where there may be some wine and bread,' Lausard remarked and the other men laughed.

'And women,' Giresse added.

'What kind of women would go near us while we are in *this* condition?' Lausard smiled and spread his arms, as if inviting his companions to inspect his wretched demeanour. He was, like most of the men, barely recognisable as a dragoon, scarcely so as a soldier of any kind. Beneath his oilskin-covered helmet he had wrapped a scarf to protect himself from the biting chill. He had not shaved for at least a week and a heavy growth of stubble covered his chin and cheeks. They bore a layer of dirt and grime that seemed as if it would resist even the strongest soap and hottest water, should any ever be found. Around his shoulders, over the top of his long, tattered, green cloak, he wore two fox skins roughly stitched together from a pair of animals he had killed days ago. Having eaten their flesh almost raw, Lausard had used the pelts like some kind of shawl in an attempt to acquire some added warmth. The fox skin was crawling with lice but even the troublesome parasites found it hard to survive in the freezing temperatures that had descended upon the countryside during the last three weeks. The stench it gave off was appalling. Beneath his cloak, in addition to his own jacket, Lausard also wore the fur-trimmed pelisse he had taken from a dead French hussar, having first torn off the gold braid and traded it for two potatoes with a deserting shoeless infantryman on the road leading into Vienna a day ago. His breeches were caked with mud, as were his boots. He wore two pairs of socks inside them as well as pieces of rag he had wrapped around his feet. At first he'd had trouble actually getting the boots on but, with wear, the leather had gradually stretched to accommodate the additions. He also wore two pairs of gloves, one taken from a captured Austrian infantry officer at Elchingen.

His companions were similarly desolate in appearance, attired in other troops' clothes in addition to their own. However, Lausard had discovered one valuable by-product of their unwashed state: their bodily secretions such as sweat and even urine, combined with the dirt, had made them waterproof. What the sergeant found even more incredible was that, despite their horrendous appearance, the dragoons were not as vile to behold as some of the other French troops he had seen during the

march from Ulm to Vienna. Many of the infantry were
without boots. Large numbers had discarded their weapons and packs. The roads leading into Vienna were strewn
with the debris of an army pushed to the limits of its
endurance. Beside those same roads, even cannon stood
abandoned and dead horses seemed to act as obscene
route markers for the advancing French. Countless men
had lost fingers, toes, even hands and feet, to frostbite and
the resultant gangrene. All were starving and exhausted.
To the residents of Vienna it must have seemed as if an
army of scarecrows had marched into their city. Lausard
gazed once more at the towering magnificence of St
Stephen's then he turned and led his men back the way
they had come.

They wandered through narrow streets, occasionally
passing other French troops who appeared as dishevelled
as the dragoons themselves. Lausard recognised one of the
figures in the small group approaching and a smile spread
across his face.

'Charnier,' he called, stepping towards the corporal.

'Alain,' the other man beamed and the two dragoons
embraced.

'Is life any easier in the third squadron?' Lausard
wanted to know.

'Life isn't easy anywhere in this damned army or this
godforsaken country,' Charnier told him.

The corporal was wearing a thick fur cloak over his
jacket. It was tied at the waist by a length of rope.
From the rope hung several strips of pork, some biscuits
threaded on to string like a necklace and two potatoes,
also skewered and attached to string. Charnier looked like
a mobile feast.

'Where did you get the food?' Lausard wanted to know.

'I've had the biscuits since we left Ulm. We found a pig a few days ago. That is all that remains.' He gestured to the strips of mouldy pork. 'The same goes for the potatoes. This city has already been ravaged by Murat's light cavalry and the Guard. You'll be lucky to find a rat that hasn't been eaten.'

'Do you want to sell some of what you have?' Lausard nodded towards the dangling morsels.

'For what, Alain?' Charnier said smiling. 'What could you possibly offer me, at the moment, that is more valuable than food? Money? What use have we for gold? We use Austrian bank notes to light our pipes.'

Lausard nodded and placed a hand gently on his companion's shoulder.

'Where are you going now?' the sergeant wanted to know. 'I thought the third squadron were billeted close to the first.'

'We were, until our horses were taken. We're to be housed with some infantry for the time being.'

'What are you talking about?'

'One third of our squadron were ordered to surrender their horses to the Guard cavalry to serve as remounts for them.'

'Who gave the order?' Lausard demanded.

'I assume the order was issued by Headquarters. Officers from the Emperor's personal bodyguard came this morning and took them. They intend to do the same with each squadron. The horse artillery are also running short of animals to pull their guns. We were told that we would be found remounts in due course. Until then, we march on foot.'

'No one is turning *my* horse into a pack animal,' rasped the sergeant.

Lausard was already pulling away from his friend, the other members of his squadron following him as he began running down the narrow street.

'What are you doing, Alain?' Charnier shouted after the sergeant. 'They have orders.'

'To hell with their orders,' Lausard bellowed without looking back.

Napoleon warmed himself beside the raging fire, his eyes scanning the reports before him. Occasionally he rocked gently back and forth on his heels but for the most part he remained as motionless as a statue. From the desk on the other side of the state room Berthier watched the Corsican's expression. The Chief of Staff returned to his correspondence every so often but his attention was constantly drawn back towards the Emperor. It was the sound of tearing paper that finally caused him to look up. Napoleon ripped the letter in half, his face contorted with rage, then balled it up and hurled it angrily into the fire.

'Our fleet has been destroyed by Nelson off the coast of Cape Trafalgar,' he snarled, watching as the paper was consumed by flame.

Berthier looked on without speaking.

Napoleon spun on his heel and headed away from the fire towards one of the huge windows that afforded him a view of the gardens of Schönbrunn Palace. In the summer, he had no doubt they were magnificent but now, deep into November, they were covered by a thin blanket of snow. But gardens were the last thing on the Corsican's mind. His eyes blazed and he turned and stalked back towards the fireplace.

'That incompetent fool Villeneuve,' he rasped, his voice

rising in volume. 'Admiral of the Fleet. I would have been better employed appointing a monkey to command my navy. Eighteen ships destroyed. Nearly six thousand men killed and another twenty thousand taken prisoner.'

There was a long silence which was finally broken by Berthier.

'It is as well you had the foresight to transfer military operations away from the coast, sire,' he said quietly.

Napoleon nodded almost imperceptibly, his fury abating somewhat.

'The English may be masters of the sea but we will be masters of Europe before the year ends,' he hissed. 'Despite Pitt's attempts to *buy* victory with tainted gold, once I have destroyed the Russians and Austrians then England will once again be isolated.' He exhaled deeply.

'There is the question of Prussia, sire. It appears likely that Frederick William will add his support to the allied cause against us. The Tsar visited him in Berlin only last month. A treaty was signed. Prussia has promised to undertake armed mediation in this war by early December.'

'And what persuaded that dilatory fool finally to commit his armies? More of Pitt's gold?'

'It was Marshal Bernadotte's march through Ansbach earlier in the campaign that angered him. He saw it as a violation of Prussian territory.'

'Something that doubtless pleased his Queen Louise. I am surprised she did not manage to persuade her husband to take arms against us sooner. She seems to be the only one in their court capable of making a decision. Little wonder they call her the only man in Prussia.' The Corsican smiled crookedly.

'That may be, sire, but the fact remains that, in practical terms, if Frederick William decides to commit forces against us, we could be facing another two hundred thousand men. We cannot permit that to happen. The army are already exhausted. The hospitals are full. There are wholesale desertions. Our lines of communication and supply are stretched to the limit. Our position is perilous enough already. Should Prussia join the war too, we could well be annihilated.'

'What are our present dispositions and those of the enemy? If we are to face yet another foe then we must move quickly to defeat those already arrayed against us.'

The Corsican crossed to the large desk next to where Berthier was seated and studied one of the maps laid out there.

'Kutusov continues to withdraw,' he mused. 'It seems he was determined to avoid a battle on the south bank of the Danube, even if it cost his allies their capital.'

'So far there have been only skirmishes with the Russians, sire,' Berthier reminded his Emperor. 'At Amstetten, Maria Zell and Dürrenstein. It seems to be only a matter of time before Kutusov joins the Tsar and General Buxhowden's reinforcements. As I mentioned previously, sire, the condition of the army must also be taken into consideration. They have been marching for almost eight weeks without rest. It is more than any man can endure.'

'It is to spare their blood I make them undergo these hardships.'

'They realise that, sire, and they are aware of your concern for them. These men would follow you to the ends of the earth. Gladly die in your name. Follow whatever orders you give but, should their present condition deteriorate any further, they may well be prevented from doing so.'

Napoleon ran his expert gaze over the map then jabbed a finger at it.

'We will advance to Brunn,' he declared. 'Once there I will order a temporary halt in operations.'

'You may have to consider another alternative, sire,' Berthier offered. 'It may be wise to retire, at least as far as Ulm.'

'Retire? Do you want me to give up all I have won in this campaign, Berthier? Do you not know me well enough by now?'

'But, sire, there are sound logistical reasons for such a movement. At least *consider* them. If we advance to Brunn we will be at the very extremity of severely extended lines of communication, potentially open to attack by troops that the Prussians are currently mobilising. If the Russians continue their withdrawal and we continue to pursue them, that will also give General Bennigsen an opportunity to attack our flank. If we decided to hold that ground then we run the very real risk of being taken on the other flank by the Austrian troops moving through the Alps and the Tyrol in this direction. It is entirely possible we could be caught between two armies, one on each of our flanks.'

'And if we withdraw as far as Ulm, do you think the countryside will support our men a second time? They scraped it clean of supplies during the advance. The army is strung out in an arc from Ulm, through Innsbruck and Graz to Vienna. Most of the army corps are barely within supporting distance of each other. Marmont reports daily that he expects to clash with the Austrians of Archduke Charles in the south.'

'Then surely, sire, you can see the sense in a strategic withdrawal.'

'Our predicament may well be the key to this entire campaign, Berthier. If I can lure the Russians and Austrians into attacking me then I can beat them. What better incentive do they need than the knowledge that the French army is starving and in rags and also outnumbered two to one? It is precisely the kind of carrot to dangle before those self-important donkeys Alexander and Francis. The Emperors of Russia and Austria are consumed by over-confidence. They will not resist the bait. Their desire to humble *me* will be their downfall.' He smiled at his Chief of Staff. 'Send orders to Murat, Soult and Lannes to advance upon this location in Moravia immediately.' He pressed a pin very slowly into the map. As Berthier looked down he saw the name of the town the Emperor had designated.

It was Austerlitz.

As Lausard reached the makeshift stables where the dragoon horses had been housed, he could already see several of his companions standing helplessly at the doors. A number of mounts had been tied together by their bridles and were being led away by half a dozen blue-uniformed horsemen. The sergeant recognised their attire. Brown fur colpacks, with red cords, covered in oilskin to protect them from the weather. Dark blue dolman jackets and pelisses, both fastened, both decorated with red lace and black fur. Blue breeches decorated with red stripes and thigh knots. The unmistakable attire of Imperial Guard horse artillery. The imperial eagle, its clawed feet planted on crossed cannon barrels, gleamed on their blue sabertaches.

'Alain, we tried to stop them,' Tigana explained as the sergeant ran up to join him.

'They said they had orders to take one third of the horses,' Carbonne added.

Lausard stepped towards the leading horseman and grabbed at his bridle.

'What the hell do you think you're doing?' he snarled.

The artilleryman tried to jerk his horse's head away from Lausard's powerful grip but the dragoon held on.

'Get off me or I'll ride you down,' hissed the gunner.

'Try,' Lausard snarled.

Delacor slid the axe from beneath his cloak.

'Yes,' he breathed, stepping forward to join the sergeant. 'Try.'

'Who is in charge here?' Lausard wanted to know.

As if to answer his question, a tall man mounted on a grey horse emerged from the stable. His pelisse was trimmed with gold braid and white fur, marking him out as an officer.

'Get away from those horses,' he shouted.

'They are *our* horses,' Lausard told him. 'I suggest you tell your men to release them, Captain.'

'You insolent bastard,' rasped the officer, guiding his horse towards Lausard. 'We have orders to procure horses for our artillery trains.'

'Orders from whom?' Lausard demanded.

'The Guard are short of horses. We need your mounts. Our unit, and most of the army, is to leave Vienna before nightfall to continue the advance. We need extra horses.'

'Show me the order.'

'I need show you nothing. You are a sergeant, I . . .'

'Your rank means nothing to me, Captain. You do not command me *or* my squadron.'

'The needs of the Imperial Guard are paramount.'

'I care nothing for *your* needs. Now return our horses to us and leave.'

The captain allowed his hand to slip to the hilt of his sabre.

Lausard quickly pulled his sword from its scabbard and pointed the tip at the artillery officer.

'You dare to threaten me?' said the captain.

'Return our horses to us now. If not, I will take yours.'

Several of the other mounted artillerymen guided their horses towards the scene of confrontation. More than one drew their sabres.

Rocheteau pulled his blade from its sheath. So did several of the other dragoons.

'If you want the horses, then take them,' Rocheteau hissed. 'If you can.'

'What is your name?' snarled the officer.

'Sergeant Alain Lausard. And yours, Captain?'

'I am Captain Bertrand Giono, officer of the horse artillery of the Imperial Guard and if you do not stand aside I will have you court-martialled.'

'On what charge? Show me your orders. Where is the piece of paper signed by the Emperor instructing you to steal our horses to drag your cannon?'

'There is no *written* order. I told you, the needs of the Guard take precedence over the needs of line troops.'

'In *your* eyes, Captain. Not in those of the rest of the army and certainly not in mine. If you want our horses you will have to produce a written order to that effect. Otherwise you will have to fight us before we allow you to take them.'

'This is treason,' snarled Giono. 'Where is your own commander?'

'Searching for food like every other man in the army,' Lausard told him. 'But even if he were here you would find him as resistant as I and my colleagues. You will not leave here with our horses, Captain. I promise you that. If you try, all you will leave behind is the corpses of your men.'

Giono glared at the sergeant then at the line of dragoons, every one now clutching a weapon of some kind. Behind him his own men hesitated. Half a dozen had drawn their sabres but some of the others looked unsure. Sonnier thumbed back the hammer on his carbine and aimed it at Giono's head.

'Leave now, Captain,' Lausard urged. 'While you still can. And take your men with you.'

For interminable seconds the two men locked gazes then Giono pulled hard on his bridle causing his horse to rear wildly before the sergeant who merely took a step back, his eyes still locked on those of the artilleryman.

'You have not heard the last of this,' Giono snarled. Then, to his men, 'Leave the horses.' He looked down at Lausard. 'Like their riders, they are poor specimens, not suited for our needs.'

Lausard watched as the horse artillery rode off.

'Good riddance,' Delacor said dismissively.

Rostov hawked loudly and spat after the retreating troops.

'He said most of the troops here were to leave before nightfall,' Bonet offered. 'No doubt that includes us.'

'Be grateful we're leaving on horseback, not on foot,' Lausard answered.

'Do you think they will be back, Alain?' Rocheteau enquired.

'We could get in trouble for not giving them what

they wanted,' Roussard added. 'As that captain said, the Guard are supposed to take precedence over line regiments.'

'They are no better than us,' Charvet said.

'What can they do to us that forced marches, hunger and exhaustion haven't already done?' Lausard wanted to know. 'And soon we are to advance again. To more hunger? To battle? If they want to come back then let them. Let them bring Bonaparte himself with them. They will not take our horses. And I will personally kill any one of them that tries.'

Twenty-Three

As he peered through his telescope, Lausard guessed there must be somewhere in the region of a thousand Austrian troops on the far bank of the river. The waters themselves, swelled by recent rain and melted snow, flowed darkly beneath the huge wooden bridge. Even from the high ridge upon which they waited, the dragoons could hear the rushing currents. The drizzle of the early afternoon, which had been an annoying accompaniment to the French troops' march out of Vienna, had given way to freezing snow that swept like a billowing blanket all across the landscape. The white-clad Austrians looked as if they had been standing in position for so long they had simply been covered in the fine powder. An army of snowmen, Lausard mused. His thoughts darkened as he saw the batteries of twelve- and six-pounders arrayed among the waiting infantry.

'It is Elchingen all over again,' murmured Lieutenant Royere. 'We will have to fight our way across.'

'If they even allow us to set foot on the bridge, Lieutenant. Look,' said Lausard, handing his telescope to the officer and indicating a number of lengths of what appeared to be string dangling from the bottom of the bridge and running beneath it.

'Mines,' muttered Royere. 'On *both* sides by the look of it.'

'As soon as we advance, they'll destroy it.'

'If they do, it'll take days for the bridging units to build anything to get us across a river of this size,' Captain Milliere sighed.

'The entire army could be stuck here until a suitable crossing is constructed,' Royere said, handing the telescope back to Lausard, who snapped it shut and pushed it back into his pocket.

Ahead of them, mounted on a magnificent white Arab horse, Marshal Joachim Murat also regarded the bridge contemplatively. The marshal was dressed in a gold-trimmed shako that sported a massive white plume. To protect him from the cold he wore a thick fur cloak over his dazzling uniform. Light blue Hungarian breeches and red Moroccan boots completed the flamboyant cavalry commander's appearance. Even his horse looked resplendant with its tiger-skin shabraque and red leather pistol holsters. He was walking his horse back and forth, deep in conversation with Marshal Jean Lannes, who, dressed in his marshal's uniform of heavily gold-embroidered blue, looked almost dowdy in comparison. Lannes took off his gold-trimmed bicorn and ran a hand through his hair, his gaze, like Murat's, fixed on the bridge.

'This will take careful planning,' he observed. 'You cannot charge across with your cavalry. They would blow you into the next world before you were half way across.'

'I am aware of that, Lannes,' Murat said sharply. 'What

had you in mind? The bridge must be taken intact. There is no other suitable crossing point.'

'If you are able to contain your exuberance for long enough then we will secure the bridge. What we do not need is another exhibition of your recklessness.'

Murat glared at his companion.

'What do you suggest then?' he sneered. 'Would you have your infantry *crawl* across the bridge in the hope that the Austrians do not see them?'

'My first suggestion is that we share our ideas. Bury our differences for the time being and use our heads to solve this problem. We must walk softly. If we give the Austrians cause to blow up the bridge then I trust we will *both* feel the wrath of the Emperor. Your family ties will not protect you should *that* happen, Murat. A brother-in-law is as open to criticism as the next man.'

The cavalry commander nodded almost imperceptibly, his eyes never leaving Lannes.

Lausard watched the two marshals as they sat astride their mounts, occasionally leaning close together conspiratorially, one or the other of them pointing at the bridge and the large detachment of Austrian troops that guarded it.

'What the hell are they doing?' Rocheteau whispered, as bewildered as the rest of the watching French soldiers.

'Working out the quickest way to get us killed,' Roussard offered.

Karim shivered in his saddle and wiped snow from his face.

'May Allah, all praise to Him, help them in their task,' the Circassian said, his voice almost lost beneath a gust of icy wind.

'Murat is headstrong,' Delacor offered. 'He will have us charging that bridge.'

'He is no fool,' Lausard interjected. 'He knows that is not the way this time.'

'There must be other crossing places, up or down river,' Giresse said, pulling his cloak more tightly around him.

'The river is impassable other than by bridges,' Lausard informed him. 'It is too deep. The current is too strong.'

'How do you know that? It might not be,' Delacor said challengingly.

'Then ride in and prove me wrong,' Lausard told him flatly.

Murat wheeled his horse and walked it back towards the waiting dragoons. He pointed a finger at Lausard, Rocheteau and Karim.

'You three. With me. Now,' he ordered and the dragoons urged their mounts forward in the direction of the marshal. 'Stay behind myself and Marshal Lannes. Do nothing unless we give the order.'

'Forgive my impertinence, sir,' said Lausard, 'but where are we going?'

Murat smiled.

'Across that bridge, Sergeant,' he told the NCO. 'Where did you think we were going?'

As the other troops watched the tiny procession heading for the ramp that led on to the bridge, many shook their heads in disbelief. Moreau crossed himself, his lips moving in silent prayer.

'This is insane,' Rocheteau muttered under his breath, his gaze drawn towards the mass of Austrian troops on the far bank.

Lausard didn't answer. He glanced down towards the fuses that trailed from the mines all around the ramp and the parapet of the bridge. There were more at the far end. Should the Austrian sappers decide to light them, the bridge and everyone on it would be blasted to atoms. From behind, he heard the unmistakable sound of marching feet and chanced a look back towards the ridge where he saw a column of French grenadiers advancing along the road that led to the bridge. Up ahead, the two marshals guided their horses slowly over the wooden structure, apparently unconcerned by the movements of their own troops behind or the files of enemy soldiers before them. Lausard, Rocheteau and Karim followed their commanders, hearts pounding that little bit faster now. They had reached the half way point of the bridge and Lausard could hear the water rushing loudly beneath them but his attention was riveted to the waiting Austrians. They stood as still as statues. Disarmingly silent. All it would take would be one order, either for the infantry to open fire or for the sappers to destroy the bridge. His horse tossed its head wildly, as if sensing the danger of the situation, but Lausard calmed it slightly with a pat of its neck.

The horsemen never altered the pace of their advance. Led by Murat and Lannes, the small procession continued on towards the far ramp of the bridge. Only when they were fifty yards from the bank did Lausard finally see movement among the white-clad ranks.

Several officers walked their horses towards the bridge. The group was led by an old man who looked distinctly uncomfortable in the saddle. He shifted back and forth in his saddle as the marshals drew nearer.

'Stop there,' he called.

Murat and Lannes continued to advance, the dragoons close behind.

Lausard saw two of the Austrian six-pounders being manoeuvred slightly by their brown-uniformed crews so that their barrels were trained on the small detachment of French horsemen.

The two marshals led their mounts down the far ramp of the bridge on to the bank. Only then did they bring the horses to a halt. Rocheteau shot Lausard a worried glance then sat still in his saddle. He was shivering slightly and he knew it wasn't just because of the icy wind.

'What do you want here?' asked the oldest of the officers. 'You realise we would be perfectly within our rights to open fire upon you? I do not think your general would be happy to lose two of his marshals so easily.'

'Why should he lose us?' Murat wanted to know. 'There is no need for you to open fire.'

'Haven't you heard of the armistice?' Lannes added. 'It has just been signed and by the terms of it, the bridge has been handed over to us.'

'I have heard of no armistice,' the older man protested. 'Show me your proof.'

'Would we have advanced into the heart of an enemy position without just cause?' Murat wanted to know. 'Two marshals and three dragoons? Did you think we hoped to storm the bridge by ourselves?' He and Lannes laughed.

The Austrian commanders merely looked on in bewilderment.

'Forgive me for not approaching you more formally,' Murat said. 'I am Marshal Joachim Murat. This is my colleague, Marshal Lannes.'

'I am Prince Auersperg of the Imperial Austrian army,' said the old man. 'And I repeat, I have heard of no armistice.'

'We approached you even without the protection of a white flag,' Lannes said. 'We came, in good faith, to bring news of a cessation of hostilities. We thought the news would be as welcome to you and your men as it is to us.'

Auersperg licked his lips and looked at his fellow officers as if for confirmation. They retained their collective look of disbelief but none spoke.

'All we require of you is that you retire from the bridge,' Murat continued. 'As stipulated by the terms of the armistice.'

Lausard saw the indecision on the Austrian commander's face, then the old man nodded.

'Very well,' he said.

'Sir, this cannot be right.'

The words came from an Austrian sergeant who had broken ranks and was pointing towards the opposite bank where a number of the French grenadiers had already reached the bridge. With them came sappers and Lausard turned in the saddle to see that the men in the dark blue uniforms were busily disarming the mines on the French side of the bridge. However, Lausard was all too aware that there was still sufficient explosive beneath the structure and on the ramp closest to them to demolish the crossing should the Austrians see through the ruse.

Murat and Lannes looked indifferently at the Austrian NCO, then back at Auersperg.

'Will you fulfil the terms of the armistice and retire from the bridge?' Lannes persisted, his voice even.

The old man hesitated once more then nodded.

The Austrian sergeant turned to the nearest file of infantry and pointed in the direction of the five Frenchmen.

'Fire,' he bellowed, stabbing a finger at them.

There was a rattle of muskets as the infantry swung their weapons up to their shoulders.

They waited, hammers thumbed back. Barrels yawning.

Lausard swallowed hard, awaiting the explosion of fire.

Murat merely shook his head.

'Is this your famous Austrian discipline?' he remarked sharply. 'Where sergeants countermand the orders of generals?'

'Lower your weapons,' Auersperg shouted indignantly. 'And arrest this man immediately.' He pointed to the perplexed sergeant.

Murat smiled at the old man.

'Respect for superior officers seems so scarce a commodity sometimes, doesn't it?' he mused.

Out of the corner of his eye Lannes noticed that one of the six-pounders was being levelled at them, a gunner reaching for the portfire.

'Yet more insubordination,' he remarked, pointing to the cannon and swinging himself out of the saddle.

As the flabbergasted Austrian gunners looked on, the marshal clambered on to the brass barrel of the six-pounder and sat there.

Lausard heard the sound of marching feet moving on to the bridge itself and turned again to see the column of French grenadiers moving swiftly across the structure. The sound of their boots reverberated through the air.

'Why are they advancing?' Auersperg demanded, indicating the oncoming French troops.

'They are not advancing at all,' Murat told him flatly. 'But the weather is so cold that they are marking time to keep their feet warm.'

Auersperg looked at Lannes as if for confirmation.

The marshal nodded.

'It is indeed a very cold day,' he offered, not a hint of emotion in his voice or expression. 'Surely you can see the sense of such movement?'

The column had practically reached the Austrian-held bank of the river by now. It marched on, over the bridge and through the motionless enemy troops who did nothing other than look on helplessly.

'I thank you for your cooperation, Prince,' Murat said, bowing his head in mock supplication.

Lausard looked back to see that the rest of the French cavalry were also advancing now. Soon, the entire force would be across the river.

Lannes patted the barrel of the six-pounder then walked back to his horse and swung himself into the saddle.

He looked at Auersperg then raised his hat in salute.

The French troops continued to march across.

'It is a desolate place, sire,' said General Rapp, pulling up the collar of his cloak in an effort to shield him from the biting wind sweeping across the open fields.

'Victory will make it glorious,' the Emperor said, gazing out over the undulating terrain.

Napoleon flicked the reins of his horse and guided the superb white charger on over the heavily frosted, bone-hard ground. His staff followed, each of them taking in details of the area that stretched both before and around them.

Close by them was a seven-hundred-foot mound of earth overlooking the main road from Brunn to Olmutz. It was known as the Santon and, as the entourage moved away from it, French troops were already dismantling an empty hut and carrying timbers from it to reinforce the side facing the enemy forces. A number of artillery positions had already been established. Gunners, sweating despite the freezing weather, lifted ammunition from caissons and dragged eight- and twelve-pounders into position in preparation for the battle they knew was imminent.

Napoleon rode south, following the line of the swiftly flowing Goldbach stream and its tributary, the Bosenitzer. Berthier's horse almost stumbled on the uneven ground as the Emperor and his staff headed towards the small cluster of buildings that made up the village of Puntowitz. The road, like the streams, flowed through steep and narrow gorges and in places it narrowed so abruptly that the horsemen were forced to guide their mounts up on to the ridges that crisscrossed the terrain so sharply. The ground rose sharply, forming a triangular shape between Puntowitz, Lapanz and Jirschikowitz. All three villages had long been abandoned.

'How high is this ground at its peak?' Napoleon wanted to know. He reined his horse to a halt as his Chief of Intelligence, General Anne Jean Marie Rene Savary, pulled a map from his portmanteau and glanced at it.

'Eight hundred and fifty feet, sire,' Savary told him. 'It is known as the Zurlan. There is a village called Bellowitz to the west.' He pointed into the distance and Napoleon saw more buildings in that direction although some were barely visible due to the light snow flurries periodically sweeping across the plains.

The Emperor nodded then urged his horse onward, south towards the villages of Kobelnitz, Zokolnitz and Telnitz. As the horsemen emerged into a gradually broadening valley, they were slowed somewhat by the marshy

fields. Even in the freezing weather, these limited movements caused mud to splash up all around the men as
their horses struggled to be free of the ooze.

'If it continues to get colder, these will freeze,' Berthier
observed. 'A number of the small lakes to the south have
already done so. The Kobelnitz pond and the Satschan
mere already comfortably take the weight of several dozen
men.'

To the west of the Goldbach stream there was another
long low ridge, but to the east the ground again rose
steeply until it finally levelled out into a plateau. Perched
on the edge of this raised ground was another small
village.

'The village of Pratzen,' Savary announced, again con-
sulting his map. 'And beyond it, the Heights. Between
nine hundred and one thousand feet above sea level, sire.
A truly commanding position.'

Napoleon stroked his chin thoughtfully.

'What is beyond the plateau?' he enquired.

'To the north and east, the villages of Blasowitz and
Krzenowitz,' the Chief of Intelligence told him. 'To
the south, the township of Aujest Markt. The town of
Austerlitz is three miles to the east, on the banks of the
Littawa river.'

'It is difficult ground, sire,' Rapp insisted.

'Unlike anything we have seen in Italy and Egypt, I
grant you,' said Napoleon. 'But it is perfect for our needs.
When I first saw this ground over a week ago, I knew it
was where I wanted to fight.'

'Let us hope that the enemy share your desire, Your
Majesty,' Rapp intoned.

'Everything we have seen so far indicates that they do,'
Napoleon continued. 'Every trap I have laid for them they

have fallen into it. Each piece of bait I have thrown, they have taken. They are convinced that we are retreating. Almost beaten before the first shots are fired.'

'Is that why you instructed Marshal Soult to abandon the Pratzen Heights, sire?' Berthier asked, his horse pawing the iron-hard ground.

'Yes. It was essential that our enemy concentrated their strength against our right flank. They have done this. They believe it will uncover our line of retreat to Vienna. They are not aware of our second centre of operations at Brunn. By concentrating their forces the way they have, they have actually exposed their *own* line of retreat. Ordering Murat to withdraw his cavalry from Wischau has further reinforced their belief that they are capable of outflanking our army. A combination of troop movements and our apparent wish for an armistice has served only to bolster their over-confidence. To them, it is no longer a question of just fighting the French army but of turning its flank and overwhelming it.'

'There appeared to be great conflict between the two sets of commanders,' Savary said. 'Only Kutusov and the Austrian Emperor advocated caution.'

'Kutusov is a wily old fox,' Berthier interjected.

'A fox preparing to be torn by hounds,' Napoleon murmured.

'The Austrian commanders are anxious to avenge what happened at Ulm,' Savary said.

'Battles are best fought with cool heads, untainted by rage,' Napoleon observed. 'That is something else in our favour. The Tsar, too, is advised by hotheads. The worst of these is Count Dolgorouki.' The Emperor's expression darkened. 'That impertinent fool who dared to come to *my* camp and lecture *me* on politics. And the letter he brought from the Tsar was addressed to "The Head of the French Government". Dolgorouki spoke and acted like a youthful trumpeter of England. When this battle is over, if he is still alive, I may well seek him out and *instruct* him in the way of things. He and his master.'

Some of the accompanying officers laughed.

'I think you should be congratulated on your restraint, sire,' said Rapp.

Napoleon smiled.

'It was difficult, but it served a purpose,' he said. 'The allies are under the impression that the French army is on the eve of its doom. I feel they are in for an unpleasant surprise come tomorrow.' Again he looked around at the length of what was to be the battlefield, using his telescope to pick out some of the more important features that he had already passed during his journey along the five-mile front. 'What are the strengths of the armies?'

'Eighty-five thousand troops face us, sire,' Savary told him. 'Four-fifths of them Russian. They are supported by two hundred and seventy-eight guns. Our own strength is presently just under sixty-seven thousand. Marshal's Davout's Third Corps will add another six thousand men to that number when it arrives shortly. We can draw upon the use of one hundred and thirty-nine cannon.'

'Send orders for Bernadotte's First Corps to take up position behind the Zurlan Height. They will then move up from behind the Santon and reform between Girschkowitz and Puntowitz, ready to launch an attack against Blasowitz. Lannes and the Fifth Corps, accompanied by Oudinot, will undertake the defence of the Santon. Soult's Fourth Corps will hold the centre. General St Hilaire and General Vandamme will occupy Puntowitz and Kobelnitz. General Legrand will hold

Zokolnitz and Telnitz. It is imperative that Legrand's division holds back the Austrian attack until the Third Corps come to its aid. Murat's cavalry and the Guard will occupy ground behind the Zurlan with the bulk of the army. I will make my command post there. At the appropriate moment, this force will be unleashed against the Pratzen Heights. It will smash through the enemy centre and destroy it.'

As Napoleon spoke, Berthier scribbled furiously on pieces of paper, his quill scratching loudly.

The Emperor looked in the direction of his opponents.

Several green-clad columns of Russian troops could already be seen moving across the Pratzen Heights. In the cold wind, occasionally masked by flurries of snow, they looked like phantoms.

'Before tomorrow evening,' he said, his voice unshakably defiant, 'this army will be mine.' He jabbed a finger in the direction of the allies. 'They are caught in a trap and hopelessly lost, even if they are three hundred thousand strong.'

The words were spoken with such conviction that none doubted his sincerity.

'I doubt if history has ever before seen a battlefield that could boast three Emperors, sire.' Rapp grinned. 'Come tomorrow, that will be the case.'

Napoleon nodded.

'Three Emperors, Rapp,' he mused. 'But only *one* victor. I trust you will be the one to bring me the news of that victory. *My* victory.'

Twenty-Four

Lausard tore off a piece of bread and pushed it into his mouth. The crust was like rock and the sergeant feared he might break his teeth on it but he chewed the food carefully, washing it down with a mouthful of wine from the bottle Rocheteau handed to him. The men huddled around their camp fire, warming themselves against the freezing night air. All along the French line, troops were gathered around raging fires, attempting to keep the cold at bay or cooking what little food they had. Charvet stirred the pot that dangled over the dragoons' camp fire, suspended as it was on a sword.

'Even the animals aren't stupid enough to venture out on a night like this,' Rocheteau said, gazing at the pot. 'Gaston and I couldn't even find a rabbit when we looked around earlier.'

Charvet continued stirring the contents of the pot with his bayonet. The men had scraped together some dried lentils, a couple of potatoes and some lumps of horsemeat they'd had for several days. All the ingredients had been put into the pot and boiled. They had little drinking water, so pieces of ice from one of the nearby frozen ponds had been heated in the pot before the food was added. Wine had been used to top up the concoction.

The ice had even covered parts of the Goldbach stream. From where he sat, Lausard could see several horses drinking from the icy water. Tigana and Karim had broken the surface coating with their sword pommels to allow the animals access to the water. Troopers led their animals to the drinking spot five at a time. Lausard and his squadron were camped about a hundred yards from the bank of the stream, close to the houses of Sokolnitz village.

'At least the dog-faces have shelter from this stinking weather,' Delacor hissed, rubbing his hands together. 'They are camped inside the houses.' He nodded in the general direction of the village. 'Why the hell couldn't *we* have been allocated some shelter?'

'Captain Milliere said that we were to fight on foot and on horseback tomorrow,' Rocheteau said, holding out his bowl as Charvet began ladling the weak-looking broth into those his companions held. 'We must be ready to move quickly, wherever we are ordered.'

'Two more ways to die,' Roussard murmured.

Lausard said nothing. His gaze was fixed on the enemy camp fires clearly visible across the valley.

'How many of them do you think there are?' Tabor mused.

'I am not God to see through a hill,' Moreau told him, crossing himself. 'Let us pray that we are spared when the fighting begins.'

'I'd rather be fighting than sitting here freezing to death,' Delacor snorted, warming his hands around his bowl before slurping greedily at the contents.

'I wonder what your countrymen have in store for us tomorrow, Rostov,' chuckled Rocheteau.

'They are no longer my countrymen,' the Russian said. 'I have told you that before. I was forced to leave Russia because of the Tsar. I have no love for him or for his troops. My family starved to death because of that Romanov bastard. France is my country now.'

'You left one country because it starved you to come to another that imprisoned you,' Lausard said quietly.

Some of the other men laughed.

'It imprisoned us all for one reason or another,' Carbonne reminded the sergeant.

'Quite true, my friend,' Lausard agreed. 'The only one among us who is here out of choice is Karim.'

'I was a slave in Egypt,' the Circassian remarked. 'As much a prisoner as any of you were in France. I was owned by the Mamelukes. I have little to thank them for.'

'Apart from your great abilities with horses, swords and other weapons,' Lausard grinned.

Again the men laughed.

'The Emperor has a regiment of them in his Imperial Guard,' Bonet offered. 'His personal bodyguard is also a Mameluke called Roustam. He goes everywhere with the Emperor. I hear he even holds his shaving mirror for him and he sleeps across the door of the imperial bedroom at night to protect Napoleon.'

'I know this man,' Karim said. 'He is a follower of Islam, as am I. His God is Allah, all praise to Him. It amuses me to hear of him spending his life as a servant, just as I did to the Mamelukes who enslaved me before I escaped.'

'I wonder if Roustam will be sleeping across the flap of

275

the Emperor's tent tonight?' mused Sonnier. 'If he does, he may well be frozen stiff come morning.'

'I would not want a man sleeping near the door of *my* bedroom,' Giresse offered. 'I would feel sorry for him. He would be kept awake all night by the sounds of pleasure issuing from the women inside with me.'

Even Lausard laughed, the sound rising into the freezing air like the leaping flames of the fire.

Joubert finished his broth and pushed more pieces of wood into the raging fire. He rubbed his mountainous belly and moved a little closer to the crackling flames. Rocheteau laid down, his head resting on his saddle, his cloak pulled tightly around him. One by one, the other men began to imitate his actions, anxious to snatch some sleep before the coming battle. Only Lausard remained crouched on his haunches, eyes constantly scanning both the lines of French camp fires and also those of the Austro-Russian army opposite. Finally he got to his feet and walked the hundred or so yards towards the banks of the Goldbach stream.

He walked back and forth, his cloak covered by fine grains of snow, his boots crunching the frost-encrusted grass and leaving footprints as he walked along the bank. Several sentries nodded a greeting as he passed. He moved on slowly, past men gathered around their fires, some sleeping, others unable to find that fleeting peace. He saw many faces that bore the all too familiar look of apprehension. It was a look Lausard had seen so many times on the night before a battle. Some men were writing letters home and he was acutely aware, as were some of those who scribbled so fastidiously, that these might well be the last communications these men ever made. Many would never see their families again. Lausard knew how they felt and a sense of desolation descended upon him, the like of which he had not experienced for a long time. The fact that he had not been plagued by memories of his murdered family surprised him. He tried to tell himself that the months of constant marching, the gnawing hunger, the terrible conditions and the perpetual exhaustion he had experienced had driven those thoughts from his mind. But he knew that was not the case. Those memories usually came, unbidden, in the small hours. The hours of the most acute loneliness. Perhaps the visit to his former home on the outskirts of Paris had helped to exorcise the thoughts that normally plagued him like demons whenever he was alone. Only now, in the hours leading up to a major battle, had those thoughts returned to jab at him like emotional needles under his skin. But he found it a little easier to drive them away as he continued on his solitary vigil along the banks of the Goldbach.

Would the coming day bring the death he had sought so keenly during the past ten years? He still believed that the only way to regain his honour was by losing his life on the battlefield. The next day might well see his desire fulfilled. But Lausard was aware of the contradiction within himself. He longed for the chance to regain honour through gallant death and yet, as ever, he would fight with unsuppressed fury to maintain a life he himself thought to be futile. It was a contradiction he was convinced he would never come to terms with. He stopped walking and turned once more to look at the enemy camp fires across the valley. An unearthly silence had descended and Lausard stood surrounded by it, lost in thought. Enveloped by the solitude, he pulled the scarf more tightly around his mouth and began walking back towards the camp fire around which his companions were gathered. He was sure it was getting colder.

Napoleon embraced Marshal Louis Nicolas Davout warmly then held him by the shoulders, a broad smile etched upon his face.

'I knew you would come,' said the Corsican. 'Where are your men?'

'General Friant and most of his men will arrive at Raigern Abbey this very night, sire,' Davout said, wiping perspiration from his forehead despite the chill of the evening. 'The remainder will be in position to support General Legrand on our right flank by eight in the morning. I rode ahead to tell you this news you so badly wanted to hear.'

Napoleon took a step back and smiled at the youngest of his marshals. Mud had spattered the commander's blue cloak and his breeches and boots were also filthy.

'A hard ride, my friend,' Napoleon said quietly. 'But it will be worth it.'

'I hope my men agree with you, sire. They have marched over eighty miles in fifty hours.'

The Emperor clapped his hands together triumphantly.

'And those fools who dare to oppose us presume to defeat men of such character,' he chuckled. He ushered Davout towards the table that had been laid inside the large green tent. Several of the Emperor's other staff were already seated around it and, once Davout joined them, they returned to their meal of potatoes and onions. Napoleon poured himself a glass of burgundy then handed the bottle to General Rapp. The ADC filled his own glass then passed the wine on to Berthier. Opposite, Savary was eating hungrily. Marshal Soult and General Duroc also consumed the food with ill-disguised relish.

'I understand a comet was sighted over Paris last night, sire,' Rapp offered.

'Surely it must be an omen of victory,' Napoleon smiled. 'The gods of war smile down upon us, gentlemen. Let us not disappoint them.'

'They have been kind to us these past ten years, sire,' Soult said. 'In Italy and Egypt and, so far, in this campaign. Let us hope they continue to smile.'

'Our fortunes in Italy and Egypt had little to do with anything other than our own abilities, Soult,' the Corsican said, sipping at his wine. 'It profits a man little to entrust his plans *solely* to the whims of gods.'

The men seated around the table laughed with genuine warmth.

'Perhaps our destiny truly lies here in Europe, sire,' Duroc said.

'I have always felt that my own destiny lay in the east. In Egypt. The land where Alexander found his greatness. There are times when I still feel drawn to that land, despite the hardships it brought.'

'We have seen hardship in many places, sire,' Duroc continued. 'Your own greatness is assured, no matter where you seek it.'

'On this battlefield tomorrow, perhaps?'

Savary sipped his wine.

'Everything has unfolded as you predicted, sire,' the Chief of Intelligence said. 'Is there any reason to think the events of the next day will be any different?'

Napoleon shook his head.

'I have seldom felt more certain of victory,' said the Corsican. 'I command the finest troops in the world. I have the best generals. It would take a miracle to defeat us. Certainly a more potent miracle than that offered by the Emperors of Imperial Austria and Holy Russia.'

Another ripple of laughter greeted his remark.

'But, it will be a hard fight, gentlemen, I have no doubt of that. What grieves me most is how many of my fine soldiers will die in pursuit of this victory we must gain.'

'Any one of them would follow you to the ends of the earth, sire,' Rapp announced.

Napoleon nodded.

'Tomorrow I will ask some of them to follow me to the end of life.' He raised his glass. 'Let us drink to their bravery and to our victory.'

The officers around the table stood up and uttered, as one, a single word:

'Victory.'

Alain Lausard stood warming himself by the fire, looking around at the other members of his squadron. Rocheteau was sound asleep. So too was Joubert, his thunderous snores reverberating around the blazing bonfire. Gaston and Roussard merely lay beneath their cloaks, gazing up at the stars that twinkled in the heavens like diamonds on black velvet. Delacor was sharpening his axe with a flat stone. Karim, sitting cross-legged on the ground, was carefully polishing the razor sharp blade of his scimitar. Tabor and Rostov were both cleaning their bayonets while Sonnier busied himself fitting a new flint to his carbine. Giresse laid his cartridges in rows on the frosted grass then carefully replaced them in his cartouche. Moreau was kneeling a little way from the fire, his head bowed, his hands clasped in prayer. Elsewhere, men found tasks to complete or slept, depending upon their state of mind;

but even the strongest entertained brief thoughts of death. Some found them harder to drive away than others but the threat of death was never far from any soldier's mind and the reality of it surfaced more predominantly on the eve of battle. Lausard waited a moment then sat down next to Giresse, slid his own sword from its sheath and began wiping the blade with an oily rag he pulled from his pocket.

'Anything moving, Alain?' Giresse asked.

'Not on our side *or* theirs,' the sergeant told him, holding up his sword and inspecting the blade in the flames of the fire. It appeared that the metal itself was ablaze. 'Neither side will risk a night attack, not in these conditions. There is a fog coming down.'

'I hope it clears before morning,' Sonnier offered. 'Otherwise we'll be shooting each other.' He wrapped a piece of rag tightly around his ramrod and pushed it down the barrel of his carbine, ensuring that there was no excess powder clogging the inside of the weapon.

'It's a pity every man in this regiment isn't as particular with his equipment as you, Sonnier,' Lausard remarked. 'Yet you lavish more attention on your carbine than you do on your sword.'

'It is my preferred weapon, Alain. Deadly at a distance. Lethal at close range with the bayonet attached.'

'I have no doubt you will be given the opportunity to put it to good use tomorrow in both circumstances,' Lausard mused.

The men looked round as they heard the sound of horses' hooves.

The rumbling stirred Rocheteau and Joubert from their slumber and the corporal instinctively reached for the loaded pistol beneath his saddle. He was on his feet in seconds, peering through the darkness towards the sound of the approaching horses.

Other men further up and down the line were also stirring now, alerted by the commotion.

Lausard was one of the first to spot the two ADCs riding down from the low ridge behind the dragoons. They were both protected from the cold by long thick blue cloaks. Both wore bicorns that sported large white plumes.

'What now?' Rocheteau grunted as the men reined in their horses.

'We bring a message from the Emperor,' called the first.

From all sides, men began to gather around the ADCs. The first pulled a rolled-up piece of paper from his portmanteau and unfurled it.

'This proclamation is being read out from one end of the line to the other so that every man in the army is aware of the Emperor's thoughts. He has taken us all into his confidence.'

There were several cheers but the ADC raised a hand for silence.

'That was probably printed on the mobile press at headquarters,' whispered Bonet. 'They have . . .'

'Just shut up and listen, schoolmaster,' Delacor snapped as the blue-clad man began to read aloud.

'"Soldiers of France, the positions that we occupy are formidable, and while the Russians march upon our batteries, I shall attack their flanks.

'"Soldiers, I shall in person direct all your battalions; I shall keep out of range if, with your accustomed bravery, you carry disorder and confusion into the ranks of the enemy; but if the victory is for a moment uncertain, you shall see your Emperor expose himself in the front rank."'

There was a sudden explosion of sound from the men and a shout of '*Vive l'Empereur!*' was joined by another and then more until the ground itself seemed to shake.

The ADC, grinning maniacally, raised his hand for silence and the roar gradually died down.

'"Note that no man shall leave the ranks under the pretext of carrying off the wounded",' he continued. '"Let every man be filled with the thought that it is vitally necessary to conquer these paid lackeys of England who so strongly hate our nation. I know you will not fail in your duty as I will not fail in mine. Your Emperor, Napoleon."'

The eruption of sound this time was almost palpable. All around, men raised their hands triumphantly into the air and the shouts of '*Vive l'Empereur!*' grew to deafening proportions. Lausard smiled and looked around at the sea of exuberant faces. Even Delacor and Karim were bellowing their approval and it was not long before Lausard himself added his own voice to those already filling the air.

Lausard had little doubt that the scene was being repeated along the entire length of the French line.

Napoleon felt the hand on his shoulder. For a moment he thought it was part of a dream. The hand was gentle at first, then more insistent.

'Sire.'

The word was whispered close to his ear.

His eyes snapped open and he was on his feet in an instant.

Savary stood before him, his head slightly bowed.

'What time is it?' Napoleon demanded, the last vestiges of sleep leaving him rapidly.

'Just after midnight, sire,' the Chief of Intelligence told him, almost apologetically. 'There is news of the enemy.'

'What news? Why didn't you wake me earlier?'

'We have only just confirmed the reports, sire. An enemy force has driven some of our troops out of the village of Telnitz, at the southern extremity of the line.'

'A night attack? Surely not.'

'The fighting seems localised in that area, sire. The numbers of men involved are small.'

'Get my horse,' snapped the Emperor, already heading for the tent flap.

Soult was waiting, already astride his own mount. Several chausseurs of the Guard, their sabres drawn, also awaited the emergence of their commander and Roustam, clad in traditional Mameluke dress, sat astride a magnificent grey, his jewel-hilted scimitar already free of its ornate scabbard. He handed the reins of Napoleon's horse to him and helped the Emperor into the saddle. The entire group moved off with Napoleon at its head, one or two of the horses struggling to keep their footing on the slippery ground.

They rode quickly, the occasional popping of musket fire echoing through the stillness of the night but there were no sustained fusillades, no thunderous roar of weapons. Finally, Napoleon reined in his horse and pulled his telescope from his pocket, training it on the village of Telnitz. In the gloom he could just make out one or two ethereal plumes of smoke rising from around the clutch of buildings. Apart from that, there was no sign of movement. The silence had descended once again.

'As I said, sire,' Savary offered, peering through his own glass. 'Initial reports indicate the fighting was localised. That seems to be the case.'

'Further evidence that our enemies have fallen into our trap,' remarked the Emperor. 'They have already sought to bring pressure to bear on our right, just as I anticipated.' He snapped his telescope shut then urged his horse on at a trot, his gaze drawn to the hundreds of enemy camp fires across the valley. His horse splashed into the icy water of the Goldbach, occasionally sinking up to its fetlocks in the mud, but the Corsican coaxed it across the stream and up on to the opposite bank. Several of his officers followed and a dozen of the chausseurs spurred their mounts across the water to surround their Emperor as he continued to stare, as if mesmerised, at the Russian and Austrian fires.

The ground became a little firmer and Napoleon pushed on.

'We should return, sire,' Soult insisted. 'There is nothing to see from here and you must not compromise your own safety.'

'Marshal Soult is right, sire,' Savary added.

As if to emphasise their concern, there was a sudden thundering of hooves away to their right.

Napoleon looked round anxiously.

Several horsemen were hurtling out of the gloom towards him, the leading two carrying long lances, both of which were levelled at the Emperor.

'Cossacks,' shouted Soult, forcing his horse in front of his Emperor's.

A number of the chasseurs pulled their carbines or pistols free and squeezed off shots. One of the leading Cossacks was catapulted from the saddle as his horse went down in an untidy heap. The gunshot seemed to reverberate around the entire valley, drumming in Napoleon's ears as he pulled on his reins and sent his horse heading back towards the Goldbach. Soult and Savary flanked him, their own mounts struggling through the mud then splashing across the stream. Behind them, more shots were fired. Muzzle flashes lit the night briefly. Napoleon heard several screams of pain and the whinnying of frightened horses began to fill the air. He heard shouts in French and Russian, all the noises mingling to form one unholy cacophony. Soult grabbed the bridle of his commander's horse as if to haul the animal physically out of the mud on the French side of the stream. Freezing water and icy mud sprayed up in geysers all around the men, some of it spattering them, but they struggled on to the firmer ground. Napoleon turned to gaze at the far bank, squinting into the gloom. He heard the ring of steel on steel as the Cossacks fought with the chausseurs. There were already half a dozen bodies lying on the hardened ground and a number of riderless horses were dashing wildly about. He saw another Cossack topple from his saddle clutching his chest. Then, as if a signal had been given, the Cossacks turned their mounts and, as one, rode away to be swallowed up by the enveloping darkness. Silence descended once again, broken only by the laboured breathing of some of the horses. All but one of the chausseurs trotted back to the safety of the French bank of the Goldbach stream. One of them was wiping blood from his sabre.

'You would be best advised to return to your bivouac, sire,' Soult said.

Napoleon suddenly swung himself out of the saddle, dropping down into the mud.

'You are right,' he agreed. 'I will walk back through the encampments of my soldiers.'

Savary nodded then also dismounted, as did Soult and

a number of the other staff officers. They set off behind the Emperor who strode along briskly, unconcerned by the chill night air and seemingly unperturbed by the brush with the Cossacks. As he reached the closest of the camp fires there were already a number of men gathered around the glowing pyre. He saw one of them point in his direction.

'Soldiers of the ninth, may I warm myself at your fire?' Napoleon asked the nearest man, smiling.

The men pushed forward to get a better look at him and the Corsican saw the exultation on their faces. Several of them reached out to touch him.

'*Vive l'Empereur*,' shouted one of the men and the cry was taken up by more and more voices.

Napoleon moved on deeper into the bivouacs, further along the French battleline, and everywhere troops gathered around him, their pleasure clearly evident.

'*C'est l'anniversaire! Vive l'Empereur!*' another shouted.

Napoleon smiled.

'A year to the day, I became Emperor of the French,' he said.

'And a glorious day it was for the nation, sire,' Savary agreed. 'These men have not forgotten, nor will they ever.'

'God willing, this coming battle will bring even more glory to France,' Soult offered. 'And to you, sire.'

'God may have little to say in the matter,' the Emperor chuckled. He continued walking. The cheering grew louder.

'It is him,' said Gaston. 'It *is* Napoleon.'

The men of the third squadron of dragoons stood watching as the small group of officers drew closer. All around them, men of other regiments, squadrons and batteries were crowding around the Emperor. Lausard could see infantrymen waving their headgear in the air. Others were waving their muskets excitedly in the air. One of the gunners from a nearby eight-pounder battery was even twirling the sponge from the cannon like a baton, such was his excitment. The roaring and cheering that swept along the line like wildfire was deafening.

The Emperor was no more than ten yards away now, his long grey overcoat open to reveal the uniform of a grenadier. His boots and breeches were spattered with mud. He looked as filthy as most of his troops. As the cheering continued he took off his bicorn and raised it into the air to acknowledge the frenzied cheering that greeted him at every turn. Even Lausard was smiling as he watched the little man draw nearer. The sergeant snatched up several handfuls of straw and twisted them into a makeshift brand, then he stuck it into the camp fire and lit it, holding the torch above his head.

Many men around him imitated the action and, in moments, it seemed that every French soldier within a hundred yards was holding one of the makeshift torches.

'*Vive l'Empereur*!' shouted Rocheteau, holding his own blazing bundle in Napoleon's direction.

Moreau crossed himself and reached out to touch the Corsican's arm.

'God bless you, sire,' he said.

All the men now held their torches aloft and, as Lausard looked to his right and left, he could see shafts of fire piercing the darkness for the entire length of the French positions. It seemed that every man in the army was holding a straw torch. He wondered what the sight must have looked like to the watching enemy troops. It must have appeared that there were hundreds of thousands of French soldiers paying homage to their leader.

'See how happy he looks,' Tigana said, remarking on the pleasure etched on the face of the Emperor.

Lausard nodded. He too could see the tears in the eyes of their commander. Napoleon looked genuinely touched by the display of emotion from his men. He stopped every now and then to shake hands with one soldier or another and Lausard found that he was closest to the Emperor. The Corsican paused, looked at the sergeant and then extended his right hand. Lausard took it and squeezed it warmly, holding the Emperor's gaze. There was strength in that imperial grip and Lausard respected it. Despite his stature, Napoleon seemed to engender the power of many within his modest frame. It was as if he had absorbed the affection pouring forth from his troops, his body swelled by that admiration his men showed for him.

'*Vive l'Empereur!*' Lausard said quietly, almost conversationally, his own tribute drowned by the cacophony of joy from the thousands of men up and down the line.

Napoleon patted him on the shoulder then moved on towards the next detachment of exultant troops. Lausard looked down at his right hand for a moment, almost as if he expected contact with the Emperor to have left some indelible mark on his flesh. Then he squeezed the hand into a fist and raised it triumphantly into the air.

'Let us hope we are cheering his name with as much enthusiasm after tomorrow's battle,' he said quietly; but his words were lost beneath the continuing wall of sound and the shouts of acclamation as Napoleon's torchlight procession continued through the ranks of his delighted men.

Twenty-Five

The fog was like a shroud, thick and impenetrable. Lausard could barely see more than a yard ahead of him. He had awoken instantly. Barely had the first notes issued from Gaston's trumpet than the sergeant was on his feet. The fire that had blazed so brightly during the night was now nothing but blackened embers. There might be a little heat at its centre but Lausard was more concerned with other things. He strapped on his sword and wandered around his men, digging the toe of his boot into those who had managed to sleep during the freezing night. A thick layer of frost covered the ground and the grass crunched beneath his boots as he moved through the thick fog. The other men stirred and responded quickly, some seeking the warmth of a fire but knowing they had neither time nor permission to build one. Joubert dug the toe of his boot into the embers and saw some glowing fragments at the centre but there was no warmth in them. He shuddered and looked around him. Lausard and his companions could hear other trumpets blaring. To the north and south of them, they even detected the rattle of

291

drums. The entire French army was stirring, rising from its slumber like some monstrous creature hidden beneath the thick blanket of mist. Lausard looked up towards the peak of the Pratzen Heights but they were hidden by the grey shroud. He could hear the gentle gurgling of the Goldbach stream but could not see it. It was as if the entire world had been condensed into an area a few yards square. Everything else was hidden by the freezing fog. He heard horses neighing to the rear and knew they were the mounts of his squadron but he could not see the animals either, many of which were also unsettled by the fog.

'How the hell are we supposed to fight in this?' Delacor wanted to know, his voice low.

Apart from the intermittent rattling of drums and the blaring of trumpets, the battlefield was relatively silent. It seemed as if the fog had also contrived to smother any sounds that might aid the men in locating their enemy. For all Lausard and his companions knew, the Russians and Austrians could be less than twenty yards away, hidden by the fog, waiting to fire into them. It was a thought the sergeant tried hurriedly to push aside. The allied troops would have to descend from higher ground to engage them, he reasoned. Their predicament must be even worse. But, for now, that nagging thought remained in his mind. Had they crept into position during the night, hoping for this cover of fog? Had their cavalry walked their horses silently into ranks on the other bank of the stream? Had their gunners manoeuvred cannon down the slopes of the valley, waiting for the right time to fire deadly salvos into their helpless opponents? He doubted it but the thought was not a pleasing one.

He glanced at his watch.

'Four o'clock,' he murmured and Rocheteau consulted

his own timepiece and nodded in agreement. 'Two hours before dawn.'

'Two hours before this fog clears,' Rocheteau grunted. 'If it does.'

Lausard nodded almost imperceptibly.

'We need some sunshine to burn it away,' he mused. 'But I can't see that happening.'

Men stumbled about in the fog-choked semi-darkness, picking up their weapons, many with shaking hands.

Some checked their cartridge cases, ensuring their ammunition had not become damp during the night. Others wiped down their swords with cloths then replaced them in the scabbards, wondering how long it would be before they were drawn again to strike at the enemy.

A little to the right, the crew of an eight-pounder readied themselves. Lausard could just make them out, shadows moving in the fog. Swarming around their gun they looked like ghosts. He saw several of them stacking ammunition close to the gun, their breath coming in gasps due to the exertion and the nervousness they were obviously feeling. One of them dipped the end of the portfire into the remains of their camp fire to light it, blowing on the end, ensuring that it glowed red. He was then forced to turn it constantly in the air to prevent it going out due to the cold.

Lausard and most of the dragoons walked to their horses and waited for the order to mount. The animals themselves were anxious, pawing at the rock-hard ground, sending small sprays of white crystals into the air. The dragoons held their bridles and waited.

Captain Milliere and Lieutenant Royere walked their mounts back and forth before the waiting dragoons, appearing and then disappearing in and out of the cloying fog. As men tried to control their increasingly nervous breathing, their breath frosted in the air before them, adding to the curtain of fog already surrounding them. They felt their hearts thudding more insistently against their ribs. The steadily growing tension clung as thickly as the fog until it was almost palpable. Many shivered, Giresse among them, and he was certain it was not merely the product of the keen air and frost-whitened ground.

'Listen,' said Lausard, holding his hand up as if to silence his companions.

They all heard it.

Drifting through the impenetrable mist. Alternately fading then growing louder.

Rocheteau licked his dry lips and tried to swallow but it was as if someone had filled his mouth with sand.

Moreau crossed himself.

More of them heard the sound.

Lausard gazed straight ahead, as if suddenly able to see the source of the steady tramping sound.

It was growing louder and it was unmistakable.

Marching feet.

The allied troops were heading down from the Pratzen Heights and across the valley.

Again Lausard looked at his watch.

Barely thirty minutes had passed since he had first consulted the timepiece. Time seemed to have become frozen, arrested by the constrictions of the fog.

He wondered how long it would be before the fighting began.

Napoleon stood on the summit of the Zurlan Height and peered through his telescope. Other than the tip of the

Santon to his left and the peak of the Pratzen Heights across the valley, little was visible.

'This fog may work to our advantage,' he said, snapping the telescope shut. 'It will hide our strength. Conceal our men until the time is right and it will hamper the enemy's movements and communications.'

'It will also hamper our own movements, sire,' General Rapp offered.

Napoleon waved away the suggestion.

'We have merely to wait,' he said. 'Let *them* come to *us*. They have chosen to attack. It is our part to allow them that privilege. By the time we strike back, this fog should have lifted.'

Napoleon moved back to his tent and emerged carrying a cup of coffee which he sipped while peering in the direction of the Pratzen Heights. Beside him, Soult and Berthier also squinted into the mist.

'I trust these relay stations will work when they are needed,' the Emperor said, nodding in the direction of three or four troops holding semaphore flags.

'Yes, sire,' Berthier assured him. 'With the coming of full daylight and the thinning of the mist, we will be able to receive and communicate information along the length of the line. There are similar stations established from here to Telnitz.'

Napoleon nodded.

'Soult.'

The shout made all three men turn and they saw the unmistakable figure of Marshal Lannes striding towards them out of the fog. Even from a distance, through the veil of mist, they could see the furious expression on his face.

'I thought you were a swordsman,' snarled Lannes, stepping close to Soult. 'I have been waiting for you.'

Napoleon looked at each of the men in bewilderment.

'Forgive my intrusion, sire,' said Lannes. 'But five days ago I sent a second to challenge this "pekinese".' He pointed angrily at Soult. 'I offered to fight him in a duel. It was a matter of honour. I have heard no reply.'

'Surely you have other matters to concern you,' Murat interjected.

'This is none of your business,' Lannes snarled at the cavalry commander. 'You were as much to blame as Soult. Perhaps I should fight you too.'

'Stop this useless squabbling at once,' snapped Napoleon. 'What the hell are you talking about, Lannes? We are about to enter battle and you are more concerned with fighting your fellow Marshals. Where are your senses?'

'Did Soult not suggest we retreat to Ulm rather than press on after Kutusov, sire?'

'It was *you* who advised caution,' Napoleon explained. 'I myself thought it odd. Never before have I heard you propose retreat.'

'That is because it was not my idea,' Lannes snarled, his attention directed back at Soult. 'It was this simpering fool and your own brother-in-law who wanted to retreat but neither had the courage to approach you with their cowardly ideas. They insisted *I* be the one to present you with such an option. Then, behind my back, they both professed surprise when you rejected that possibility. They sought to make *me* the scapegoat for their cowardice.'

'You insolent peasant,' snarled Murat, taking a step forward. 'How dare you speak this way?'

'How do you respond to these allegations, Soult?' Lannes rasped. 'Am I to have satisfaction? I repeat my challenge.'

'We have more important things to occupy our attention just now,' Soult replied haughtily.

Lannes held his adversary's gaze for a moment then hawked and spat at his feet.

'Son of a whore,' he cried then turned his back and stalked away into the mist, disappearing like the last remnant of a dream.

'I command school children, not Generals.' Napoleon shrugged. 'Leave your petty differences until after the battle.' He shook his head. 'Am I to assume the first crisis of the day has been averted?'

Soult nodded.

'Then let us hope there are no more,' the Emperor mused. He reached for his watch. 'The time, gentlemen, is five thirty. Take your posts.'

The collection of marshals and generals swung themselves into their saddles and rode off to join their designated units. Only Berthier, Soult, a group of aides-de-camp and some orderly officers remained close to the Emperor.

Once again, he checked his watch.

He too heard the sound of marching feet from the opposite side of the valley, rising through the fog like some terrifying, invisible portent.

Lausard looked at his watch then up into the sky. It was after six a.m. but the dank, freezing fog was delaying the coming of dawn, depriving the dragoons of the light they needed to see their oncoming foe. Captain Milliere and Lieutenant Royere continued to walk their horses back and forth, both officers also glancing at their timepieces, peering through their telescopes into the swirling mist or occasionally exchanging words.

'You should have asked your God for a clear morning,' Delacor hissed, prodding Moreau in the ribs.

Moreau did not speak. He was staring into the thick mist as if mesmerised. He was not alone. Many of the dragoons waited silently, eyes looking ahead even though they had no hope of catching sight of their approaching enemies.

Moments later they heard the blaring of trumpets and the rattle of drums.

From the depths of the fog, away to the south, a band exploded into life, its martial music an accompaniment to the steadily growing crescendo of marching feet from the as yet invisible Austrian column bearing down on the French right.

Lausard sighed in frustration.

'They must be close to Telnitz now,' he murmured.

The words had hardly left his mouth when an all too familiar sound began to fill the air.

Several volleys of musket fire shattered the relative stillness of the morning. They were followed by more and then the thunderous roar of cannon also began to multiply.

'It sounds as if "the Emperor's cousins" have just been woken,' Rocheteau remarked. 'I hope they stand.'

'The Corsican Legion are good men,' Bonet offered, gazing off in the direction of the gunfire. 'They will not give ground unless they have too.'

'If only we could see what was happening,' said Giresse anxiously.

'We'll see in good time,' Lausard told him, glancing up at the fog-laden sky once more. 'The first time we view the enemy will be when they come at us through this mist.'

The salvos of gunfire from the direction of Telnitz were

growing in ferocity and the men could also hear shouts and screams drifting up the valley.

Horses, as nervous and impatient as their riders, pawed the ground repeatedly. Several even reared, almost ejecting troopers from their saddles.

'Hold steady,' called Captain Milliere, still guiding his own mount back and forth. Every so often he would lead the bay towards the bank of the Goldbach stream, as if being closer to the water would enable him to see what was happening round about. Lausard heard the animal's hooves splashing in the icy water. Each time he returned to his endless vigil, no clearer about the dispositions of the enemy or how much closer they were to the rest of the French line.

Lausard could see the crew of the nearby eight-pounder checking and rechecking their ammunition. The man with the sponge dipped the implement into the bucket of water he'd taken from the Goldbach, waiting to swab out the barrel after each round had been fired. The other gunners stood relatively still for as long as the biting air would permit. The gunner holding the portfire continued to turn it slowly in his hand. The corporal didn't even bother to check the angle of the barrel. He, like his companions, had no idea whether they would be firing point blank into advancing infantry coming out of the fog just yards away, or lobbing shells into formations hundreds of yards away. One of the men repeatedly patted the bronze barrel of the cannon as if seeking reassurance. Lausard himself found that his hand kept falling to the hilt of his sword; perhaps, he told himself, for a similar reason.

From the south, the sound of battle continued to grow ever more dominant.

★   ★   ★

Napoleon paced agitatedly back and forth close to the camp fire, occasionally sipping at his coffee, sometimes pausing to squint through his telescope. His musings were interrupted by the sound of a horse's hooves. He looked up to see a staff officer, his uniform spattered with blood, hurtling up the precipitous incline of the Zurlan Height. The officer dragged hard on his reins and brought his mount to a halt then he swung himself out of the saddle, almost stumbling as he landed on the hard ground. Napoleon saw that he had a wound on his right thigh. It had been hastily bandaged but blood was soaking through the gauze. He winced as he made his way towards the Emperor. Soult put out a hand to steady the injured man. The officer saluted and handed a piece of crumpled paper to the Emperor who read it swiftly.

'The Corsican Legion has managed to link up with Friant's men,' said Napoleon. 'They have driven the Austrians out of Telnitz again.'

'The mist is causing much confusion, sire,' the staff officer said. 'Two of our regiments have already fired on each other. Fourteen squadrons of Austrian cavalry have bypassed Telnitz and crossed the Goldbach stream.'

'Are Friant's division still in possession of the village?' Napoleon wanted to know.

'They are badly outnumbered, sire, but they still hold it. However, more enemy troops are now closing in on Sokolnitz village and the castle beyond. It seems only a matter of time before they push us back. There must be close to forty thousand allied troops on our right flank now.'

Napoleon managed a faint smile.

'It is as I predicted,' he said triumphantly. 'They are

preparing to turn our right but, by so doing, they will expose their own centre.'

'And what if our right flank *is* pushed back, sire?' Soult wanted to know.

'Space I may recover,' said Napoleon flatly. 'Time, never.' He peered again through his telescope. The mist was at last beginning to lift slightly. The plateau of the Pratzen Heights was visible from his high vantage point. Through the glass he could see yet more unwieldy columns of green-clad Russian troops moving south. 'They move like a torrent, away from their own centre. We must ensure the timing is right. We must allow them to clear their centre before we strike. A minute too early and all will be lost. One drop of water can cause the full bucket to overflow.' Without taking his eye from the steadily marching enemy troops, Napoleon touched Soult gently on the shoulder. 'How long will it take you to move your divisions to the top of the Pratzen Heights?'

'Less than twenty minutes, sire,' Soult assured him. 'My troops are hidden at the foot of the valley, hidden by fog and camp fire smoke.'

Napoleon nodded.

'In that case,' he said, checking his watch again, 'we will wait a further quarter of an hour.' He snapped the telescope shut.

Twenty-Six

Lausard heard the sound and recognised it immediately. The loud bang, the high-pitched screech and the rending of air.

The first roundshot struck the iron-hard ground close to the French side of the Goldbach, spun up and flew into the air before landing two or three yards away. He watched the lethal six-pound lead ball roll across the frosty surface then finally come to a halt.

It was followed by another. Then another. Suddenly the air was riven by a fusillade of musket fire and the all too familiar roar of artillery. Moreau crossed himself.

Lausard ducked involuntarily as another deadly projectile screamed over. It struck two horses close by, obliterated them then thudded into the earth. Blood from the dead animals sprayed in all directions. One of their riders was also sent hurtling from his saddle as if jerked by invisible wires. Bullets too began to part the air around the dragoons. Lausard felt something slam against the side of his helmet and looked down to see that it was a spent musket ball. Rocheteau cursed as another bullet tore off the knee cuff of his boot.

'Fight on foot,' bellowed Captain Milliere and the dragoons dismounted, following their officer through the fog towards the outlying buildings of Sokolnitz. Other troopers took charge of the horses and dashed to the rear with them, keeping them out of danger until they were needed. Lausard saw his own magnificent chestnut disappear into the mist but his mind was more concerned with the oncoming enemy troops.

Two of the buildings nearest the dragoons were already ablaze and the fire at least gave some much needed light as the men hurried to find cover amidst the primitive wooden huts. However, thick black smoke from the fire mingled with the fog to create an even more noxious curtain, one that was further added to by the sulphurous smoke from cannons and muskets now steadily spreading across the length of the French line.

Lausard saw French infantrymen sheltering inside the buildings, many of them already firing in the direction from which they knew the enemy would come.

He dashed into a house followed by Rocheteau, Giresse, Rostov and Tabor and all five men took up firing positions in the windows of the house, waiting for their enemy to come into view.

The fog was finally beginning to clear, the dawn gradually forcing its way upwards from beneath the blanket of mist. The sergeant could even see a hint of watery sunlight struggling to escape the confines of the clouds. And in that new-found light he finally saw the mass of green-clad Russian troops advancing towards the village, a huge column led by mounted officers and drummer boys and trumpeters who beat the charge and drove the leviathan onwards. Bayonets glinted in the sunlight. Flags waved in the crisp breeze as the Russians drew nearer. The dragoons, now ensconced in houses all through Sokolnitz waited, hammers cocked.

The Russians marched straight into the freezing water of the Goldbach, struggled through it then scrambled up the bank, trying to reform as they approached the waiting French.

'Fire!' roared Milliere.

Hundreds of carbines opened up.

Lausard pulled his own tightly into his shoulder to absorb the recoil.

A withering salvo hit the leading Russian troops and Lausard saw dozens hit the ground but their comrades merely struggled on, blasted in the flank now by the fire of the infantry and the even more devastating discharges of the battery of eight-pounders the dragoons had been close to. The French gunners poured caseshot into the tight-packed formation, sweeping away entire files of men as if they were corn falling to a scythe.

Lausard tore the top from another cartridge and reloaded, spitting the ball down the barrel, feeling the heat from the metal on his lips.

Beside him, Rocheteau did the same as he watched the dense Russian column drawing nearer.

An officer leading the men was simply blasted from his horse by several of the two-ounce balls spewing from the mouths of the eight-pounders. The constant salvos were continued with incredible efficiency as sweating gunners shoved canisters into barrels that were already growing hot.

The leading two ranks of the Russian column slowed their pace slightly then fired.

A choking cloud of smoke erupted from the muzzles along with their lead balls and Lausard ducked as the projectiles tore into the houses of Sokolnitz. They were followed by more and more and the louder discharges of Russian artillery began to eclipse the outnumbered French batteries as they pounded away at the village and the French troops occupying it.

Lausard ducked as a portion of the roof collapsed, pieces of timber crashing down into the building. Tabor cursed as a lump of wood fell across his leg but he shoved it away, relieved that no damage had been done other than a large rip in his breeches.

Dust and smoke filled the air as the dragoons prepared to fire one more volley before their enemies reached the village. Each man took careful aim and fired. Lausard saw more Russians fall but then they broke into a run as they closed on the houses held by the French. Like the sea breaking on rocks, the Russian column smashed into Sokolnitz. Green-clad troops hurled themselves at the houses, the leading ones throwing their weight against doors to try and force entry. A gigantic sapper, swinging a huge axe, stove in the door of the house where Lausard and his companions sheltered. He stumbled in, swinging the lethal weapon with incredible strength but Lausard ducked beneath his swing and drove his bayonet upwards into the man's stomach, tearing it free to slide the fifteen-inch blade into the Russian's throat. Rostov used the butt of the carbine as a club, shattering the front teeth of his opponent before stepping over him and smashing another man's jaw. Rocheteau stabbed one man before hacking madly at another with his knife, laying the cheek open to the bone. Tabor, using his enormous strength, drove his bayonet so deeply into his foe that it pierced the man's stomach, tore through his body and erupted from his back. As Tabor pulled at it, the steel came free, remaining in the Russian as he fell backwards, blood spraying from the wound. Tabor drew his sword and slammed the hilt into another man's face, using the blade to finish him off.

Lausard, realising they were hopelessly trapped inside the building, drew his own sword and hacked his way through two more Russians out into the street, followed by his companions.

The same scenario was being repeated all over the village. French and Russian troops were fighting hand-to-hand all over Sokolnitz. Some of the French were escaping via windows in the back of buildings, others had been forced to cut their way through their foe into the street like Lausard and his men. The air was now full of the stench of sulphur, gunpowder, sweat and blood. Bodies already clogged the streets and artillery fire from both sides poured into the village, killing friend and foe alike. Lausard hacked madly with his sword, striking to right and left, rasping in pain and rage when a Russian grenadier drove a bayonet into his shin. The leather of his boot was split easily as the blade cut through his flesh but only scraped his bone. The sergeant caught his assailant with a savage backhand blow that sheared off his left ear and most of that side of his face.

Tabor picked up a Russian with one hand, crushing his windpipe in his massive grip then tossing the body aside.

Lausard saw Karim emerge from another house close by, wielding his scimitar to lethal effect. He avoided a bayonet thrust then struck at his opponent's arm, catching him just above the elbow and slicing the limb off with one blow. The Circassian immediately spun and caught a charging corporal with a back-hand swipe that cut through his skull as easily as if it had been a coconut.

Moreau, his face splashed with blood, was standing back-to-back with Tigana, both of them hacking at the Russian infantry.

Sonnier had clambered on to the roof of one of the buildings and was calmly loading and reloading, shooting down Russians with unerring accuracy. His face was blackened by powder and he could barely breathe from the constant clouds of smoke. His mouth was filled with the coarse powder but he kept up his fire with mechanical precision.

Lieutenant Royere stepped in front of a bayonet thrust meant for Joubert's back, deflected the steel then cut the infantryman down. Joubert nodded in thanks then caught a Russian by the head and twisted sharply, using his strength to break the man's neck.

Through the rapidly clearing mist, Lausard could see the castle of Sokolnitz away to the north, smoke rising around it as the Russians and Austrians attacked there too. He was gasping for breath, both from his exertions and also because the air now tasted like a furnace. Buildings had been set alight by mortar fire and the smoke from artillery and muskets mingled with the stench of burning wood and the more sickly sweet odour of incinerated flesh. More and more Russian troops were pouring across the Goldbach stream and already many of the blue-jacketed French infantry were beginning to withdraw.

'Captain, look,' Lausard shouted, trying to attract Milliere's attention as the officer drove his sword into the chest of an attacking Russian. 'The infantry are pulling back.'

A roundshot suddenly hurtled over and Lausard saw that it was heading straight for the officer but, as he prepared to watch his commander blasted apart, the nine-pound ball spun away at an angle off the rock hard ground and pulverised two Russians. Blood sprayed the officer who sank to his knees momentarily, sweat pouring from his face. Lausard ran across to him and noticed a slight wound in his right side. He slapped a hand to the injury but Milliere brushed it away.

'The ball went straight through,' he gasped through clenched teeth.

Lausard held his gaze for a moment but the officer nodded.

'Get the men out of here,' Milliere said, getting back to his feet. 'Lieutenant, withdraw; we're overrun.'

Royere struck at another Russian then signalled to Gaston who blasted the notes of recall as loudly as he could, struggling to summon enough lung power to make himself heard above the incessant roar of weapons, raging flames and the screams and curses of men. But he continued blowing and many of the dragoons obeyed the call.

Lausard stopped a dozen men and drew them around him. They were all still holding their carbines and Lausard swiftly reloaded. Rocheteau and Sonnier joined him, then a dozen more men. Royere too swung his Charleville up to his shoulder and aimed as more Russian troops advanced towards the waiting dragoons.

'Fire!' roared the lieutenant and the volley tore into its target.

The Russians were stopped in their tracks long enough to allow the dragoons to join their comrades who were already spilling out of the village towards the castle and walled pheasantry beyond.

Lausard saw more Russian columns advancing across the Goldbach towards the castle and also in the direction of Kobelnitz further to the north of the French battleline. The fighting looked as though it had spread along almost the entire extent of the front by now.

'To horse,' roared Milliere and the dragoons ran towards their waiting mounts and swung themselves into the saddle. Lausard looked to his right and left. To the south, Telnitz and Sokolnitz were in enemy hands, palls of smoke rising over both of them. To the north, Russian infantry were pouring over the Goldbach and he could see that fighting had already begun around Kobelnitz. Allied artillery fire was still raking the French positions. Several of the gunners crewing the eight-pounder close to the French were already dead. One of them stood beside the trail of the gun, his face stained with smoke and blood, his right arm having been severed at the elbow. He was holding the shattered limb in his good hand and staring at it in bewilderment. A number of the horses used to pull the limber were also dead in their harnesses. The battery seemed doomed to remain on the bank of the stream whether they liked it or not. Lausard looked on blankly as the remaining men swabbed the barrel, pushed in fresh rounds and continued firing, already deafened by the thunderous discharges that came with every shot.

Captain Milliere, his side bleeding freely, rode back and forth glancing occasionally towards his men then at the battlefield now mostly visible with the clearing of the mist.

He looked at Lausard and the two men locked eyes.

'What now, Captain?' Lausard asked breathlessly.

Milliere had no answer.

★   ★   ★

Napoleon looked up at the blood-red orb of the winter sun. It had finally forced its way into the sky, burning away the worst of the fog and rising slowly into the boiling sky. Sunlight glinted on bayonets and swords but the Corsican was more concerned with what was happening on the battlefield before him. He checked dispositions on the maps spread out on the icy ground then glanced from one end of his line to the other.

Soult and Berthier also ran appraising eyes over the situation.

'It seems that Marshal Lannes has succeeded in isolating the allied left flank, sire,' Berthier observed, pointing to the columns of infantry and swarms of cavalry moving to and fro between the Santon and the Pratzen Heights. The ground between the two imposing ridges was strewn with dead men and horses and clouds of smoke drifted back and forth at the whim of the cold breeze.

'It is not the left that concerns me, Berthier,' Napoleon offered. 'It is the centre.' He jabbed his telescope towards the Pratzen Heights. 'Once that is taken, the battle is ours.'

'Once taken, it must be held, sire,' Soult added.

'Quite right, Soult.' He turned to Berthier. 'Send an order to Marshal Bernadotte that the village of Blasewitz must be held at all costs. Situated at the base of the Pratzen Heights as it is, it is crucial to our position. Have Marshal Murat support him with cavalry.'

Berthier scribbled quickly and then snapped his fingers. A staff officer ran across, took the order from him and swung himself into the saddle, putting spurs to his horse and hurtling away to deliver the order.

Napoleon turned to Soult, his piercing gaze never leaving that of the marshal.

'One sharp blow and the war is over,' he said flatly. 'I have no need to tell you what has to be done.'

Soult was already clambering aboard his horse, guiding the animal towards the valley floor.

'The enemy is more numerous than ourselves,' Napoleon mused as if his comments were not directed at anyone in particular. Only Berthier and some staff officers standing nearby heard his words. 'They expect to attack me and vanquish me. No, it's more. Not only to beat us; they desire to cut us off from Vienna and round up the French army!' His voice rose in volume. 'They think I am a novice! Well, they'll come to regret it. I will put an end to this campaign with a crash of thunder that will stun the enemy.'

Berthier was the first to notice the horseman riding hard up the slope towards the Emperor. The man wore the uniform of an ADC and, from its gleeful flamboyance, was most likely attached to Murat's command. But the white pelisse and dolman jacket, the light-blue breeches and red boots were so heavily spattered with blood it was difficult to make out any kind of uniform at all. Even the horse he rode, a magnificent grey, was covered in blood, some of it from two bad wounds it had sustained. Part of the aide's red shabraque had been torn away and another corner was badly burned. He had lost a stirrup and Berthier noticed several bullet holes in his pistol holsters. One had even ripped away a spur.

The horseman pulled hard on the reins and looked almost imploringly at Napoleon.

'Sire,' he gasped, wincing as he spoke. 'Prince Murat requests cavalry reinforcements immediately or we will be destroyed. Some of General Kellermann's light cavalry have already been scattered. Prince Murat says the situation is critical.' He had barely spoken the last word when he slipped from the saddle and landed heavily at Napoleon's feet.

A number of officers ran forward to help the wounded ADC.

Napoleon pulled out his telescope again and trained it on the area where he knew Murat's cavalry were concentrated.

'Send him the men he needs, Berthier,' the Corsican snapped. 'Quickly.'

The Chief of Staff was already scribbling the orders. Other riders waited to dash off with them.

Napoleon looked up towards the newly emerged sun, still spilling its brilliant colour across the sky. He couldn't help but think the blazing orb looked like a wound in the heavens. His heart began to beat a little faster.

The dragoons moved northwards at a canter and Lausard could see that the battle had indeed now spread along the entire length of the French line. Up on the Pratzen Heights he saw the eagles of Soult's men glittering in the sunlight and a number of the dragoons raised their fists in salute as they saw that the infantry had taken the most prominent piece of high ground on the battlefield. Smoke now drifted over the terrain almost as thickly as the fog had done in the early hours of the morning and, all around, Lausard could hear the incessant roaring of cannon fire and musketry. There were bodies everywhere. The wounded, where possible, were dragging themselves towards the dressing stations in the rear of the French lines and many of the bandsmen acted as medical attendants to aid those most savagely injured. But for the most part those too badly wounded died where they lay. On more than one occasion Lausard had to guide his horse around bodies.

'First they want us as infantry, now as cavalry,' Delacor grunted, ducking his head involuntarily as a volley of cannon fire erupted from a battery of eight-pounders nearby.

'We were told we'd be used as both today,' Rocheteau reminded him.

'We left enough men back in Sokolnitz,' Carbonne offered, his own cheek badly gashed by a metal splinter.

'And we'll leave plenty more on the field before the day is finished,' Roussard interjected.

Lausard ignored the mutterings and rode up alongside Captain Milliere and Lieutenant Royere. The captain had pressed a piece of gauze to his injured side and bound it with some strips of cloth he'd torn from a discarded shabraque. Blood was seeping steadily into the gauze and he winced occasionally.

'What exactly were our orders, Captain?' Lausard asked.

'To join the cavalry reserve of Marshal Murat as quickly as possible,' the officer told him. 'The other two squadrons are already there.'

Lausard could already see three columns of French horsemen forming up around the base of the Santon. Hussars, chausseurs and more dragoons all waited for orders while, to the rear, mounted on huge black horses, solid phalanxes of cuirassiers, carabiniers and horse grenadiers waited patiently.

'So, we're to be sacrificed while the "big boots" stay behind to take the glory,' Delacor said, looking disdainfully at the heavy cavalry.

As the dragoons formed into lines, Lausard could feel

his heart beating quicker. The adrenalin he always felt surging through his veins before a charge seemed to make his senses keener. Every sound was amplified. Every smell was more easily detected. The sweat of nervous men and horses. The stench of excrement and horse dung. The coppery odour of blood. The stinging fumes from so many weapons.

Riderless horses careered about, both French and Russian, and Lausard saw a number of men trying to catch them to use as remounts. The ground ahead of the dragoons was relatively flat and clear, better terrain for cavalry than the gulley-riddled fields further to the south. He glanced around him at the other men. Some were staring ahead, trying to see who their opponents were to be. Others, like him, were gazing around at their companions. Some merely sat motionless in the saddle staring at the ground. Every man had his own thoughts. Every emotion from stark terror to exultation spread through the ranks. Moreau was mouthing a silent prayer. Charvet flexed his fingers, clenching them into fists over and over again. Lausard himself took off his helmet briefly and ran a hand through his long brown hair. He was sweating profusely. Carbonne dabbed at his injured cheek then licked at the blood defiantly.

On either side of the cavalry, Lausard saw infantry regiments formed into squares to protect themselves from attack by enemy horsemen. One of the squares had opened its outer side to allow two four-pounders to fire from within. They kept up a steady fire while the mounted troops continued to move into formation.

'Where the hell are the enemy?' Delacor hissed.

As if to answer his question, Lausard pointed at several ranks of Austrian and Russian hussars who were drawn up not more than a thousand yards away from the French, their presence suddenly revealed by a strong gust of wind that dispersed the smoke swathing them.

Seconds later, Lausard heard trumpets blaring and, within moments, the enemy hussars began to advance, first at a walk, then a trot and then a canter.

'Draw swords,' roared Captain Milliere and the order was echoed around every French cavalry unit in the vicinity. The sound of steel leaving scabbards reminded Lausard of thousands of hissing snakes.

The French cavalry moved forward at a walk but broke almost immediately into a gallop. At four hundred and eighty paces a minute they swept towards the oncoming allied horsemen who had also increased their speed by now.

'Charge,' roared Milliere and a dozen other officers and trumpeters blasted the notes that increased the speed of the advance to six hundred paces a minute and sent the two sets of riders hurtling towards each other at something approaching twenty-five miles an hour.

Lausard roared his defiance and lifted his sword above his head for a second before lowering it slightly so that the point was aimed at the oncoming enemy cavalry. The two sets of horsemen were closing with incredible speed. Lausard could almost make out the features of men before him and he saw doubt on some of those faces. Delacor, the reins gripped in his teeth, held his axe in one hand and his sword in the other. Karim swung his scimitar above his head, the blade swishing as it parted the air. Other men urged their mounts on and the horses responded as if infected with the same fury as their riders.

The horsemen were less than two hundred yards apart now.

Lausard still bellowed as loudly as he could, anxious only to be amongst his enemies. His mind was a blank. All he could see before him was men he must kill. All he was aware of was the thundering of thousands of hooves. All he felt was the sword gripped tightly in his fist.

One hundred yards.

It had probably taken less than a minute for the two groups of cavalry to come within range of each other but, for Lausard, it was as if his every movement was exaggeratedly slow. His horse neighed loudly, chewing savagely on the bit, eyes rolling in their sockets.

Fifty yards.

Now he could clearly see the faces of the men who opposed him. One in particular, no older than himself, looked pale and wan. To Lausard, it seemed as if the man barely had the strength to lift his sword.

And then they collided.

The shock was incredible.

Some men were catapulted from their saddles purely by the impact. Horses crashed to the ground. Troopers on both sides began hacking madly at the nearest foe. The world was narrowed down to a few square yards of life or death. Lausard struck madly with his sword and brought down first a Russian hussar corporal then a trooper. He drove onwards, into the second rank, striking with a power and ferocity that smacked of madness. And, all along the line, both sets of horsemen behaved the same way. Limbs were hacked off. Bodies pierced or slashed. Faces were gouged and cut. Hands were sliced from arms. Weapons began to rain down on to the dark earth, men fell from their saddles. The lucky ones were dead before they hit the ground, many were trampled to death by the churning hooves of the horses. Lausard saw

Karim decapitate a Russian officer then swing left with his wickedly sharp scimitar and take another man's arm off at the shoulder. Delacor drove his axe into the head of a Russian dragoon, carving his way straight through the leather of the man's helmet and cleaving the skull. With his other hand he drove his sword into the stomach of another opponent. Charvet cut down two men then sent another hurtling from his saddle with a punch that broke his jaw. Captain Milliere cut a standard bearer across the face, shattering the bridge of his nose. As the man clapped both hands to his face, the officer drew a pistol and shot him in the back of the head. Lieutenant Royere shouted in pain as a sabre cut him across the right forearm but he managed to turn in his saddle and drive his long straight sword into his opponent's back.

All around him, Lausard knew personal duels such as these were taking place. He had seen them so many times on so many battlefields during the last ten years but all he was concerned with was the men he himself faced. He cut two more down then rode over a Russian hussar who had lost his horse. The sound of splintering bone was audible even above the cacophony of clashing steel and agonised shrieks.

'Fall back!'

Lausard looked round and saw that Captain Milliere had bellowed the order.

The French cavalry were already beginning to retire, extricating themselves with ease from a foe who looked beaten. Lausard turned his horse almost reluctantly and raced back towards the blue-clad French infantry who had advanced a few hundred yards to the rear of their cavalry. They stood in unbroken lines, muskets lowered. Lausard watched in amazement as they parted, opening up at intervals as assuredly as if they had been on parade. The French cavalry streamed through the gaps which were immediately closed again. The pursuing Russian horsemen tried to halt as they realised what was happening. But before they could wheel their exhausted mounts, Lausard turned to see the infantry open up with volley after volley of musket fire. Entire ranks of enemy cavalry crashed to the ground, dying horses rolling on their riders. Men dead in the saddle, holed by dozens of bullets, were carried on by their mounts. A vast pall of sulphurous smoke swept across the field once more and, when it cleared, Lausard could see that the enemy horsemen were either dead or retreating.

Again the French infantry parted and this time their reformed cavalry swept through them once more. Moving at a canter, they rode after the fleeing Russians. Lausard saw the unmistakable figure of Marshal Murat guiding his horse along just behind the front rank of dragoons. To his left he saw General Kellermann, standing in his stirrups as he rode, urging his men on.

'Alain, look,' said Rocheteau and the sergeant glanced to his right.

Wave after wave of green- and blue-clad hussars and dragoons were bearing down upon the advancing French horsemen. The leading ranks crashed into them and, once more, Lausard found himself locked in a series of hand-to-hand contests. The French cavalry wheeled slightly to meet the charge head on but the Russians had the impetus of attacking downhill and it gave their charge an added ferocity that took the dragoons by surprise. Lausard saw several men around him cut down. Many more were wounded by the onslaught. Sonnier didn't even have time to pull his carbine from its boot on his saddle. He merely swivelled the weapon upright and fired; the ball smashed into the face of his opponent, driving his teeth back into his mouth. He had no time to reload and hacked at the next man with his sword.

Charvet drove a fist into the face of one man and knocked him from his mount. Another he caught by the throat, jerking him from his saddle with such ferocity he broke the Russian's neck. Bonet and Roussard cut wildly at their opponents with their swords, driving the wickedly sharp points home when they could.

Tigana skewered a Russian hussar through the ribs but cursed as the dying man fell from his horse with the blade still embedded in his chest. Tigana snatched another sword from the hand of a French dragoon who had slumped forward in his saddle, bleeding badly from two wounds to his face and chest.

All along the line, Lausard saw that the allied cavalry were forcing their way through the French lines by sheer weight of numbers. He saw Marshal Murat draw his own sabre to strike at a Russian dragoon and send him falling from the saddle with his throat gashed open. The marshal's aides gathered round to protect their commander but Murat fought with the same ferocity as his men. But, Lausard realised as the Russian cavalry continued to slam into them, it was rapidly becoming a frenzy born of desperation. Beyond the lines of troops he could see a large column of enemy horsemen preparing to join the combat, flags flying proudly over their tight-packed formation. He suddenly felt pain in his left thigh and spun round to deflect a second cut. The first had torn through his breeches and into his thigh but, fortunately, not too deeply. He struck back at his attacker, driving his blade into the Russian's chest and stomach.

Delacor and Gaston, both spattered with blood, were being forced backwards by the combined attack of five Russian dragoons. Lausard spurred his horse a couple of yards to their aid, driving his blade into the back of one man and catching another with a tremendous backhand stroke that almost severed his arm. Delacor finished another with his axe. Gaston swung so hard he shattered the first Russian's collarbone then gutted the other with two swift incisions.

All three men were gasping for breath and Lausard could only gesture wearily towards the massive column of horsemen about to smash into the already outnumbered French.

'We'll all be killed,' Sonnier gasped, his face a crimson mask, black powder staining his lips and tongue.

The sound that reached their ears next was like rolling thunder.

Lausard looked down as if expecting to see the very earth itself moving. He heard the notes of the charge being blasted from away to his right and then, moving at incredible speed, a column of French carabiniers hurtled towards the onrushing Russian column.

The impact was fearful.

Like a battering ram, the French ploughed into the lighter Russian horsemen, followed, moments later, by the awesome mass of the cuirassiers. Lausard saw the sunlight glinting on their steel helmets and breastplates as they drove into the enemy troops, their long swords held above their heads. The collision drove the Russians back several yards at a time. Unable to cope with the sheer power of the French heavy cavalry, they buckled under the onslaught.

Lausard, his uniform drenched with sweat and blood,

his mouth parched, his eyes streaming and his throat raw, gripped his sword more tightly and watched the savage combat for a moment. He even managed a smile when the head of the Russian column collapsed under the force of the heavy cavalry's charge. Like a shaft of hot steel into butter, the carabiniers and cuirassiers moved effortlessly through their foe, leaving hundreds dead or dying. As the dragoons looked on, the enemy horsemen turned and fled. The watching French infantry cheered delightedly.

Captain Milliere was gathering the remnants of the squadron around him, forming them up into a column. Lausard urged his horse across to join his companions. He looked down at the gash on his thigh but paid it no heed. His breath was already coming in gasps, his heart hammering against his ribs due to his recent exertions and the adrenalin pumping through his veins so furiously. He saw Rocheteau and the corporal nodded as something passed, unseen, between the two men. Lausard managed a smile.

The column moved on over the bodies of dead and dying men and horses, over a field stained with the blood of so many. He glanced southwards and saw that the entire length of the French line was wreathed in smoke. Eagles still waved defiantly on top of the Pratzen Heights but now, to his delight, Lausard saw, through the choking smoke, that some allied troops were beginning to fall back. However, his attention was suddenly caught by the unmistakable roar of cannons, the savage detonations of the Emperor's "beautiful daughters", the twelve-pounders. Dozens, it seemed, had opened up simultaneously and the deafening fusillades continued. The eagles he had seen brandished so proudly atop the Pratzen Heights were suddenly hidden by smoke so dense it was almost palpable.

Almost immediately, the column of dragoons moved to the right, towards the steeply sloping ground that led to this most crucial part of the battlefield. Lausard tried to swallow but his throat was too dry. He wiped his face with the back of his hand and urged his horse on. The animal was as exhausted as its rider.

Ahead of them the cannon continued to roar.

Napoleon shielded his eyes momentarily from the clouds of smoke that swept across the Pratzen Heights. Millions of tiny cinders filled the air like a swarm of insects and the Emperor brushed them away with his bicorn.

'The Russian Chevalier Guard, sire,' Berthier said, nodding in the direction of a mass of mounted green-clad troops advancing steadily through the smoke. Big men on big horses, they presented a fearful sight. 'They are the last obstacle to our victory.'

'Then let us remove that obstacle,' the Corsican said flatly. But, even as he spoke, he saw hundreds of French troops rushing towards him, fleeing in the wake of the oncoming Russians. Many of the French had abandoned their packs and weapons to make their escape more easily. Savary rode forward and held up a hand as if to halt the terrified tide. More staff officers joined him but the infantry had no intention of stopping.

'Let them go,' said Napoleon, a slight smile on his face.

'But, sire, we will be overrun,' Savary protested. 'At least three infantry regiments have already either been destroyed or have broken.'

'Bessiéres,' the Corsican called and his Guard commander moved closer. 'Deal with this situation.'

Marshal Bessiéres smiled and swung himself into the

saddle. He walked his horse back and forth before the waiting ranks of mounted grenadiers. Every man sat astride a black horse.

'Men,' he shouted. 'The horsemen before you are the Tsar's personal bodyguard. Every squadron leader is a prince. Every trooper is of gentle birth. I suggest we teach them some humility.' He pulled his sword from its scabbard to a deafening roar from the watching men.

Napoleon watched as the mounted grenadiers rode off to meet the oncoming Russian cavalry.

Lausard drove his horse the last few yards up the sharp incline that finally levelled out on to the plateau of Pratzen.

More and more dragoons spilled on to the high ground and began to form up into ranks under Captain Milliere's watchful eye. Lausard could see a savage battle being fought three or four hundred yards ahead, the familiar bearskins of the mounted grenadiers clearly visible in the maelstrom. He also saw chausseurs and Mamelukes among the cluster of horsemen. All were intent on hacking down their opponents and he could see hundreds of Russian horsemen already lying dead on the grass. Riderless horses were dashing about wildly; others still carried dead riders in their saddles. It was a scene of utter devastation and pandemonium, something the sergeant had come to know well during the last few years. He tried to suck in a breath but every lungful tasted of blood and gunpowder. He coughed and spat, trying to drive the taste from his mouth.

Lausard saw General Rapp riding towards Napoleon, blood pouring from a cut on his head. Behind him, a stream of prisoners marched mournfully past. Some, Lausard noticed, were in tears.

'The Chevalier Guard are defeated, sire,' shouted Rapp triumphantly.

'Many fine ladies of St Petersburg will lament this day,' Napoleon mused.

Some of the dragoons who heard his comment laughed and the Emperor turned and raised a hand in their direction.

The exhausted men roared out '*Vive l'Empereur!*' with as much energy as they could muster and Napoleon nodded gratefully.

He reached for his telescope and swept it back and forth along the entire length of the line. Everywhere, the allies were retreating. French troops were surging forward to regain ground they had lost or relinquished earlier in the day.

'What time is it?' the Emperor asked and Berthier fumbled for his watch.

'Three p.m., sire,' his Chief of Staff told him.

Napoleon merely nodded.

'The Russians are retreating towards the frozen lakes,' Napoleon observed, squinting through his telescope once more to see that thousands of green-clad troops were piling on to the Satschan mere, desperate to escape, seemingly oblivious of the fact that the ice could break at any moment under their weight. 'Order a battery to open fire on them. Break the ice.'

Berthier hesitated for a moment.

'Do it,' snapped the Corsican. 'This victory must be total. Do you think they would have spared any of *our* men had the situation been reversed? And send a message to Davout and his Third Corps. No prisoners.'

Staff officers hurried over to take the orders. Lausard watched as they galloped off into the reeking smoke that covered the battlefield from north to south.

Captain Milliere, his breath coming in gasps, turned to Lausard.

'It would appear your war is over, Sergeant,' he wheezed.

Lausard held the officer's gaze, his own face a bloody mask.

'Yes, Captain,' he murmured. '*This* one.'

Twenty-Seven

———>-0-<———

The night was cold. Frost turned the grass white once more and those wounded unlucky enough to be left on the field froze to death. Napoleon sat in his room inside the Posoritz post-house, close to the fire, his face still grimey with powder from the conflict. He gazed at the piece of paper General Rapp had handed him.

'Eleven thousand dead Russians, four thousand dead Austrians. Twelve thousand prisoners, one hundred and eighty guns and fifty colours and standards taken.' He smiled. 'That's good news to slap on the walls of Paris, my friend.'

Rapp grinned.

'What of our own casualties?' Napoleon wanted to know.

'Around one thousand three hundred killed and nearly seven thousand wounded, sire,' the general told him.

Napoleon's smile faded slightly.

'I feel the loss of each of them personally, Rapp,' he murmured.

'The numbers would have been far greater if not for your genius, sire.'

'That may be. But I still weep for *one* lost man. At least we have the victory we wanted. The Austrian Emperor will visit me tomorrow to sue for peace. The Tsar and his army are in flight back to Russia.'

'I heard one of our cavalry patrols came across him sobbing like a child at the roadside but he escaped before they could seize him.'

'Let him go. I have no desire for revenge against that insolent upstart. We have dealt him a blow he will not easily recover from.' The Emperor got to his feet and put one hand on Rapp's shoulder, glancing at the bandage around the officer's head. 'It is time for you to rest, my friend. It is time for us all to enjoy the fruits of our victory.'

'This day will live forever in the minds of those who fought here, sire.'

'And those who did not. I have decided to provide pensions for the widows of those who died and also formally to adopt the orphaned children. They will be permitted to add "Napoleon" to their baptismal names. All will be found places in state schools. Boys will be found posts, girls will be found husbands and awarded dowries at state expense. I will not allow the memory of this day to die.'

Rapp saluted and turned smartly out of the tent.

Napoleon returned to his desk, to the letter he had been writing when the general disturbed him. He ran appraising eyes over it, aware that his own exhaustion would prevent him from writing anymore:

My dearest Josephine,
    I have beaten the Austro-Russian army commanded by the two Emperors. I am a little weary. I have camped

*in the open for eight days and as many freezing nights.
Tomorrow I shall be able to rest in the castle of Prince
Kaunitz and I should be able to snatch two or three
hours sleep there. The Russian army is not only beaten
but destroyed.*

I embrace you.

He took up the quill once more and scratched one last
word at the bottom of the letter:

Napoleon.

Alain Lausard walked the battlefield slowly, his cloak
wrapped tightly around him to protect him against the
chill night air. Most of the bodies had been removed.
Burial parties had hauled the corpses into mass graves,
the wounded of both sides had either been transported
away or left to die where they lay. There were discarded
weapons everywhere. Lausard could see the camp fires
of his squadron high up on the Pratzen Heights. They
had gone through the discarded packs of their defeated
foes and scavenged whatever food they could find. Black
bread, made from straw and bran, had been found among
the abandoned possessions of the Austrians. Lausard
had eaten his fill of that and of the chunks of pork
and horsemeat they'd collected. Now he walked the
silent gulleys and ravines alone. The clouds were still
thick in the sky and snow had been falling intermittently
since darkness cast its pall over the field. The sergeant
wandered on, over ground that had seen so many men
fall during the day. He paused to look at the gurgling
Goldbach stream, still stained with blood in places.

'Come back to the fire, Alain.'

The voice made him turn and he saw Rocheteau standing there, a cup in his hand. He offered it to Lausard.

'Brandy,' the corporal told him.

'Austrian or Russian?' Lausard grinned then swallowed some of the fiery liquid.

'Charvet has cooked up some more broth,' Rocheteau told him. 'And Rostov took several bottles of vodka from a dead Russian officer. Come and share it with us.'

'I needed some time on my own,' Lausard said, looking out across the night-shrouded field once more. 'Time to think.'

'What is there to think about except that we are alive?'

Lausard turned and looked at his companion.

'It is a simple philosophy.' He smiled. 'But a good one. I will join you shortly.'

Rocheteau hesitated a moment then disappeared into the darkness.

Lausard stood motionless, listening to the wind whistling over the open fields and gulleys. Snow stung his face as if to remind him that he *was* still alive. And, for the first time in many years, it was a feeling he savoured.

He turned and made his way back up the hill.